What the Children Said

1) Norwood
2) Zachary
3) Baker
4) Baton Rouge
5) Lafayette
6) St Martinville
7) New Orleans
8) Metairie
9) Chalmette
10) Violet
11) Gretna
12) Algiers

Acadiana

CULTURES OF CHILDHOOD

Cultures of Childhood Series

What the Children Said

CHILD LORE OF SOUTH LOUISIANA

Jeanne Pitre Soileau

University Press of Mississippi / Jackson

The University Press of Mississippi is the scholarly publishing agency of
the Mississippi Institutions of Higher Learning: Alcorn State University,
Delta State University, Jackson State University, Mississippi State University,
Mississippi University for Women, Mississippi Valley State University,
University of Mississippi, and University of Southern Mississippi.

www.upress.state.ms.us

The University Press of Mississippi is a member
of the Association of University Presses.

In this book, some quoted material contains racial slurs.
While those words have been retained, this is in no way an
endorsement of the use of such slurs outside a scholarly context.

First printing 2021
∞

Library of Congress Cataloging-in-Publication Data

Names: Soileau, Jeanne Pitre, author.
Title: What the children said: child lore of south Louisiana / Jeanne
Pitre Soileau.
Description: Jackson: University Press of Mississippi, 2021. | Series:
Cultures of childhood | Includes bibliographical references and index.
Identifiers: LCCN 2021013955 (print) | LCCN 2021013956 (ebook) | ISBN
978-1-4968-3573-4 (hardback) | ISBN 978-1-4968-3574-1 (trade paperback) | ISBN
978-1-4968-3575-8 (epub) | ISBN 978-1-4968-3576-5 (epub) | ISBN 978-1-4968-3577-2
(pdf) | ISBN 978-1-4968-3578-9 (pdf)
Subjects: LCSH: Folklore and children—Research. | Folklore and
children—Louisiana. | Children—Folklore. |
Children—Louisiana—Folklore. | Counting-out rhymes—Louisiana. |
Circle games—Louisiana. | Jump rope rhymes—Louisiana. | Hand games. |
Rhyming games—Louisiana. | Wit and humor, Juvenile. |
Children—Juvenile humor.
Classification: LCC GR43.C4 S65 2021 (print) | LCC GR43.C4 (ebook) | DDC
398.209763/4—dc23
LC record available at https://lccn.loc.gov/2021013955
LC ebook record available at https://lccn.loc.gov/2021013956

British Library Cataloging-in-Publication Data available

Being a little person in a big world with nobody taking you very seriously is tough.
—*Barbara Kingsolver,* Prodigal Summer

DEDICATION

To the children of south Louisiana who might now be mothers and fathers, and in some cases, grandparents—thank you for sharing. To my own teachers at all grade levels, many who encouraged my limitless reading and patiently answered my endless questions. To my children, who helped me gather lore from their friends.

Contents

Preface

A little preparation. What does a children's folklorist do? In my case, I gather together groups of children and ask them a series of questions. The questions and the children's answers to them are recorded, transcribed, and used for lectures, articles, book content, and as part of the syllabus for courses I used to teach before I retired.

My method of collection is by question. The questions include:

1. How do you choose who is "it"?
2. What kind of hand-clapping games do you play?
3. Do you play ring games?
4. What tag games (or running games) do you play?
5. Can you tell me a joke?
6. What do you say to tease someone?
7. What speeches do you make on the playground?
8. What do you say when you play jump rope?
9. What cheers do you know?

This questionnaire has to be flexible. Alternate questions depend on what children were doing when I arrived to interview them. If they were playing on a computer, I might ask what games they were playing, and who had introduced the games to them. If they were engaged in wild running games, I might observe first, and then gather the children together and get them to describe what tag games they were playing. Sometimes girls could dominate an entire tape session, leaving me to simply go "Uh huh" and "Oh, really?" while they competed with one another to recite a half hour of hand-clapping games.

On rare occasions, I might walk into a recording session well prepared, with two working tape recorders, extra tapes, extra batteries, and a carefully planned questionnaire, only to have the kids take over, the planned questions go out the window, and the children run amok. Boys are the least predictable.

What the Children Said

Introduction

I entered the classroom and set up my tape recorder on a windowsill. Then I plugged in my microphone and set it next to the tape recorder. While I was doing this, the teacher in the classroom came over to me and said in a low voice, "I don't think you're going to get much from these kids. You know, children don't play any more. Half of these kids barely speak English."

I smiled, and then I turned on the tape recorder. I asked the first question of my list of usual questions, "How do you choose who is 'it'?" The fifth and sixth graders swarmed forward shouting, "I know one! I know one!" And this was the beginning of a collecting session that lasted ninety minutes. It was held at John Dibert Elementary School in New Orleans in 1979. By the time I finished that ninety minutes, I had an audio tape filled with jump-rope jingles, hand-clapping rhymes, jokes, scary stories, and counting-out formulas. This was a pretty typical collecting session. And I collected for fifty years.

It seems that children in south Louisiana were playing in the 1970s, and are still playing well into the twenty-first century, *whenever they have the chance*. Many spoken rhymes and stories they pass on to their siblings and peers make up a body of lore that children have shared for at least two hundred years.[1] They play old, folkloric games inherited from English-speaking roots. They play in new ways, sending images of themselves to one another on phones, parodying television commercials, and re-enacting movie scripts. They concentrate their eyes on computers while playing video games and stretch their imaginations writing and acting out videos for YouTube.[2]

As my collection of children's lore grew, my appreciation of the power of children's speech grew. The reader will note, as he or she examines the transcripts of recorded tapes that make up much of this book, that children teach one another. Children speak to one another in a hierarchical fashion, the strongest speaker often out-shouting the less voluble. Older schoolchildren perform schoolyard speech events for the entertainment of younger students, and both old and young benefit from the interchange. Children as young as three and four listen to, and memorize, long passages of schoolyard lore, and while they may make some initial errors, transmit jump-rope jingles, handclaps, and teases and taunts, almost verbatim from one century to the next.

I look back, and I feel very lucky to have been an intense collector of child lore in south Louisiana. I spent from 1969 to 2019 amassing a file cabinet full of audio and videotapes filled with the voices of children as they entertained themselves and their friends with what folklorists call "child lore." Those fifty years have enriched my life with an unexpected indoctrination into the secretive world of children's play. Here are a few of the things I learned:

Children seldom share their schoolyard games with adults. They are not likely to invite an adult to join in on a wild tag game. Girls playing a hand clap will probably invite their immediate friends to join in but ignore the teacher observing them on yard duty.

The few adults I interviewed often remembered playing certain games only after prompting. I framed my questions using "reminders," such as "Did you ever use the rhyme 'Eenie meenie minie moe?'" This almost always got a response, leading the adults to even further memories.

By simply using the few questions in my questionnaire, I could elicit more than six hundred examples of childhood verbal lore. (See index of first lines at the back of the book.)

A careful count of my sources included in this book revealed that I had cited 290 African American children's contributions and 360 games, rhymes, and songs provided by white children and adults.

There were distinct differences between the way African American and white children interacted. African American boys and girls used Black English vernacular when they engaged in play. African American boys jostled and poked at one another more than their white counterparts while they spoke. Physical distance between girl players, their clapping patterns, body motions, mimetics, and facial and eye movements remained clearly African American during the fifty years of my tapings.

White boys and girls used white dialect, and depending on their ages sometimes utilized street grammar. White children's voices can be clearly distinguished from African American children's voices by cadence, usage, and accent, and they seldom imitated the African American modes of expression they heard all around them on the playground. I found it interesting that even over fifty years of integration, on the school grounds, African American and white speech modalities remained idiosyncratic.

Children of both races and sexes learned racism and sexism early. An attentive reading of what the children say to one another, and how they say it, reveals that by the second and third grades boys and girls are already willing to be recorded calling one another pejorative names and using racist slurs.

Presented in the following book are play and verbal interactions collected in small, controlled situations in schoolyards and playgrounds of south Louisiana. Sometimes I recorded only one or two volunteers. Other times a crowd pressed in from all directions, clamoring to be heard, and I had to select out only the most insistent.

The areas I visited were New Orleans and its suburbs, Baton Rouge (and the small towns that surround it), and Lafayette, the "Hub City" of Acadiana.

The organization of this book consists of several elements—transcripts, or partial transcripts; examples of schoolyard lore as reported by students; and lists of sources (schools, birthday parties, day camps, bingo babysitting).

Chapter 1, "Counting-Out," explores methods children used to select who would be "it." As in all of the following chapters, the counting-out formulas are given, followed by sources and notes.

Chapter 2, "Ring Games," presents chants and songs children employ while holding hands or forming a ring. Some circle games south Louisiana children played can be traced directly to England, as chapter notes will attest.

Chapter 3, "Jump Rope," played on the schoolgrounds where principals permit it, has been popular in south Louisiana since at least the early 1900s. Adults who were interviewed recalled "skipping rope" in Mid-City at Crossman Elementary School in the 1920s.

Chapter 4, "Hand Games," includes a variety of games played with the hands, from clapping, which utilizes rhymes and songs, to "Hot Hands," where players attempt to smack the hands of their partner as hard as they can.

Chapter 5, "Rhymes and Songs," has several sections. There are rhymes and nursery rhymes, which are usually chanted, rather than sung. Section 2 is schoolyard songs, mostly parodies of well-known tunes like "Battle Hymn of the Republic" or "Row Row Row Your Boat." And section 3 features camp songs.

Chapter 6, "Running and Imaginative Games," includes a transcript of a taped session made at Gates of Prayer Hebrew Synagogue. The transcript is lengthy, but it demonstrates that even in a classroom designed to teach religious fundamentals, the children become highly animated when recalling folk games. Part 2 of "Running Games" records about forty-eight running and chasing games boys and girls told of playing in New Orleans alone. Parts 3 and 4 include variants of running games with strict rules and dramatic play with a story line. The games involving a "wolf" can be traced directly to Europe.

Chapter 7, "Teases," contains rhymes almost every adult I recorded remembered.

Chapter 8, "Jokes," records children of all ages struggling with the elements of logical order, precise timing, and entertaining delivery.

The following pages contain the reproduction, to the best of my ability, of the recorded sound and patterns of children's speech, as well as mine. In order to demonstrate various speech modes and oralities, I have presented careful transcriptions of portions of taped sessions with children. I offer the recording transcripts for a couple of reasons. One, I know that in some sessions I made interviewer's errors, some glaring. I sometimes interposed my own opinions or interrupted the flow of the children's narratives. Aspiring collectors could learn from those mistakes. Two, I want to present the flow of a taping session, so that others can see how such recording events transpire and how they might wander off into sometimes unexpected areas.

I begin with the following transcribed passage in which three boys speak and, indeed, wander off into unexpected areas. This is one of the few interviews where the speakers came from a rural setting. Most of the other tapes were made in urban localities. The reader might detect where the interview departs from the planned questionnaire and where the departure led.

It had been more than a year since I had armed myself with a tape recorder and sallied forth to collect the lore of south Louisiana children. Then, on April 11, 2017, a friend of mine called and suggested that I interview three little boys, ages seven, seven, and nine, who were "bored and restless." Translation: the boys were driving my friend, and other residents of the nursing home where he lived, nuts. For some reason the boys were not in school. They were being "baby-sat" at Landmark of Acadiana, a sprawling home for the aged and infirm in St. Martinville, Louisiana. I drove down Louisiana Highway 182, otherwise known as "The Old Spanish Trail," and met with Mrs. Smith,[3] the hairdresser for the nursing home. She introduced the three boys as "My son and his two cousins." Her son, aged seven, a tall, robust child, was part African American. The two cousins, one seven, the other nine, were white, blond, blue-eyed, and small for their ages. I herded the boys, who smelled deliciously of sweat and sunshine, down the hall and to a small patio decorated with a three-tiered water fountain and several wooden rocking chairs. They arranged themselves—Tony, the part African American child, stood on the left side of the patio. He leaned his shoulder up against a red brick pillar and cast his eyes down shyly. The two tow-headed boys, Matt and Jr., clambered into the oversized wooden rockers and began immediately to scoot and rock. They excitedly challenged one another to see how far they could rock the chairs back and then shuffle them forward.

I had a carefully prepared questionnaire in hand. I was hoping to see if these three boys played the same types of ball games, tag games, and teasing and taunting games I had recorded forty years ago. I was not prepared for the direction this taping session would take us all. Following is a transcript, somewhat edited, of the seventeen minutes I spent with the three boys:

(JS) This is April 11, 2017, and I am interviewing Tony, Matt, and Jr. They are going to talk to me about some of the games they play at school—maybe. OK. First question: When you play a game, how do you choose who is it?

(Tony) (Softly.) By counting . . .

(JS) How do you count? What do you say?

(Jr. pointing to Tony.) *He* always chooses . . .

(Tony laughs, and looks down bashfully.)

(JS) How do *you* choose? (I speak to Jr.)

(Jr.) Eenie meenie minie . . .

(Tony leans forward and breaks in.) Eenie meenie minie moe / Catch a tiger by the toe / If he hollers let him go / Eenie meenie minie moe. (Then he leans his shoulder back against the brick pillar.)

(JS) What do you do? Do you use your feet? Do you use your hands?

(Jr.) We touch head. *He* always does it. (Points at Tony.) And I go (Jr. puts his hands out and laces his fingers.)

(JS) Do you count on your fingers?

(Jr.) No.

(JS) Is there any way other than that that you choose who is it?

(Everybody looks blank, so I change tactic.)

(JS) All right—what games do you play on the playground at school?

(Jr.) We play kick ball. We kick a ball around at recess.

(JS) Do you bring your own ball?

(Matt and Jr. in one voice.) Nooo! We use the ball at school.

(Tony) It's a school ball.

(Jr.) I bring one from home.

(JS) Oh, do you go to different schools?

(All boys) Yes!!

(JS) OK, what do *you* play on the school ground? (I turn to Matt.)

(Matt) I don't go to school. I got kicked out.

(JS) You what?

(Matt) I got kicked out.

(JS) You got kicked out? Do you want to tell that story?

(Matt) Yeah.

(JS) OK. What happened?

(Matt) (Mumbles.) I brought a pill to school.

(JS) You what?

(Matt) (Says softly.) I brought a pill to school.

(JS) Whose pill was it?

(Matt) Mine.

(JS) Well, you can't bring a pill to school anymore.

(Jr. breaks in.) Well, *I* brought five pills in my pocket. I didn't get in trouble.

(JS) You had five pills in your pocket, and you took them to school? Where did you get the pills?

(Jr.) From my house.

(JS) What did you do with the pills?

(Jr.) I shared them.

(JS) Oh really? So it was your own medicine? The medicine you were supposed to be taking?

(Matt) Yeah, me and Jr.—we both on Adderall.

(Slight pause)

(Matt) I got kicked out of school . . .

(JS) And you? (I look at Jr.) You didn't get kicked out of school? They didn't know you had them, huh? Do they have a lot of kids at school on Adderall?

(While the Adderall discussion has been underway, the boys have begun rocking their chairs all the way back, then tipping them forward until they almost fall over. The rocking gets more frenetic as the interview proceeds.)

(Tony) (Still leaning on the brick pillar.) There's one more kid who is on Adderall in my school. His name is Justice, and he's in my class.

(JS) Oh, OK—all right—let me ask you another question, then. (I take a few seconds to fiddle with the recorder, to make sure it is on and recording all this. In the short time it takes to poke at the recorder, Matt and Jr. begin a rocking chair war. Jr. topples his chair over onto Matt. Matt fends off the rocking chair back with his elbow but bops Jr. on the head. "Ow!" Matt and Jr. begin to shout and tussle. Jr.'s rocking chair falls forward, and he scrambles out from under it.)

(JS) OK, well, can you tell me a joke?

(Jr. from across the patio where he has scooted his rocker.) You got to tell me what kind of joke.

(Tony stands against the pillar, looking amused, watching and silent. Jr. wiggles out from under his rocker and rights it.)

(JS) You gotta come closer because this is not gonna pick you up waaay across there. Tell me a joke.

(Jr.) Why did the banana eat a banana?

(JS) Why did the banana eat a . . . what?

(Jr.) Why did the banana eat a banana?

(JS) OK. Why *did* the banana eat a banana?

(Jr.) To get more bananery.

(Tony laughs. I chortle.)

(JS turns to Matt) OK. Do you know a joke?

(Matt) Why is seven . . . Why is six scared of seven?

(JS) Why?

(Matt) Because seven eight nine.

(JS) (I chuckle.) OK, that's a good one.

(Jr.) I know one.

(JS) OK. Tell me another joke.

(Jr. speaks softly from several feet away. He is rocking his chair rapidly backwards.)

(JS) You gotta come closer, because from way over there I can't hear you, and neither can my recorder.

(Jr. comes closer dragging his rocking chair with him.)

(JS) Uh—and what's your joke?

(Jr.) I don't have a joke.

(JS) You don't have a joke? You just want to bring the rocker over? (Jr. is concentrating on scooting the rocker with himself in it closer to me.) OK, can you tell me a scary story?

(Tony leans forward, and says softly.) I know one.

(JS) You know a scary story? C'mon, tell me your scary story.

(Tony) I was at Jr.'s house, and I was playing a video game, and (Matt and Jr. become quite still. The mad rocking ceases.) I was playing, and a pictures fell off the wall by itself. I mean a picture fell off the wall.

(Jr.) I was playing on my Play Station, and the pictures fell, and then, like, it broke, and more pictures kept falling, and we ran to my mom and dad's room, and they said we was the one making them fall. And they just kept falling!

(Tony) And . . . and they . . . they said we made 'em fall.

(Jr.) And we ran back, and it looked like glass all over, and the pictures were back up.

(JS) Oh, that's wild.

(Jr.) That was creepy, that's what! (Jr. flips the rocking chair over all the way onto the chair Matt is sitting in.)

(Matt) Ouch!

(JS) (I turn to the side, and there is Matt, sprawling.) Oh, you're underneath that chair there. How you feelin'?

(Matt) I feel good.

(JS laughs.) OK—ummm—You sing any songs when you are on the playground that are silly songs?

(Jr.) Sometimes I'm singing on the playground while I'm waiting . . .

(JS) OK, c'mon, let's hear you sing.

(Matt and Jr. suddenly launch their rocking chairs over on each other and butt heads. Much grunting and muttering.)

(Jr.) Ow!!

(JS) (In an attempt to gain control.) OK, let's hear you sing . . .

(Matt, on his back under the chair.) I'm a la la toodle dee dooo . . . Don't kill me please.

(JS) (I am not sure if "Don't kill me please" is a song or directed at Jr.) Don't kill me please? Is that a song? How does it go?

(Jr.) Yes. "Born on Tuesday . . ." (Giggles.) (Sings a few notes.)

(JS) How does it go?

(The three boys together.) "Oh, don't kill me . . ." (Suddenly Matt and Jr. flip their chairs up and engage in a joust, rocking their chairs wildly, poking each other with the chair knobs. They giggle hysterically. Tony steps back flat against the brick pillar, watching.)

(JS) (I have lost control of Matt and Jr., who are engaged now in battering one another with the rocking chairs, looking one another in the eye. They are at this point aware only of themselves.) (I address Tony, who is serenely observing Matt and Jr.'s escalating battle.) OK, when you are at home, do you play video games? (Matt and Jr. from the floor under their chairs.) Yeah!

(JS) What video games do you play?

(Tony) Lego Batman.

(JS) Are you good at it? Lego Batman? And what other games do you play?

(Tony shrugs.)

(JS) You get to play on the Play Station in the house?

(Tony) Yeah.

(Matt) I have a Play Station!

(JS) Y'all both have a Play Station? Do you live in the same house?

(Boys all together.) Noooo . . . no.

(JS) You don't all live in the same house?

(Boys all together.) We live on the same street. He lives somewhere . . . down the road . . . he lives close to me . . .

(Jr.) EEeeeyah! He lives on Romero . . . I live on Comeaux lot . . . My middle name is Anthony . . .

(JS) Your middle name is Anthony?

(Jr.) My daddy's middle name is Anthony. (The jousting continues and is getting fiercer. Grunts and groans get louder.)

(JS addresses the boys as they struggle under the chairs.) Is there anything that you can tell me about anything else that you play?

(Matt) I can play all of my games. I can shoot my BB gun all the time.

(JS) Tell me about your BB gun.

(Matt) We shoot at trees. We shoot cans. One time we go walk in the field. Jacob shot me with the BB gun. I laughed.

(Jr. stops wrestling, sits back in his rocker.) And one time me, and Matt, Tony, Cade, and uh—we went by some kind of kayoke, you know, that river. Um, Cade, Tony, and Matt went walking toward the (Mumble).

(JS) So, who gave you the gun? Who gave you the BB gun?

(Jr.) I . . . I wasn't there when he got shot that time . . .

(JS) Who gave you the BB gun?

(Matt) My dad. My dad gave me the BB gun. Me and Jacob, we were taking a walk—we go out there—I have two BB guns, so I gave one to Jacob. I let him have it 'cuz the other one that I gave him, it was old—and I gave it to him because it was old. So I got a brand new one, and I didn't need it. I would go walk in the field, and he shot me with a BB gun. I was mad. And we went with my dad shooting it a couple of times, and days, and then he trusted us—he trusted us. We come to a—and we go shoot. And one time—um—we saw a farmer. And we shoot at him, first because we didn't know he was a farmer. We were in the woods . . . (Jr. tries to break in here, but is ignored. Jr. then signals for Matt to stop talking.)

(JS) Did you shoot at him?

(Matt) We were . . . we were raised back there . . .

(JS) So, you were walking in the woods, in a field . . .

(Matt) Field—

(JS) Field—when you saw a farmer and you *didn't* shoot at him?

(Matt looks at Jr.) No, we didn't shoot him. Sooo . . .

(Jr.) When we was walking back, when the truck passed, we shot his *truck*—we shot the truck.

(Matt gives Jr. a look.) We tried to shoot the tires . . .

(Jr. to Matt.) Why didn't you shoot the tires? Or just the metal?

(Matt) And when we were walkin' back, Jacob kept sayin', "I'm gonna shoot you. I got a BB gun, Boy." And then I got a aim at him, and I got a bead on him. It wasn't cocked. So when I run, and he cocked it, he shot me here (Points to ankle.), and right there (Points to calf.). And when I ran, and I tried to hide, he shot me again.

(JS) Did it hurt?

(Matt) Not that much. I think one time Jacob shot me in the butt.

(Jr.) Jacob shot *me* in the butt, too.

(JS) (Looks at Tony.) Do you have a BB gun?

(Tony) Yes.

(JS) What do *you* shoot at?

(Tony) I shoot at . . . I shoot at cans . . . the same thing as him—cans.

(Matt) Um—I was at my friend's house . . .

(JS) Uh huh.

(Matt) We were one day riding a four-wheeler . . .

(JS) Yeah?

(Matt) We was ridin' a four-wheeler, and he was shooting, and then I starting shooting . . . and then we got an idea. We was shooting, and we was shooting at houses . . . people's houses, and people's cars. We were in the woods. If I didn't do it, he would have dropped me off in the middle of the woods—so, like, good, I'm gonna do it. So we was shootin' people's houses.

(JS) Uh huh? Did anybody notice?

(Matt) No. They were all gone.

(Jr.) Did you do it?

(Matt) (Excitedly.) We shot a truck . . . an old truck . . .

(Jr.) We shot an (Mumbles softly.).

(Matt) Shot . . . yeah, we shot one . . . yeah, the four-wheeler . . . I drove the four-wheeler, and it ran out of gas, and then we went go get on a dirt bike, and we went home.

(Jr.) We . . . when the dirt bike . . .

(Matt interrupts breathlessly.) Yeah, when I put my foot down, my ankle . . . it wouldn't stop. When I was riding it by myself, I put my foot down, and I busted my toe . . . (Unintelligible.).

(JS) Yeah, it doesn't stop when you put your foot down.

(Matt) Yeah, I was on the dirt bike when I busted my toe.

(JS) Do you have a four-wheeler?

(Jr.) His mom and dad won't let him ride a four-wheeler. When we ride 'em they don't know it.

(JS) Oh, his mom and dad won't let him?

(Matt) No, we ride a bike.

(JS) Where do you ride a bike?

(Jr.) In the road.

(Matt) I ride in the road, too. And we got a teenager that comes to my house, and I get to ride a dirt bike. My mom doesn't know it.

(Tony) And I went, too.

(Matt) *He* never rode it! Tony sat on the dirt bike, too, but he never *rode* it.

(Jr. breaks in.) *You* never rode it. And Tony, he rode the . . . he never *drove* it, but he rode it!

(Matt) Did too! I drove the four-wheeler *and* the dirt bike.

(JS) And how old were you when you were doing all this?

(Matt) Nine.

(JS) Nine?

(Matt) Actually, I was eight when I drove the—uh—the four-wheeler.

(Jr.) I'm seven.

(JS) And you're seven!

(Jr.) In one more month I'll be eight.

(JS turns to Tony, who is taller and heavier than the other two.) And you're a big boy. Do you play football?

(Jr.) I'm on the twenty-fourth of April.

(Tony) No, I played football.

(JS) You played football?

(Tony says something soft and unintelligible.)

(JS turns to Jr.) Where do you play football?

(Jr.) I play football in the park, and I play basketball.

(JS) Oh, yes, you're tall.

(Matt) I used to play football in the park. I play basketball now. I don't play football.

(JS) Oh well . . .

(Matt) I used to play soccer, but a girl kicked the ball and hit me in my wrong spot.

(JS) Ouch!

(Matt) I quit. And then I quit football. Then I quit basketball. I started doing basketball. I never quit basketball yet.

(JS) Uh huh? Where do y'all live?

(Jr.) I live almost by Matt, but not by him. You know, you go down that road, and you keep going, and you make a curve, and then you see a brick house.

(JS) A brick house. Is that in Broussard, Cade, Lafayette, Youngsville?

(Matt) I don't know. I live on the highway.

(JS) On the highway—oh, OK, that's why you have fields around, huh?

(Matt) Yeah.

(JS addressing Tony.) Where do you live?

(Tony) I live by him. (He points to Matt.)

(Matt) Yeah, he lives by me.

(JS) Let's see if I can think of anything else I can ask you. I want to know if you tease people at school?

(Jr.) Yeah, I do—a lot.

(JS) What do you say when you tease them?

(Jr.) I say, "Oh, go play with the dogs."

(JS) Do they like that?

(Matt) I tease people at school.

(JS) You tease people at school? Like what?

(Matt) I tell them they a burnt cookie.

(Tony, who is part African American, looks down at his feet.)

(JS) A what?

(Matt) A burnt cookie. I say, "You stayed in the oven too long."

(Tony) Yeah, you a burnt cookie if you are too black. You take off the burnt, and you could be white.

(Matt) You take a burnt cookie, and you can't take off the crust. Hey—they left overnight in the oven too long!

(JS) (Laughs.) You a burnt cookie—you left in the oven too long? I never heard that one.

(Jr.) You heard that a lot?

(JS) Oh, sure, I've heard all kinds of things from kids, but I never heard that one before . . . well . . .

(Jr.) You heard a lot of people?

(JS) Oh, sure. Go play with the dogs? Sure. I hear all kinds of things from kids.

(Jr.) Go play with the chickens! Or the cats!—Or a worm! (He pokes Matt with his index finger.) What a worm! You look like a worm!

(Matt) Excuse me!

(Jr.) (Giggles.) Sometimes me, Tony, and Matt are fighting—he grab me by the arm and he slam me—he squeeze me by the arm and hurt me—(Matt and Jr. suddenly flop forward in their rocking chairs, and Matt grabs Jr. by the arm. They tussle. The chairs tip forward, and the tops of the chairs clash together.) (Hysterical giggling.)

(JS) Oh no . . . wait . . . wait . . . you might gouge out each other's eyeballs!

(Boys continue to wrestle, crash chairs together, and squeal even more
  hysterically.)

(Jr.) No—I gonna get on the bottom and pay back—(Giggling madly—trying to
  pinch Matt's arm.)

(JS) How come?

(Jr. and Matt squeeze each other's arms and do not let go of each other—scuf-
  fling under the chairs—tipping and rocking the chairs against each other.
  Tony remains standing, watching from about two feet away.)

(Jr.) I know I won!

(Matt, not letting go of Jr.'s arms—giggles.)

(Jr.) (Growling almost unintelligibly.) I got him on the seat—on the bus—I did
  that on the seat (Pfffft.) like that—on the bus!

(Both boys struggle, squeezing, pinching, rocking. They end up on the ground,
  the rocking chairs on top of them.)

(JS) I'll bet that was fun.

(Jr.) I got him in the eyes though—I gotta get him his payback though.

(Matt) (Mumbles while struggling against Jr. under his rocking chair.)

(Jr.) I'll jump on you, and get my payback!

(Jr. and Matt wrestle one another mightily from under the overturned wooden
  rockers.)

(Jr. and Matt together.) I'll get you! I'll get my payback!

(JS) Well—(Turning to Tony who is still leaning against the brick pillar.) While
  they are doing that—do you have any stories you want to tell me?

(Tony) Uh uh.

(JS) Nothing at all?

(Jr. and Matt continue to writhe against one another, muttering about "pay back"
  and "get even.")

(JS) Oh, well—I guess this is it—seventeen minutes.

Tape off.

This is the last interview I recorded before sitting down to write this book. I
walked into the Landmark of Acadiana prepared to ask a set number of questions the purpose of which was to find out if boys in the twenty-first century
still passed on the school-yard lore boys of the twentieth century engaged in.
Did they still utilize counting-out rhymes to choose who is it? It seems they
do. The boys knew the most commonly used formula collected by me, and
other folklorists, for the last hundred years—"Eenie meenie minie moe . . ."

"What games do you play on the playground at school?" elicited the answer, "We play kick ball. We kick a ball around at recess." Most groups of boys I interviewed from the 1970s to 2018 named ball games as their most often played school-yard activities.

"Can you tell me a joke?" The answers to this question—"Why did the banana eat a banana?" and "Why is six scared of seven?" are both quite typical of jokes in my collection told by seven-year-olds.

The question "Can you tell me a scary story?" was answered by the three boys excitedly relating an incident where pictures unexpectedly fell off a wall while they were playing video games. This type of story falls in with other seven-year-olds' depictions of rocking chairs rocking all by themselves and spooky noises in closets at night.

"You sing any songs while you play on the playground that are silly songs?" went only partially answered. This was in part due to the boys' rambunctious play, and partly because the boys did not strain too hard to think of one. They did come up with the line "Born on Tuesday." I went to YouTube and typed in "Born on Tuesday," and up popped a song by Drake. Listed on YouTube as "Tuesday ft. Makonnen (Lyrics)" September 26, 2018, the song had 2,569,503 views and featured a chant about sex, drugs (pills), and posturing.

The question "Do you tease people on the playground?" gave me a glimpse of the kind of interplay between Tony and his two cousins. The tease Matt supplied, "I tell them they a burnt cookie," made Tony visibly uncomfortable. Matt's repetition, "A burnt cookie. I say, 'You stayed in the oven too long,'" prompted Tony to explain, "Yeah, you a burnt cookie if you are too black. You take off the burnt and you could be white." Matt immediately retorted, "You take a burnt cookie, and you can't take off the crust. Hey—they left overnight in the oven too long." It seems from this interchange that racism is still alive, even in a closely related family.

I had expected, interviewing three boys under ten, to get quite a lot of video game lore. They did speak of playing on Play Station and playing Lego Batman. However, they seemed to engage in more outdoor activity than I had expected.

What I had not planned for was the extended discussion of BB gun activity. Jr. and Matt became focused and acutely verbal when recounting their gun-related exploits. They started by saying, "We shoot trees. We shoot cans." Then they sat forward, became intent, and went into an account of shooting at each other, farmers, farmers' trucks, people's houses, and finally, back to shooting at each other. Matt states that his dad gave him the BB gun, went shooting with him a "couple of times," and then "he trusted us." Interestingly, I can remember almost the same BB gun pursuits when I was a tomboy in the early 1950s. My mother and father handed my brother and me BB guns and then paid no attention to what we did with them. And, yes, my brother and I shot at cans, various people, neighbor's windows, and each other.

I had also not foreseen the Adderall discussion. Two of the boys, Matt (nine) and Jr. (seven) brought up Adderall and how it had affected their lives. One had been "kicked out" of school, and the other had taken his medicine to school and shared it with his friends. The trend of medicated children is a thread that wandered through my nearly fifty years of classroom experiences. Children have been dosed on amphetamines, depressants, opioids, antihistamines, and other drugs, obtained legally and illegally. In the main, it is the parents or older siblings who provided the medications. I walked into a university freshman English class in 2007 and encountered one of my female students handing out her Adderall to her friends, collecting money from them, and stuffing it in her handbag. She laughed when she saw my face. "I get my prescription filled, and I make my fun money selling Adderall," she grinned.

What I learned from my seventeen-minute discussion with the three boys at Landmark of Acadiana is this:

Though I had only a small sampling of three seven- and nine-year-old boys, they were still proponents of folklore shared by a network of children from as long ago as 1969, when I first began my child lore collection in south Louisiana. These young boys use counting out to choose who is it. They pass on silly, age-appropriate jokes. Video games are hugely popular with them. Two of the boys engaged in intense physical bouts, wrestling one another and straining to attain dominance.

Racism is alive and festering in south Louisiana, even in closely related families.

Guns and gun lore make for exciting conversation.

Drugs are very much an active part of some children's lives.

This seventeen-minute taping session solidified my belief that young male children are conserving much of the lore that defines south Louisiana childhood.

I often feel that my taped sessions with young people present a window to youthful verbal expressiveness and the rites of passage that the young formulate for themselves. For adults, that window might more correctly be identified as a mirror. I recalled, listening to Matt and Jr., how my brother and

I played with a BB gun as children. Other readers, seeing the songs, rhymes, teases, jokes, and tag games, might experience memories of what they, too, played as children.

The following chapters contain extensive examples from the collection I have made over the years. Some samples come from as early as 1970, and others from as late as 2019. All are transcriptions from oral tapes and scribbled notes and reflect my attempt to capture the mode and expression of the speakers. The children stutter, speak in dialect, and use fractured grammar, partial sentences, and lapses in logic. An examination of tweets on Twitter reveals that this is the manner in which ordinary people often communicate.

This is also a collection of verbal interactions between children that take place primarily on the school grounds. Schoolyard lore is distinct from nursery rhymes. An adult playing a nursery rhyme with a child will possibly twiddle the child's toes and say, "This little piggy went to market / This little piggy stayed home . . ." A child remembers this and perhaps plays it with his or her sibling. That same child might recall the nursery rhyme years later as an adult, and play "This Little Piggy" with his / her own children. In the schoolyard, however, it would be unseemly for a child to remove another child's shoes and play with his toes. It would be just as unlikely for a child to walk up to an adult, offer a jump rope, and say, "Let's do 'Cinderella dressed in yella / Went upstairs to kiss a fella / Made a mistake and kissed a snake . . .'" Jump rope rhymes are for friends one's own age. Schoolyard lore is by children, for children.

Elizabeth Tucker, in *Children's Folklore: A Handbook*, refers to the way children learn and share as "the childhood underground . . . a network of children that transmits children's folklore . . ."[4] No one really knows exactly how the network functions or how children pass on games they learn in grade school. Perhaps it is by watching and listening while others play. Perhaps an older child recruits a younger one into the play circle, and actively demonstrates the game. All collectors like me can know is that the process happens. I recorded three- and four-year-olds clapping hands and chanting long and involved songs I had also recorded from older students at schools across New Orleans, Baton Rouge, and Lafayette, Louisiana. I recorded songs in New Orleans that were played simultaneously in New York, London, and New Zealand. There were boys I taped who, at three and four, already knew street boasts and dozens. I was not present at the stage where these children acquired their lore. I, like other active folklorists, simply recorded what was shared with me.

No folklorist can get it all. I look back on my years of collecting and envisage my work as a series of small "time capsules." Each time I visited a school, a recreation center, or city park and switched on my tape recorder, a crowd of children formed. Out of the crowd, only a few stepped forward and volunteered to share their knowledge. There might be thirty children in the group. Every child knew *something*, but only the most courageous spoke up. I recorded for maybe half an hour and then departed, and the crowd dispersed to go out and play all those games they knew—games that I had missed! I took my recordings home and transcribed them. In the end, the result is several hundred pages of typescript, representing only a smattering of what swirls around in the children's network.

Children might be classed as a secretive society. Their playground lore is private, special, reserved for children alone. It is also ranked by age. Elementary school children play handclaps, ring games, tag, hide and seek. Once advanced to middle school, many girls drop handclaps and jump-rope rhymes, and instead, begin to share make-up secrets, sex lore, and phone and Facebook and YouTube play. Boys in middle school often switch from marbles and wild running games to telling jokes and stories and more organized physical play. By the end of high school, many informants are able to recount only fragments of the rhymes they had played so joyfully only a few years before. By the end of high school, many girls have to be prompted with first lines in order to launch into a once-familiar jump-rope jingle.

The games of childhood are not, however, truly forgotten. They get filed away somewhere is a special recess in the human brain, where they lie dormant. Their memory can be sparked. First lines such as "I like coffee / I like tea" and "Say say say playmate / Come out and play with me," when shared with adult women, often elicit instant recognition. "Oh, yeah! I played that when I was in third grade." Adult men can sometimes name every marble in the wooden marble box I open. "That's an aggie," "That's a shooter," "I used to have one like that; it was called a 'peewee.'"

Schoolyard lore gets passed around quickly. A child might participate in a jump-rope session and then pass on the jump-rope jingle she memorized to her friends within minutes. Folklore collectors have noted how consistent the transmission remains. Children's play is not only rapidly spread, but complex. It is influenced by many things: popular culture, current songs on the top one hundred charts, television programs, video games, movies the children see. At the same time, children's play conserves chants and formulas ranging from the times of the Greeks and Romans to modern parodies of instantly recognizable commercials. The game "Knucklebones," identified as modern

Jacks, is depicted on ancient Greek vases. "Blind Man's Buff" or "Bluff," is recorded in eighteenth-century paintings and in schoolbook illustrations from China in 1912.[5] So, children's play is both innovative and conservative. The same boys and girls who start a counting-out rhyme with the antique "Eenie meenie minie moe," can later sing, "McDonald's is your kinda place / They serve you happiness / French fries up your nose . . ."

What you are about to read is a distinctly south Louisiana collection of folk rhymes, silly songs, jokes, jump-rope jingles, counting-out formulas, and handclaps. A quick check of the number of entries showed that I had included 360 items of lore given by white children and two hundred and ninety items shared by African American children.

Most of my recordings were made on the playgrounds of public schools, where the preponderance of informants were African American. And yet, many readers from anywhere in the English-speaking world might recognize some of the key lines. They might say, "Good Heavens! I remember that awful joke!" "I remember saying that insensitive taunt." "Geez—does my granddaughter say that?"

A final note before the children's voices are heard: This study is unique. What makes it so special is that it concentrates on a small triangle of cities centered in south Louisiana, and it continued for nearly fifty years. The triangle consists of Baton Rouge, New Orleans, and Lafayette, Louisiana, and their environs. I collected most of the material myself, carrying my hand-held tape recorder. I began collecting in the late 1960s, when I jotted down hand games I heard girls playing on the school grounds in New Orleans. I moved to Baton Rouge in 1973, where I taught at Louisiana State University for two years. It was in Baton Rouge that I began tape recording. In the earliest stages, two Baton Rouge teachers, Ethel Bridges and Janice Pierce, contributed games in the form of written material from their seventh-grade classrooms. They had asked their seventh graders to take home questionnaires and to interview their siblings and parents. In 1975, I moved back to New Orleans and continued to collect through the 1980s. In 1990, I moved to Lafayette, Louisiana, the "hub city" of Louisiana, as well as the center of Cajun culture. It was in Lafayette that I pursued my doctoral degree in English / folklore at University of Louisiana at Lafayette. My biggest regret looking back over those fifty years of collecting is that I did not manage to record more.

CHAPTER 1

Counting Out

When I asked children to tell me how they chose who was "it," I was surprised to see them point to their feet to count. In my childhood, every time we counted out, we used our fists or the tops of our heads. The children in south Louisiana consistently pointed to their feet. Counting out, or choosing who's "it," is as much a part of most games as the game itself. I watched boys spend their entire twenty-minute recess period negotiating who would be "it," and what game they would play—then the bell rang. This is one aspect of boys' play that sometimes contravenes the ideas of teachers and other adults. The adult mind says, "Get on with it!" The boys' minds say, "Hey, we could be Cylons, and you could be Dracons. And I'm gonna be head of the Cylons, and you can carry the spear. And all you other guys chase us. And . . ." Then an argument erupts over who, and what, and how—and soon the bell rings—and the boys walk off still arguing. Adults see this as unnecessary arguing. The boys see it as satisfying communication.

There are many ways of choosing who is "it," and children all over the world engage in it.[1] For south Louisiana children, both African American and other, the most popular count-out formula from the 1970s to 2017 was:

Eenie meenie minie moe
Catch a fella (monkey, ******, teacher, tiger)
By the toe
If he hollers let him go
Eenie meenie minie moe.[2]

—St. Joan of Arc bingo, African American girls; Andrew Jackson Elementary, 3rd-grade African American girls; Charles Gayarre Elementary, African American 3rd-grade boys; John Dibert Elementary, 5th- and 6th-grade African American and white girls and boys; Lusher Elementary, 3rd-grade white girl; Adolph Meyer Elementary, African American 3rd-grade boy; Eisenhower Elementary, 5th-grade African American boy, New Orleans[3]

At John Dibert, the girls in the fifth grade added, "Out go the cat / out go the rat / out go the lady in the big, blue hat." At both Lusher and Adolph Meyer, the fourth line was, "If he hollers make him pay / fifty dollars every day."

At Happy Face Nursery School in Chalmette, Louisiana (1977), second-grade white girls from St. Robert Bellarmine School chanted:

> Eenie meenie minie moe
> Catch a fella by the toe
> If he hollers let him go
> Eenie meenie minie moe.

Then they launched right into:

> Engine, engine number nine
> Going down Chicago line
> If the train goes off the track
> Do you want your money back?[4]

(JS) All right. And then do you do your hands? Or do you do your feet?
(Child) Feet, and whoever it lands on you gotta say, "Yes," and spell y-e-s, and say
   "with a dirty dish rag turned inside out."

What do children see in these formulas? It is no longer fashionable for folklorists to try to link them with ancient pagan rites or with secret Masonic passwords, as nineteenth century collectors sometimes did; but for children they are just as important as any magic formula or super-secret password. They satisfy a need for children to feel that they are fairly chosen for an unwelcome task—that of being "it."[5]

Some rhymes used for choosing "it" are also used for handclaps, for example:

> My mama and your mama
> Were hangin' out clothes
> My mama punched your mama
> Right in the nose.
> What color was the blood?
> Green
> G-R-E-E-N and you are not it.
> —John Dibert Elementary, 5th- and 6th-grade African American and white boys and girls;
> Andrew Jackson Elementary, 6th-grade African American girls, New Orleans

Another version of "My mama and your mama," was collected at McKinley Junior High School in Baton Rouge, Louisiana, in 1974. Again, it was used as both a handclap and a count out:

> My mama your mama
> Live across the street
> 1618 Beeston Street
> Every night they have a fight
> And this is what they say
> Boys are rotten just like cotton
> Girls are dandy just like candy
> Itsy bitsy soda water
> Itsy bitsy pooh
> Itsy bitsy soda water
> Out goes you.
> —*African American 7th-grade girls, Baton Rouge*

Short phrases used in nearly every New Orleans school included:

> Boy scout, camp out.
> —*John Dibert, 6th-grade African American girls; Andrew Jackson 3rd-grade African American girls,*
> *New Orleans*

> Girl scout, camp out.
> —*John Dibert Elementary, 6th-grade African American and white girls, New Orleans*

> Cub scout, camp out.
> —*Andrew Jackson Elementary, 3rd-grade African American girls, New Orleans*

Below are two counting-out formulas used both in New Orleans, and in Lafayette, Louisiana, in the nineteen forties when I was in grade school:

> One potato two potato three potato four
> Five potato six potato seven potato more.
> —*Eisenhower Elementary, 5th-grade African American boys and girls; Lusher, 5th-grade white girl; Beauregard*
> *Junior High, 7th-grade African American boys and girls—New Orleans; St. Genevieve Elementary, 3rd-grade white*
> *boys and girls, Lafayette; Ruthanna B. (white) Tulane Freshman student (learned in Cooperstown, New York)*

Engine engine number nine
Going down Chicago line
If your train goes off the track
Do you want your money back?
Yes
Y-E-S and you are truly not it.
—*John Dibert Elementary, 5th- and 6th-grade African American girls; Eisenhower Elementary, 5th-grade African American girls, New Orleans; Adolph Meyer Elementary, 5th-grade African American girls, Algiers, La.; St. Genevieve Elementary, 3rd-grade white boys and girls, Lafayette, La.*

One girl added to the end of "Engine engine," "With a dirty dishrag turned inside, outside, double-side out." This particular ending is very old and was reported to me by my parents, who lived in New Orleans as children, and by one of my English professors at the University of New Orleans, who recalled that it was used in the City Park area of New Orleans when he was a boy in the late 1920s. Henry Carrington Bolton, in *The Counting-Out Rhymes of Children*, cited twelve references to "dish clout."[6] "Engine engine" is sometimes used for jump rope and is also said in an abbreviated variant at times:

If your train goes off the track
Do you want your money back?
No
N-O spells no and you are truly not it.
—*St. Joan of Arc bingo, African American teenage girls; Beauregard Junior High, 7th-grade African American boys and girls, New Orleans*

Note that the shorter version above was collected from older children. As with handclap games, teenagers often forget the first part of counting-out formulas and remember only the key phrases or the chorus.

Many count outs are basically two-liners:

Bubblegum bubblegum in a dish
How many bubblegums do you wish?
Three
T-H-R-E-E and you are not it.
—*John Dibert Elementary, 6th-grade African American and white boys and girls; Eisenhower Elementary, 5th-grade African American boys and girls; Beauregard Junior High, 7th-grade African American boys and girls, New Orleans*

Popsicle popsicle in a dish
How many popsicles do you wish?
Two
T-W-O and you are not it.
—*Adolph Meyer Elementary, 5th-grade African American boys, Algiers, La.*

Itch bitch don't shit
Just because you're not it.
—*John Dibert, 5th-grade African American and white boys, New Orleans*

It bit don't shit
'Cause you know you're not it.
—*Charles Gayarre Elementary, 4th- and 5th-grade African American girls, New Orleans*

Ushy dushy ice cream
Ushy dushy out.
—*John Dibert Elementary, 5th- and 6th-grade African American girls, New Orleans*

I struck a match and the wind blew it out.
—*Adolph Meyer Elementary, 5th-grade African American girls, Algiers; Andrew Jackson Elementary, 3rd-grade African American girls, New Orleans*

Johnny struck a match and the wind blew it out.
—*Andrew Jackson Elementary, African American 3rd-grade girls, New Orleans*

Three horses in a stable
One jumped out.
—*Lacoste Elementary, white 4th-grade boys, Chalmette, La.*

I struck a match and the match went out.
—*St. Joan of Arc bingo, African American teenagers, New Orleans*

Tarzan climbed a tree and Tarzan fell out.
—*John Dibert Elementary African American and white 5th and 6th graders, New Orleans*

Mickey Mouse was building a house
How many nails did he use?
Ten
T-E-N with a dirty dishrag turned inside, double-side, triple-side out.
—*John Dibert Elementary, African American and white 6th-grade girls and boys, New Orleans;*
Lacoste Elementary, white 4th-grade boy, Chalmette, La.

Mickey Mouse built a house
How many nails did he use?
Five
F-I-V-E- spells five and you are truly it
With a dirty dishrag turned inside out and outside in
Around your neck.
—*St. Catherine of Siena Girl Scout Troop (1977), 7 white and 1 African American girl, Metairie, La.*

The following rhyme was given to me at one time as a handclap. Then it was chanted twice again as a count out:

2–4–6–8
Johnny had a rattlesnake
Snake died, Johnny cried
2–4–6–8.
—*Charles Gayarre Elementary African American and white 5th-grade girls; John Dibert Elementary,*
African American and white 6th-grade boys, New Orleans

Inky dinky donkey
Mary had a donkey
Donkey died, Mary cried
Inky dinky donkey.
—*John Dibert Elementary, African American and white 5th- and 6th-grade boys and girls, New Orleans*

Years later, in 1997, I recorded third-grade boys at J. W. Faulk Elementary School in Lafayette, Louisiana, telling me how to choose who is "it," using much the same formula:

(The single white boy.) We put our foot in, and we just count 'em out, and 'til the
last person who has their foot in is it.
(JS) OK Do you say anything when you do that?

(Boy) No—we just say—a little song.
(JS) How does that song go?
(Boy) Like—

> Icky picky ponky
> Daddy bought a donkey . . .

(He begins again.)

> Icky picky ponky
> Daddy bought a donkey
> Donkey died
> Daddy cried
> Icky picky ponky[7]
> And that—and that person has your finger on . . . on . . . your foot—um—

(Another boy.) You gotta take your foot out . . . your foot out, and makes you not
  it . . .

—*J. W. Faulk Elementary, white 3rd-grade boy, Lafayette, La.*

My aunt, who was a child in Eunice, Louisiana, in the 1920s, remembers
saying the following count out:

> Ipsy bipsy soda cracker
> Does your father chew tobacco
> Yes, my father chews tobacco
> Ipsy bipsy soda cracker
> O-U-T spells out.

It showed up again, slightly shortened, in New Orleans fifty-two years later:

> Itsy bitsy (or "icky picky") soda cracker
> Does you mama chew tobacco
> Yes.

—*Andrew Jackson Elementary, 3rd- and 4th-grade African American girls, New Orleans*

While it seems that there are threads of continuity in counting-out rhymes,
which lend similarity across time, children do like to introduce other ideas
as well:

Ike and Tina Turner
Ike and Tina boo
Ike and Tina Turner
Out goes you.
—*Charles Gayarre Elementary, 5th-grade African American girls, New Orleans*

At John Dibert Elementary, in a mixed class, a white boy recited:

Some people say that blacks don't steal
Caught one in my watermelon fiel'
Eatin' that watermelon, throwin' away the rime (sic)
Got my shotgun just on time—Boom!

Across town from John Dibert Elementary, a group of African American girls at Beauregard Junior High were videotaped singing the same counting-out formula, only this time they chanted the first line:

Some people say that *preachers* don't steal . . .

At the St. Joan of Arc bingo babysitting group an African American seven-year-old boy caused lots of giggling and hooting when he said:

I went to King Kong's house
And he kicked my black ass
OUT!
—*St. Joan of Arc bingo, African American 1st-grade boy, New Orleans*

At Adolph Meyer Elementary, another African American child chanted, "I went to King Kong's house / and he kicked me out." The whole class burst out laughing at the child who said it, and they yelled, "That ain't the way it goes!" They refused, however, to tell me the real way it went in front of their teacher. Over the years I have spent collecting folklore in classrooms, I have seen very few cases where the students felt totally free to speak out in the presence of their teachers.

There are various ways of choosing who is "it" without a verbal formula. Some children at John Dibert Elementary told me that they flipped a coin for "heads" or "tails." In some cases, the group ran to a designated place, the last one to arrive was then "it" (*John Dibert 5th- and 6th-grade boys*). Andrew

Jackson Elementary third-grade girls said, "When Florida go out to play, she point, and that person 'it.'" Sometimes everybody shouts "not it," and the last person to shout, is "it." A sixth-grade African American girl at Andrew Jackson Elementary once told me, "I always tell 'em who gonna be 'it' and they 'it,' 'cause if they not, I beats 'em up."

In this chapter, and those that follow, the material is presented in two ways. Some rhymes and games appear alone, followed by a tag denoting the source. Each chapter also contains some example of direct transcript. These transcribed passages feature my voice, (JS), and the voices of children being interviewed.

I include the transcripts for two reasons. One, each child's speech is noticeably individualized and of interest to anyone who might wish to study speech patterns. And, two, as I pointed out in the introduction, I made mistakes while interviewing. Sometimes I talked too much. Sometimes I barreled on and missed an opportunity to draw certain speakers out more. Reading the transcripts could help future interviewers to avoid my mistakes.

One of the recordings I made was at St. Genevieve School, Lafayette, Louisiana (1997). I was familiar with the school, as I had attended St. Genevieve School from kindergarten to eighth grade back in the late nineteen-forties and early nineteen-fifties. The informants were three white second-grade girls, three white second-grade boys, and one black second-grade boy. Toward the end of the tape, three fourth-grade white girls, two white fourth-grade boys, and three sixth-grade white girls joined us.

The following transcription, included almost in its entirety, illustrates the manner in which many recording sessions proceeded. I appeared, introduced myself, and set up my tape recorder. In this case, I set up on a table in an echoing cafeteria, where the children gathered and organized themselves into two groups. Girls, with a self-appointed lead girl, and boys with a self-appointed lead boy, stepped forward. The first lead girl, a second grader, began the session by interviewing *me*:

(JS) The microphone is very small.
(Lead girl) A microphone?
(JS) Yes. This is February 21, 1997, and I am recording at St. Genevieve School, Lafayette, Louisiana.
(Lead girl) Why do you want us?
(JS) Why do I want you? That's a good question. The reason I'm asking you to be my interviewees is that I went to school here when I was a kid.

(Lead girl) How long will this take?

(JS) I don't know. I don't know how long exactly it's gonna take, but what I want
    you to do . . .

(Lead girl) How old were you when you came here?

(Me) I was—hum—let's see—I started out—OK—it was a long time ago, be-
    cause I started out, I was in kindergarten, and I came here all the way to the
    eighth grade . . .

(Lead girl) That's when me and Alison started.

(JS) Yeah.

(Lead girl) You was in eighth grade here?

(JS) Yes, I graduated from the eighth grade here, and then I went to Teurlings. I
    finished up at Teurlings.

(Lead girl) There was—now there is only the sixth grade.

(JS) Huh.

(Lead girl) Because they . . .

(JS) OK. This is what I want to know. When y'all go outside, and play any kind of
    game; how do you choose who is "it"? What do you say?

(Lead boy) We put our—we put our feet . . . we put our two feet in, and we say,
    "Mickey Mouse stuck his finger up his butt / How many inches did it go?
    (Laughter.) And then you say . . .

(JS) Would you repeat that one? I've never heard it before. Say it again?

(Lead boy) Mickey Mouse stuck his finger up his butt / How many inches did it go?

(JS) And you count out?

(Lead boy) You pick how many inches you want, and you count, and you say,
    "You are surely not it for the rest of your life." And wherever it lands on, you
    could take a . . . and you do it over and over until the last one, and the last
    one left is "it." (Noise level rises as boys begin to shout in background.)

(JS) Boys, I can't do anything if you are gonna scream and holler—hold it—

(Tape off)

(Tape on)

(JS) We are going to begin again. You—you had another way of choose—of
    counting out? Or choosing who's gonna be "it"?

(Boy) We have another one.

(JS) How does yours go?

(Boy) Mickey Mouse built a house / What color was it?

(JS) And then what?

(Boy) And then, like, purple—like—p-u-r-p-l-e, and then—you are not it—we—
    whoever is left—whoever it lands on, is not "it."

(JS) OK And what is your other one?

(Boy) King Cut had a butt / What color was it?

(Another boy corrects him.) King KONG had a butt / What color was it? Any color, and then you do sumpin' like we did for Mickey Mouse—stuck his finger up his butt . . .

(Laughter from the boys, and giggles from the girls.) Yeah!

(JS) What was the first one? King Cut?

(Boy) King Cut . . .

(Another boy) KING KONG! King KONG had a butt / What color was it? Whatever color . . . then you are not "it" for the rest of your life, life, life!

(JS) OK Then how do you do it?

(Boy) You say King Kong had a butt / What color was it? And then you say p-u-r-p-l-e.

(JS) Is that what you do? And whoever it lands on, then they are "it"?

(Lead boy) It's what color is it. We go what color is it, you see, and you pick a color, then you spell that color, then you go "life, life, life, life."

(JS) Life, life, life, life—how many times?

(Lead boy) About three.

(JS) OK.

(Another boy) Bubblegum bubblegum in a dish / How many pieces do you wish? Then you say a number—then you go 1–2–3, and you are not "it," and then . . .

(Screaming starts in the background.)

(JS) Excuse me for just a moment—I'm sorry, but you are going to have to go outside because I cannot record if you are making that much noise. (I shoo people out.)

(Girls) We have another one, and it goes "Ink pink, you stink," and there's another one . . ."Girl Scouts / Camp out" . . .

(Boys) We have another one for us—"Boy Scouts camp out / Girls chicken out."

(JS) Girls chicken out? OK. All right, when you go to play marbles, how do you choose who's gonna be the first one to play marbles?

(The interview wanders away from counting out here, but I let it go on because it includes primary examples of struggle for domination between the second-grade boys and girls.)

(Boy) We don't play marbles—we can only play it on Friday—like today—we can play marbles . . . we don't always have a little piece of chalk, so we take a rock, and it's white, and we make sure it does, and we just draw.

(JS) Where do you make the circle when you play marbles?

(Boy) Either over there, or over there . . . (indicating two hard surfaces—a concrete walkway, and the asphalt parking area beside St. Genevieve Church.)

(Boy) Yeah, usually right there.

(JS) It's on a concrete surface? You play marbles on the concrete?

(Boy) Yeah. We don't really . . . we don't really think about playing in the dirt. We
    don't want to get dirty.

(Girl) We don't really play marbles.

(JS) How do you lag?

(Boy) What do you mean, "lag"?

(JS) You don't lag to play marbles? What are the rules when you play marbles?

(Boy) Well, since we never really play, we have rules, like, you can't take the
    marble and throw it at the balls. You can flick it, or just kinda push it, but you
    can't run in the circle, and knock 'em out whenever they not looking.

(JS) OK. So you have to . . . how do you shoot?

(Boy) You shoot . . . you put your fingers (The boys show the traditional marble
    placed against index finger and middle finger / thumb, push off from there,
    method.) You put it like this—or you put it like this (He demonstrates the
    shoot the marble off the end of the index finger with the thumb method.)

(JS) All right. What is another game y'all have? (I face the girls.)

(Girls look lost) We have . . . we have . . . um . . .

(JS) Do you do handclaps?

(Girls) Uh . . . yeah.

(JS) Show me one—stand up—OK, guys, let them do. (As the girls stood, the
    boys' noise level rose.)

(Girls)

> Mailman mailman do your duty
> I've got a big sister 'Merican beauty
> She can do the pom pom
> She can do the twist
> But most of all she can kiss kiss kiss
> K-i-s-s-kiss kiss[8]

(The girls fall into side splits.)

(Girls) Oh! Ow o wow!

(JS) So when they say, "kiss," they do a split sideways. Does the one that hit the
    ground win? Or is there any kind of rule here?

(Lead girl) No!

(Second girl) Whoever doesn't hit the ground first they . . . whoever hits the
    ground last they win. (?)

(Lead girl) We have another one that . . . put in the foot . . . when put their foot
    they say:

> Boys go to Jupiter
> To get more stupider.

(Boys) No! Never! We say girls go to . . .
(Girls) We have a . . . we have another one!
(Boys) You shut up! . . . WE have another . . .
(Girls) Girls go to . . .
(Boys) You shut up! . . . Man! Boys go . . .
(Another boy, hurriedly.)

> Boys go to college
> To get more knowledge—YES!

(Lead boy)

> Girls go to marbles
> To get more barbles.

(Girls giggle)
(Boy in the back of the room shouts.) Yeah! Formalatoo!
(JS) OK, enough.
(Giggling from the girls.)
(Boy)

> Y'ALL go to Jupiter
> To get more stupider.

(Girls continue to giggle while they try to think.)
(Boy)

> Y'all go to Jupiter
> And get more loopiter . . .

(Girls)

> Boys are rotten
> Made out of cotton
> Girls are sexy
> Made out of Pepsi!

(JS) Girls are sexy / Made out of Pepsi?

(Wild giggling from the girls.)

(JS) All right . . . let's get something from the boys. (The boys are straining forward and elbowing the girls out of the way.) All right, guys, what's one of the songs that y'all can sing?

(Girls) I know one!

(JS, facing the boys.) You don't sing any songs?

(Lead boy) We don't do like the girls—we different—we play football, sports—but we don't do nuttin' . . .

(JS) Do you play tag games?

(Lead boy) Yeah! "Chinese Freeze Tag"!

(JS) OK. Tell me.

(Lead boy) That's our main game! "Chinese Freeze Tag" is if you get somebody—if you get 'em three times, they frozen.

(Lots of noise in background.)

(JS) OK. So how do you choose who is "it" for "Chinese Freeze Tag"?

(Boy) The same thing.

(JS) OK. One of those Micky Mouse things?

(Boy) It's not like Mickey Mouse—It's like he said—King Kong had a butt / What color was it?

(Another boy) No, it wasn't like that either.

(Noisy argument breaks out—unintelligible for a few seconds. I hear "Chase—three times—".)

(JS) And then who is "it"—who has to chase you? And he has to hit you three times?

(Boy, hurriedly) No, it's like a bubble . . . No, one time like this . . . he's froze . . . then another time (Someone says, "Freeze, freeze, freeze, freeze.")—They have to go under his legs. They have to go under his legs, and tap him right by the legs. (Laughter from the listeners.)

(Boy) Tap him under his legs, or go under his legs . . .

(JS) You're it? You touch him, and he's frozen . . .

(Boy) Yeah! Yeah!

(JS) How does he . . . you go under his legs?

(Boy) No, I don't—I don't go under somebody—that's not—"IT" goes under his legs.

(Second boy) Somebody that's NOT "it" goes under his legs.

(JS) So, while he's frozen—I've got to get this straight, because . . .

(Lead boy) We go like this—we tap him, and he's frozen. Then they go under his legs.

(JS) While he's frozen—the people who are NOT "it" go under his legs, and when he goes under your legs, then you're free? (I am beginning to feel like this sounds like a Monty Python skit.)

(Lead boy) Yeah.

(JS) And what about tapping him three times?

(Lead boy) After you're unfrozen—if he taps you two more times—you "it."

(JS) OK. I got it.

(The noise level rises. The girls are clamoring to be heard, and the boys are physically restraining them by edging closer and closer to me.)

(JS) All right—just a minute—I want to get the girls.

(The girls are ready with a variant of a handclap featuring "Miss Suzy".)

> Miss Suzy had a steamboat
> The steamboat had a bell
> Miss Suzy went to heaven
> The steamboat went to hel-
> Lo operator, give me number nine
> And if you disconnect me, I kick
> You in the
> Behind the refrigerator
> There was a piece of glass
> Miss Suzy sat upon it
> And broke her big fat
> Ask me no more questions
> And tell me no more lies
> Miss Suzy's in the bathtub
> With fifty other guys
> Eating chocolate pies
> Zipping up their flies.[9]

(Girls break up giggling.)

(Boys shouting) We want to say something!

(Giggles continue among girls.)

(JS) Yes? The boys want to say something.

(The boys, desperate to be heard, shout.) King Cut had a (Mumble.) / What color was it?

(Loud giggles from girls.)

(JS) I can't hear you now . . .

(Boys, louder) King Cut had a house (?) / What color was it?

(JS) Has a what?

(Boy) Just like a-s-s.

(JS) Oh, like a "butt." What color was it?

(Boy) Yeah—we told you that one. We told you that, but this is sort of like a different one.

(Lead boy shouts) King Kong had a butt / What color was his HEAD?

(Boys, all out-shouting the girls, who are clamoring to offer a new game.) Hey— we got another one!

(JS) OK. What?

(Boy) "TV Freeze Tag."

(JS) OK what's "TV Freeze Tag"?

(Boy) Like, you say the name of a show—and then, you duck. You say the name of a show and then you duck—and then—and then—you—they can't get you. But after ten seconds, you gotta get up, and then you gotta keep on runnin' les' you . . .

(Here the girls interrupt, and insist on playing the handclap "Miss Suzy" again.) Soon the bell rings and the session ends.

    —St. Genevieve Elementary School, 2nd-, 3rd-, 4th-grade white boys and girls, Lafayette, La.

This is one taping incident where I allowed the boys and girls to yell louder than each other and muscle in on the space in front of the microphone. In some sessions I exercised more control over elbowing and pushing forward to get to the front. In this case, it seemed that the struggle to be heard was so much a part of the group dynamics, that I taped it all.

Things I gathered from re-reading the first part of the counting-out chapter: It seems that half the fun for kids rests in a desire to shock. Using formulas like "It bit don't shit / Just because you're not 'it.'" And "I went to King Kong's house / And he kicked my black ass / OUT!" the children from New Orleans and Chalmette elicited a giggling, hand over the mouth, response; naughtiness that made the speaker stand out.

In the transcript from St. Genevieve second graders, I extrapolated a few added items: The St. Genevieve respondents were eight and nine years old, and like the children in New Orleans, they, too, enjoyed shocking the hearer. The first count out offered by the lead boy, was "Mickey Mouse stuck his finger up his butt / How many inches did it go?" This caused the boys in the background to begin to "scream and holler" so much that the tape recorder had to be turned off for a minute.

The St. Genevieve second-grade boys and girls were articulate, quick witted, and confrontational.

At their early age, the second-grade boys and girls from St. Genevieve were already engaged in responding to one another in combative ways. When given a chance, the girls challenged the boys with words and wit and giggles; while the boys resorted repeatedly to shouts, loud noise, insults, and physical gestures.

In summary, the varied counting-out formulas above give some semblance of fairness to choosing "it," but most children soon learn how to manipulate the rhymes so that the count lands on whom they want. The chooser can skip a beat, add a line, or simply pass over his friend's fists or toes while counting, so the counting out ends on the person he has chosen.

The last entry for counting out comes from a freshman student I interviewed at Tulane University. Ruthanna, who is white, was from Cooperstown, New York, and she recalled more than an hour's worth of schoolyard lore. I asked her, "When you were playing chase games or outside, how did you choose the first person to be 'it'?" Her answer was, "Um . . . well, sometimes we just said the youngest one was going to be 'it,' because that was usually me, and I couldn't run as fast as the others. Sometimes we would say, um, we would say . . . Last person to holler 'I' is 'it,' and the last person to holler got to be 'it.' And there were counting things . . . 'One potato, two potato, three potato four—five potato, six potato, seven potato, more;'[10] and then we had, um, 'Engine engine number nine, going down Chicago line, if the train goes off the track, do you want your money back?' and we had with the girls . . . we had . . . 'My mother punched your mother right in the nose' . . . no . . . how did it go? 'My mother and your mother were hanging out clothes. My mother punched your mother right in the nose. What color was the blood? R-E-D spells red and you are 'it.' Those are the basic ones we did."

Ruthanna was nineteen years old at the time I collected from her, and these counting-out rhymes were almost word for word the same as those used by second and third graders in and around New Orleans and Lafayette, Louisiana, hundreds of miles from Cooperstown, New York. Further memories from Ruthanna reflect more negotiations around being "it."

(JS) Was there any argument among the kids about who was "it"?

(Ruthanna) Always. ALWAYS. You couldn't have it any other way. And usually my older brother, who was always the oldest, would say, "OK calm down. I'll be 'it,'" just to shut us up. And I always got caught anyway, because I was the youngest. My two brothers were older than me, and all the others in the area; all of them in the block were usually two years older than me. And if anybody got adamant about not wanting to be "it," they would say, "Let *me* be 'it,' because we are all gonna catch Ruthanna anyway . . ." (Laughs.) Which was true. I always got caught first. And then my brothers would always end up helping me because I never could catch anybody. I was just a short, stubby little kid, and I could not run . . . very fast . . . and, uh, and I would get very upset because I would run and run, and I could never catch anybody. My oldest brother . . . usually my oldest brother . . . would say, "Well, I'll help you *this* time." And we'd catch everybody. (Laughs.)

—*Ruthanna B. white freshman Tulane student from Cooperstown, NY, taped in New Orleans*

JUST FOR FUN

Out of curiosity, I "Googled" "Eenie meenie minie moe" on January 28, 2020. "Wikipedia" popped up immediately with several pages of information, including 1. Current versions / 2. Origins / 3. American and British versions / 4. Variations / 5. Controversies / 6. Popular culture [6.1 Music / 6.2 Literature / 6.3 Film and television] / 7. See also / 8. References.

Interestingly, under "Origins," references to "divining," "oracle," and "heathen priest song" appeared. It is up to the reader to decide whether these origins might be factual.

CHAPTER 2

Ring Games

Ring games are played in a circle, standing or sitting. Like counting out and handclaps, there is a lot of interchange; the same game one set of girls play in a circle, can, with another group, become a handclap or be played in a line. Very small children often enjoy circle games. They give the players a sense of security since everyone holds hands, and they are often easily memorized.

The first one is from St. Rita Catholic School and was collected at the International Year of the Child Celebration held in Lafayette Square, New Orleans, 1979:

> Round in a circle, round again
> Round in a circle, say your name,
> Rhonda,
> Richard,
> Kelly,
> Paul . . .
> —*2nd-grade white boys and girls, St. Rita Catholic School, New Orleans*

In 1974, a group of African American girls from McKinley Junior High School in Baton Rouge performed their circle game. The girls began by holding hands and stepping to the right for "Round in circles / Each one goes." Then they dropped their hands and stepped back one step for the motions which followed:

> Round in circles
> Each one goes
> Borrow nice (*Reach hands grasping toward sky.*)
> Borrow twice (*Grasp twice towards sky.*)
> Bend down and plant some rice (*Bend down as though planting.*)

Run your hands into the sky (*Reach hands again towards sky.*)
Let them down and move your (thigh?) (*Shake hips.*)
Clap your hands
Stomp your feet
Simple clap and that's complete.

The same Junior High girls remained in the circle and continued:

A tootsie tootsie a tootsie roll
I say—a tootsie tootsie a tootsie roll
We touch the ground (*All touch the ground.*)
A tootsie tootsie a tootsie roll
We turn around (*All turn.*)
A tootsie tootsie a tootsie roll
We come sides (*All shuffle to side.*)
A tootsie tootsie a tootsie roll
We do the fish (*All make swimming motion.*)
A tootsie tootsie a tootsie roll
We do the jerk (*All dance the "jerk."*)
A tootsie tootsie a tootsie roll
And the popcorn (*Dance with hands pumping up.*)
A tootsie tootsie a tootsie roll.

(*This can be extended as long as the caller can think of things to do.*)
—*McKinley Junior High School, African American girls, Baton Rouge*

A group of third graders at Andrew Jackson Elementary played another circle game, one that is very old and a favorite with kindergarten teachers:

A-tisket a-tasket a green and yellow basket
I wrote a letter to my mother
And on the way I dropped it
A little girl picked it up and she put it in her pocket
Her pocket.
—*Andrew Jackson Elementary, 3rd-grade African American girls, New Orleans; St. Genevieve Elementary, white girls (1940s), Lafayette, La.*

The players sat in a circle and one player went around skipping. She dropped the "letter," usually a handkerchief or a folded note, behind one player, who then got up, and chased her around the circle. If the one who dropped the object was caught, she then had to get in the center of the circle as a prisoner. "A-Tisket a- Tasket" was also popular on the playgrounds at St. Genevieve School, Lafayette, Louisiana, in the 1940s. The nun who taught kindergarten utilized it for rainy day play, and the children carried it onto the outdoor play spaces.[1]

> Motorboat, motorboat, go so slow
> Motorboat, motorboat, go so fast
> Motorboat, motorboat, step on the gas!
> —*White kindergarteners, Lacoste Elementary, Chalmette, La.*

The children made a circle, holding hands. They moved in the circle, slow, then faster, then as fast as they could, and all fell down laughing.[2]

> Roller coaster, roller coaster, go so fast
> Roller coaster, roller coaster, step on the gas
> We go round in a circle and we dance
> And when you fall—You OUT!
> —*John Dibert Elementary, 6th-grade African American girls, New Orleans*

The girls played "Roller coaster" in a circle, and when they said, "You out!" the girls in the circle suddenly sat down. The last person to "fall," had to get out of the circle.

The white seven-year-old girls at St. Rita Catholic School, and the African American third graders at Andrew Jackson Elementary all played the "Hoky Poky." This game is a great favorite with kindergarten teachers. I collected it as part of supervised playtime activities, as well as unsupervised recess play, on the playground. The New Orleans children sang:

> Here we go loopty loo
> Here we go loopty lie
> Here we go loopty loo
> All on a Saturday night.
> You put your right foot in
> You take your right foot out
> You put your right foot in and
> You shake it all about
> You do the hoky poky

And you turn yourself around
That's what it's all about.

(Then you repeat the pattern again, using left foot, right arm, left arm, head, back-
side, entire body.)[3]
—*St. Rita Catholic School, 1st-grade white girls; Andrew Jackson Elementary,*
3rd-grade African American girls, New Orleans

"Who stole the cookie," which follows, is usually played by small children. It was, however, one of the favorites for African American third-grade girls at Andrew Jackson Elementary. They quickly arranged themselves into a circle, and one girl appointed herself leader:

(*Girl starts*) Who stole the cookie from the cookie jar?
(*Second girl*) Number one stole the cookie from the cookie jar.
(*Third girl*) Who me?
(*All girls*) Yes you!
(*Third girl*) Couldn't be.
(*All girls*) Then who?
(*First girl*) Number two stole the cookie from the cookie jar.
(*Fourth girl*) Who me?
(All girls) Yes you! (*And so on around the circle of girls playing and clapping from side
to side.*)[4]
—*Andrew Jackson Elementary, 3rd-grade African American girls, New Orleans*

"Casserella," which follows, was played in a circle, with one central player doing the motions, and all the girls making the ring as imitators. The game was videotaped at Beauregard Junior High, and collected on audiotape at McDonogh High School, Andrew Jackson Elementary (3rd and 6th graders), John Dibert Elementary (5th graders), and at the St. Joan of Arc bingo babysitting venue. The following example was performed by African American third and sixth graders, at Andrew Jackson Elementary, New Orleans:

Look who's here Casserella Casserella

(*All girls circle and clap while center girl claps with them; then, on "What can you do"
center girl does a dance step and all girls imitate her.*)
Look who's here Casserella it's you.
What can you do Casserella Casserella

What can you do Casserella it's you.
We can do it too Casserella Casserella
We can do it too
Casserella it's you.
Choose your partner Casserella Casserella
Choose your partner Casserella it's you. (*Center girl closes eyes, spins and chooses new center girl.*)[5]

—*Beauregard Junior High School, African American girls; McDonogh High School, African American teenagers; Andrew Jackson Elementary 3rd- and 6th-grade African American girls; St. Joan of Arc bingo, African American teenagers, New Orleans*

When the Andrew Jackson girls played "Casserella," they made comments on the center performer while they clapped and sang. If they liked her performance, there were grunts, and remarks of approval. If she moved badly, there were statements like "She can't dance" or "She move bad." As each new partner was chosen, the number of girls in the center doubled (1, then 2, then 4, then 8). All the girls in the center were supposed to move identically on "What can you do Casserella." There was some dissention among the players over what steps to do.

The sixth-grade African American girls at Andrew Jackson Elementary made a large circle and played "Step Back Sally." There was no central performer in this play; all girls in the circle moved in unison:

Let's go zoodio zoodio zoodio (*Clap for first two lines.*)
Let's go zoodio all night long
Oh you step back Sally Sally Sally (*Step back together.*)
Walkin' through the alley alley alley (*Walk into the circle together.*)
I peep through the window (*Put hands to face.*)
And what do I see (*Hand on forehead.*)
A big fat man from Tennessee (*Hands held wide.*)
My mama called the Doctor and the Doctor said
I got a pain in my tummy (*Hold stomach.*)
Oo chee ah!
I got a pain in my head (*Hands to head.*)
(Boy shouts, "I got a pain in my nose!")
Oo chee ah!
I got a pain in my leg (*Hold leg.*)
Oo chee ah!
I got a pain in my arm (*Hold arm.*)

Oo chee ah!
I got a pain everywhere (*Shimmy all over.*)
Oo chee ah!
—*Andrew Jackson Elementary, 6th-grade African American girls, New Orleans*

The sixth-grade boys, who had so far been trying their best to disrupt the play, gave up, and now joined the circle. Boys and girls together continued with this chant:

We gonna kick over (*Kick forward.*)
Side to side (*Kick right leg to side.*)
We gonna kick under (*Kick backward.*)
Side to side (*Kick left leg to side.*)
We gonna kick over (*Kick forward.*)
Side to side (*Kick right leg to side.*)
Round and round (*Swivel hips.*)
We gonna kick over (*Kick forward.*)
Round and round (*Swivel hips.*)
We gonna kick over (*Kick forward.*)
Round and round. (*Swivel hips.*)

(The girls keep up with each other, kicking and circling their hips, while the boys clown around and do anything to confuse the play.)
—*Andrew Jackson Elementary, 6th-grade African American girls and boys, New Orleans*

The same sixth-grade girls from Andrew Jackson began to chant "This-a-way that-a-way," and the boys interrupted, shouting, "Y'all shouldn't play that!" The girls continued:

This-a-way that–a-way (*Girls rock hips backward and forward.*)
This-a-way that-a-way
This-a-way that-a-way
All night long
Try miss it miss it (*Hop back, then thrust hips forward.*)
Try miss it miss it
All night long

(The boys began to squeal and shout like they did when someone was saying something naughty.)

We got another one
Just like the other one
This-a-way that-a-way
This-a-way that-a-way
This-a-way that-a-way
All night long
Try miss it miss it
Try miss it miss it (*Boys shouted and broke in and stopped the chant.*)

(Boy) Oooooh Lawd! Try miss it miss it / Try miss it miss it!
(Another boy) Y'all shouldn't play that!

Girls in the ring broke up laughing and stood aside for the next group to be recorded.

—*African American 6th-grade boys and girls, Andrew Jackson Elementary, New Orleans*

This next game can be played either as a handclap, a line game, or, as in this case, a circle game. Here, the Andrew Jackson African American third graders stood in a circle, and clapped their hands while they chanted:

My name is Jean (*Single player steps to center.*)
Check (*Chorus of players.*)
Then come-a Dinette
Check
I in the dirt
Check
I'm nine years old
Check
My sign is Scorpio
Check
My bad Scorpio
Check
Some chirrun don't like me
Check
They stay to fight me
Check
And I'm a bad bad bad bad bad one
Check (*Center player steps back and joins the circle.*)
My name is Terry (*New girl steps in.*)

Check
I goin' to Jackson
Check
I'm a Libra
Check
So check me out
Check.

(The players stopped in confusion.)
—*Andrew Jackson Elementary, 3rd-grade African American girls, New Orleans*

As soon as the third graders stopped, the sixth-grade girls were ready to perform again. They bustled about and arranged all the boys and the girls into two lines. They then began to clap and sing, "Soul Train, Soul Train," while players paired off and danced down the center between the two rows. The group clapped hands and shouted and grunted and laughed in encouragement as the dancers processed two by two down the center space. The boys joined in but made a lot of noise about it. Wow, this was a fifteen-minute riotous dance fest, and I did not have a video camera at that time!

Soul Train Soul Train
Da da da da da da da da
Da da da da da da da da
Soul train Soul train
Da da da da da da da da
Da da da da da da da da
Oh da da da duh da da
Oh da da da duh da da.

(Repeated as long as the performers continued, with constant comment on dancers from the sidelines.)[6]
—*Andrew Jackson Elementary, 6th-grade African American girls and boys, New Orleans*

At Eisenhower Elementary School, in Algiers, Louisiana, a suburb of New Orleans on the west bank of the Mississippi River, the girls played another circle game where there was a center player who did the motions, and all the other players imitated her:

Mary had a party (*Leader—Clapping, and stepping side to side.*)
Pizza pizza daddy-o (*Chorus.*)
How you know it? (*Leader.*)
Pizza pizza daddy-o
'Cause you tole me
Pizza pizza daddy-o
You're a (unclear)
Pizza pizza daddy-o
You're another one
Pizza pizza daddy-o
Do the front swim (*Center player does front swim motion*
Pizza pizza daddy-o (*with arms.*) (*All imitate.*)
Do the backwards (*Back swim motion with arms.*)
Pizza pizza daddy-o (*All imitate.*)
Do it underwater (*Hold nose, shimmy, raise one arm.*)
Pizza pizza daddy-o (*All imitate.*)
Do it on top of water (*Swim front again.*)
Pizza pizza daddy-o (*All imitate.*)
Do the monkey (*Dance steps.*)
Pizza pizza daddy-o
Now turn aroun' and touch the groun'.

(A girl explains, "And they have to go around, and whoever they pointing at when they stop, they have to go to the center of the circle.")
—*Eisenhower Elementary, 4th-grade African American girls, Algiers, La.*

Across the Mississippi River, in New Orleans, near City Park, the fifth-grade girls at John Dibert Elementary also played "Pizza Pizza":

Mary havin' a baby (*Single caller.*)
Pizza pizza daddy-o (*All chant.*)
How you know it? (*Group asks.*)
Pizza pizza daddy-o (*All chant.*)
'Cuz she tole me (*Single caller.*)
Pizza pizza daddy-o (*All chant.*)
You a liar (*Single caller.*)
Pizza pizza daddy-o (*All chant.*)
You another one (*Second caller.*)
Pizza pizza daddy-o (*All chant.*)

Backstroke (*Caller "backstrokes."*)
Pizza pizza daddy-o (*All imitate.*)
Underwater (*Caller does breaststroke motion.*)
Pizza pizza daddy-o (*All imitate.*)
Do the dog (*Caller does jerky dance.*)
Pizza pizza daddy-o (*All imitate.*)
Front stroke. (*Puts arms out in Australian crawl.*)
—*African American and white girls, John Dibert, New Orleans*

The girls from John Dibert stopped at this point, and one African American girl then went on to explain the next circle game. I taped this conversation:

(Girl) Here comes Dana walking near the street . . .
(A girl interrupts.) Oh, I know that!
(JS) Wait, let her say it.
(The first girl continues with this detailed explanation.)
Here she stops right in front of you, and she starts to dancin', and you do the
     same thing she does, and then the person who stopped in front of you, you
     have to go, um, have to go walk, you gotta walk around the circle, and go
     stop in front of another person, and do the same thing.
(JS) Do you play that in a line or a ring?
(The informant says.) We play it in a circle, and at school, and at home.
(JS) How does it go?
(First girl)

Here comes Dana walkin' down the street
She didn't know what to do so she stopped in front of you.

(The girl then explains.) All right then, she does something, a dance.
(JS) And you have to imitate what she's doing?
(Girl) Yeah, you gotta walk around the circle and do it again.
—*John Dibert Elementary, 5th-grade African American girls, New Orleans*

Some chants can be performed in a line as well as in a circle. The following used two lines facing each other, with the leader chanting and demonstrating the leg motions:

Ching Chong Chinaman (*Jump—clap—jump.*)
Sitting on a fence (*Jump—clap—jump.*)

Tryin' to make a dollar (*Jump—clap—jump.*)
Out of fifty-nine cents (*Jump—clap—jump.*)
He missed, he missed, he missed like this.

(The girls jumped up and down, crossing their legs in various poses. The leader set the pattern. If any girl did not follow the set pattern, she missed.)[7]
—*St. Catherine of Siena Girl Scouts (1977), Metairie, La. (7 white, 1 African American)*

At McKinley Junior High School in Baton Rouge (1974), the girls also lined up in two lines, faced one another, and chanted:

Chinese checkerboard sittin' on a fence
Tryin' to make a dollar out of fifteen cents
He missed, he missed, he missed like this!

(This was repeated over and over, and each time the feet were moved in a different pattern. Each girl took her turn and stepped up as leader. All followed the leader's pattern, which, as the game went on, became faster and faster—the one girl who managed to follow all steps "won.")
—*McKinley Junior High, African American girls, Baton Rouge*

The next ring game comes from three- and four-year-olds at Louise Day Care Center in New Orleans (1977). This is a camp song, a nursery school song, and, obviously, a schoolyard song as well:

If you're happy and you know it clap your hands (*Clap clap.*)
If you're happy and you know it clap your hands (*Clap clap.*)
If you're happy and you know it
Then you really oughta show it
If you're happy and you know it clap your hands (*Clap clap.*)
(Go through the same thing and "stomp your feet" (*Stomp stomp.*); shout "hooray!"
(*Hooray hooray.*); then you "shake your head" (*Shake shake.*) End with "Shout hooray.
(HOORAY!")
—*Louise Day Care Center 3- and 4-year-old African American girls, New Orleans*

"Concentration" and "Categories," are types of games where the players sit or stand in a circle and keep a steady rhythm of clap, clap, snap snap (*the fingers*), slap slap (*the thighs*), while supplying various topics to specific headings.[8] These games are closely related to the next handclap. Here a group of sixth

graders from Andrew Jackson Elementary in New Orleans, stood, made a
circle, and clapped side to side:

> Hands up to eighty-five (*Clap clap.*)
> You gonna git it (*Clap clap.*)
> Name some (*Clap clap.*)
> Girls (*Clap clap.*)
> Wanna piece (*Clap clap.*)
> We loraleese (*Clap clap.*)
> My agitation (*Clap clap.*)
> My destination (*Clap clap.*)
> Rhonda (*Clap clap.*)
> Sheila (*Clap clap.*)
> Denise. (*Clap clap.*)

When a girl hesitated before naming someone, she was out.

Then the Andrew Jackson Elementary African American third grade girls
stepped up and played their variant of "Hands Up to Eighty-Five":

> Hands up to eighty-five (*Clap clap.*)
> Gonna get it (*Clap clap.*)
> That's a (*Clap clap.*)
> Girl (*Clap clap.*)
> Wanna piece (*Clap clap.*)
> Dolora leece (*clap clap*)
> Your allocation (*Clap clap.*)
> Your destination (*Clap clap.*)
> No hesitation (*Clap clap.*)
> Glenda (*Clap clap.*)
> Margaret (*Clap clap.*)
> Felicia (*Clap clap.*)

> Uh—wait—(*Girls giggle and point, "You out!"*)
> —*Andrew Jackson Elementary, 3rd- and 6th-grade African American girls, New Orleans*

The next circle game comes from African American kindergarten and first-
grade girls at Beechwood Elementary School in Baton Rouge (1975). It is
familiar to me because I remember playing the identical game in the late
1940s at St. Genevieve School in Lafayette, Louisiana:

Head and shoulders, Baby (*Touch head and shoulders.*)

1–2–3 (*Head, shoulders, head.*)

Head and shoulders, Baby (*Touch head and shoulders.*)

1–2–3 (*Head, shoulders, head.*)

Head and shoulders, head and shoulders, head and shoulders, Baby

1–2–3

Knees and ankles, Baby (*Tap knees and ankles.*)

1–2–3

Knees and ankles, Baby

1–2–3

Knees and ankles, knees and ankles, knees and ankles, Baby

1–2–3

Waist and thighs, Baby (*Tap waist and thighs.*)

1–2–3

Waist and thighs, Baby

1–2–3

Waist and thighs, waist and thighs, waist and thighs, Baby

1–2–3

Push the baby, Baby (*Pretend pushing a baby carriage.*)

1–2–3

Push the baby, Baby

1–2–3

Push the baby, Baby, push the baby, Baby, push the baby, Baby

1–2–3

Boogie woogie, Baby (*Dance jauntily.*)

1–2–3

Boogie woogie, Baby

1–2–3

Boogie woogie, Baby, boogie woogie, Baby, boogie woogie, Baby

1–2–3.

—*Beechwood Elementary, kindergarten and 1st-grade African American girls (1975), Baton Rouge;*
St. Genevieve School 3rd-grade white girls (1940s), Lafayette, La.

The Beechwood Elementary girls continued with another ring play. This time they enlarged the ring, and appointed one girl to take a center role. She demonstrated the moves, and the other girls followed, clapping their hands to the rhythm:

When I was a baby baby baby
When I was a baby
This what I do
Unh unh unh unh unh (*Thumb in mouth.*)
All day long (*All imitate.*)
All day long
When I was a girl girl girl
When I was a girl
This what I do
Stomp stomp stomp stomp stomp (*Stamp feet loudly each time she says "Stomp."*)
All day long (*All imitate.*)
All day long
When I was a teenager a teenager a teenager
When I was a teenager
This what I do
Woomp woomp woomp woomp woomp (*Shake hips from side to side.*)
All day long (*All imitate.*)
All day long
When I was a lady lady lady
When I was a lady
This what I do
Swish swish swish swish swish (*Sweeping motion.*)
All day long (*All sweep.*)
All day long
When I got married married married
When I got married
This what I do
Smack smack smack smack smack (*Kissing motion from side to side.*)
All day long
All day long (*Loud smacking and laughter.*)
When I had a baby a baby a baby
When I had a baby
This what I do
Unh unh unh unh unh (*Snuggle an imaginary baby close in the arms.*)
All day long (*All imitate holding baby.*)
All day long
When my husband died died died
When my husband died
This what I do

Hooray hooray hooray hooray hooray (*Jump up and down with arms raised.*)
All day long (*All jump, waving arms.*)
All day long
When my baby died died died
When my baby died
This what I do
Boo-hoo boo-hoo boo-hoo boo-hoo boo-hoo (*Put hands over face.*)
All day long (*All cover face and boo hoo.*)
All day long
When I died died died
When I died
This what I do
UNH UNH unh unh unh.[9] (*Slowly collapse in a heap.*)

The girls ended up flailing around in a pile, laughing and poking at one another.

—*Beechwood Elementary, kindergarten and 1st-grade African American girls, Baton Rouge*

Beechwood Elementary, where I first recorded the game above, is in Baton Rouge, La. Two years later (1977), an hour and a half south from Beechwood, I recorded a group of white second graders at Happy Face Nursery School in Chalmette, Louisiana, singing their variation of "When I Was a Baby":

When Courtney was a baby a baby a baby
When Courtney was a baby she acted just like this
Waa waa (*Put hands over face and cry.*)
When Courtney was a child a child a child
When Courtney was a child
She acted just like this
Brush your teeth and go to bed
Brush your teeth and go to bed ("*Brush*" *teeth, put clasped hands on side of face.*)
When Courtney was a teenager a teenager a teenager
When Courtney was a teenager
She acted just like this
Oh, my beautiful hair
Oh, my beautiful hair (*Sweep hand, push back hair dramatically.*)
When Courtney was a mother a mother a mother
When Courtney was a mother
She acted just like this

Brush your teeth and comb your hair (*Shake finger at "child."*)
Brush your teeth and comb your hair
When Courtney was a grandma a grandma a grandma
When Courtney was a grandma
She acted just like this (*Hand on back, bend over.*)
Oh my aching back (*Creep forward, holding back.*)
Will you hand me my pillow?
When Courtney was dead dead dead
When Courtney was dead
She acted just like this
Look at those people (*Hand to forehead to shade eyes.*)
In cars passing by
When Courtney went to heaven heaven heaven
When Courtney went to heaven
She acted just like this
Look at those pretty little houses
With children in them . . . (*Pause.*) . . .
—*Happy Face Nursery School, white 2nd-grade girls, Chalmette, La.*

(JS) Look at those pretty little houses with children them . . . does it go on?
(Girl) I learned it from my cousin at school.
(JS) And where did your cousin learn it?
(Child) She just made it up.
(JS) She made it up? Where does your cousin go to school?
(Girl) St. Louise. (St. Louise de Marillac Catholic School in Arabi, Louisiana).
(JS) Oh, she goes to St. Louise. OK. Do you know any more? Ah, then I can go to
    the teacher . . .

The girls walked away, chatting together. The interview, for them, had finished. Their version of "When I Was a Baby," sung by girls in the second grade, and in a suburban setting, eerily consists of imitative actions of different events of their lives, seen from their perspective. Lady Alice B. Gomme, writing in 1898, had noted that boys and girls, when playing this game, had relived different events in their nineteenth-century lives.

Clearly, the ring game form offers many opportunities for girls to explore socially significant activities they see demonstrated around them. For very small children "Round in a circle," "Roller coaster," and "Motorboat" engage the players in a hand-holding, supportive togetherness, where they can perform certain actions in unison and strengthen their sense of belonging to their small "circle."

"Casserella," and "Mary Havin' a Baby / Pizza Pizza Daddy-O," and other games where there is a central player, allow for much more complexity in the interaction of the girls; and a more demanding performance from the girls singled out to be in the center of the ring. "Casserella" allows each girl who demonstrates actions to become a leader, to "strut her stuff," and to be as daring as she pleases while she is the center of attention. This central performer is either rewarded or made fun of by the girls in the outer circle, and these other girls can make the performer feel either special or intimidated by their continuing commentary on her improvisations.

Forming a ring, facing one another, and closing out the world around them gives children a greater sense of community and allows them to relate to each other in ways that only occur in this setting. Ring games contain some of the most vivid satire on adult life, as well as the most concentrated personal interactions in children's folk games.

JUST FOR FUN

YouTube.com. Kidspot. "How to Play Apple on a Stick clapping game" 198,154 views, May 23, 2013, two white girls demonstrate the game.

YouTube.com. MyLorgan. "Anne and Virginia playing "Say Say My Playmate" 303,627 views, Dec. 26, 2013. This video includes several extra stanzas the children in New Orleans did not seem to know. I really enjoyed reading the comments that followed this video.

Type in a favorite handclap you remember, and see if YouTube players perform it, and if they add extra verses. Maybe you can make a YouTube video of a favorite handclap of your own.

JUST FOR FUN

archive.org, Halliwell Phillips, J. O. The Nursery Rhymes of England. This collection was done in 1886. See how many of the rhymes you are familiar with.

CHAPTER 3

Jump Rope

South Louisiana is a wonderful place for children to play outdoors. It is warm most of the year, and young people of all ethnicities traditionally "run the streets." Unfortunately, as the cities get more crowded and crime statistics soar, upper- and middle-class youngsters become more confined, entering cocoons of air conditioning and meeting for planned play dates. It is the working-class and poor children who still experience much of their playing lives outdoors.[1] Boys fill the playgrounds every evening bouncing basketballs, throwing footballs, and working their muscles at running games. Girls play hopscotch, tetherball, and tag or do cheers and play jump rope, all on the "banquettes."

I collected jump-rope rhymes at schools and at summer camps. Skipping rope was prohibited at some schools. It was up to the principal whether to permit it or not. Where the activity took place, the girls jumped singly or in groups, using one rope or two or even long strings of rubber bands fastened together to make "Chinese" jump ropes. The words to jump rope jingles don't have to make sense. As long as the players know what the game was, everything was fine.

The following examples come from New Orleans, Baton Rouge, Lafayette, and summer camps and New Orleans Recreation Department sites. At every public school, the majority of contributors were African American. There were white and black respondents at the Girl Scout meeting and at Ursaline Academy and summer camps.

WBOK

WBOK

—Andrew Jackson, 3rd-, 6th-grade African American girls, New Orleans; Adolph Meyer,
African American 5th-grade girls, Algiers, La.

[WBOK 1230 AM, as of 2017, was a broadcasting station with a Christian radio format. In the 1960s, it had an R&B format.]

Curly Larry Moe
Open up the do'
Tic tac toe.

—Andrew Jackson Elementary, African American 3rd- and 5th-grade girls, New Orleans

The following game is related to "Curly Larry Moe" only because the fifth-grade girl used the three stooges at the beginning of her jingle:

1 stooge 2 stooge 3 stooge (*Then she explains, "Three people jump, like one stooge, two stooge, 'til three is in, and then one jumps back out, and they say,"*)
I walk to the store (*She continues, "Then the other one jump in and say,"*)
I went in the door (*"And then the other one jump in and say,"*)
I walked out the door
(*"And one jump out, and then when they got two people in they go,"*)
Cat, the rat, the baseball bat
Cat, the rat, the baseball bat
Cat, the rat, the baseball bat.

"And then one person is in, and he gets 'hots' (fast turning), then he gets 'slacks' (*dragging the rope slowly on the ground.*)"

—John Dibert, African American 5th-grade girl, New Orleans

Other players used a shortened version:

Cat, the rat, the baseball bat
Cat, the rat, the baseball bat.

(*Repeat faster and faster.*)

—Andrew Jackson, African American 3rd-grade girls; John Dibert, African American 5th-grade girls; Magrauder Center Desire Project, African American 6th-grade girls, New Orleans

Kindergartners and first graders at Beechwood Elementary in Baker, Louisiana, a small town not far from Baton Rouge, jumped to repetitions of:

M-i-s-s-i-s-s-i-p-p-i[2]

In New Orleans the third-grade girls at Andrew Jackson spent entire recesses chanting:

Ice cream
Ice cream
H-O-T stands for hots!

(*One girl explained," Then you start stingin' they legs up."*)
—*Andrew Jackson Elementary, African American 3rd- and 6th-grade girls, New Orleans*

Children of every ethnicity chanted the following as they jumped rope. It was played at John Dibert, Andrew Jackson, Eisenhower, and the St. Joan of Arc babysitting group, in New Orleans, where older and younger informants all knew it well:

I like coffee
I like tea
I like Tina to jump in with me (*Tina jumps in.*)
I hate coffee
I hate tea
I hate Tina to jump out with me. (*Tina jumps out.*)

I recorded "I Like Coffee" played by two girls; one turned the rope, and the other jumped in and out with her. At other locations the game was played by larger groups of friends.[3]
—*Desire Project Magrauder Center, African American girls; John Dibert Elementary, 5th- and 6th-grade African American and white girls, New Orleans; Adolph Meyer Elementary, African American 5th-grade girls, Algiers, La.*

"Red, White, and Blue," which follows, was very popular when I was a girl in the 1940s and 50s. It was played the same way the African American girls from Andrew Jackson played it, with the exception of the last line:

Red, white, and blue
She's the prettiest (*Girl jumps in and jumps four times.*)
Stars all over you (*Crouch down while turners turn the rope over jumper's head three times.*)
She's the dirtiest (*Begin jumping again.*)
What colors?
All colors

'Cept red.
Red, white, and blue
Yo' mama don't have no shoes! (*Jump out and new player jumps in.*)

The sixth-grade girls at Andrew Jackson also jumped rope to:

1–2 buckle my shoe (*Lean over and touch shoe.*)
3–4 shut the door (*Turn in place while jumping.*)
5–6 pick up sticks (*Reach down and touch ground for each syllable.*)
7–8–lay them straight (*Pantomime laying sticks down.*)
9–10 a big fat hen. (*Jump with hands on hips.*)[4]
—*Andrew Jackson Elementary, African American 6th-grade girls, New Orleans*

The following five games are variants of skipping rhymes with the line "Fives into Twosies." Each respondent recalled the game played slightly differently:

Fives into twosies
Lends into miss
Oh! 1–2–3–4–5–6 . . .

The players explained, "We go, like, 1–2—I jump in, and she go 3–4, while I jump out, and then another one go 4–5." So each player jumps in, jumps twice, then another girl jumps in on the third beat, while the first player is jumping out.
—*Lusher Elementary, African American and white 5th-grade girls, New Orleans*

Fives into ones is ladies in a miss
Oh 1 (*One jumps in.*)
Oh 1–2 (*First jumps out as second jumps in.*)
Oh 1–2
Oh 1–2–3 (*Second jumps out as third jumps in.*)
Oh 1–2–3
Oh 1–2–3–4 (*New exchange.*)
Oh 1–2–3–4
Oh 1–2–3–4–5 (*New exchange.*)
Oh 1 oh 1 oh 1 oh 1 oh 1. (*One girl explained, "And then you say what number you want to go to, but it has to be more than five."*)
—*Andrew Jackson Elementary, African American 6th-grade girls, New Orleans*

At Adolph Meyer an African American girl in the fifth grade explained the following variant of "Fives into Twosies" in this way: "Fives in the numbers / Ladies in a miss / Go 1 . . . Then everybody in line takes one, and then the first person goes and takes two, and then everybody else takes two, and then the first person takes three, and so, like, follow the leader."

Fives into twosies

Ladies in a miss

Go 1–2–3–4–5–6–7–8–9–10–11–12–13–14–15

Hey spot! Your booty ain't hot!

—Adolph Meyer Elementary, African American 5th-grade girl, Algiers, La.

From school to school, the jumping pattern of "Fives into Twosies" varied. The players at St. Joan of Arc bingo were teenagers, and they explained "Five into Twosies" in a slightly different way, "People jump in *two at a time*, two at 1–2, then, as these two jump out, two more jump in at 3–4, and so on." At John Dibert, the words were the same as at Adolph Meyer, but the players said, "We jump in 1–2, one player, then 3–4, a new player, and so on . . ."

The following three are very short jump-rope rhymes, and all came from Adolph Meyer Elementary:

Little girl little girl

How old are you? (*One informant explained, "You jump 1–2–3–4–5–6 . . . 'til you can't jump no more, and that's how old you are."*)

H Doctor Pepper D HOTS! (*On "Hots" the turner gives "Peppers."*)

H-E-L-P

One girl explained, "If you miss on H, you get 'high waters,' and the rope don't touch the ground. If you miss on E, you get to jump with ya eyes closed. L, you get 'low waters,' with the rope touching the ground; and P, you get 'peppers,' that's hots."

—Adolph Meyer Elementary African American 5th-grade girl, Algiers; Same version of "Help" also recorded at St. Catherine of Siena Girl Scout meeting, Metairie, La., white girls, and Ursaline Academy, white and one African American high school girls, New Orleans, 1977

Three Girl Scouts, who were white, contributed a version of "Helicopter" similar to the one my schoolmates and I played in Lafayette, La., in the 1950s:

Helicopter, helicopter, please come down
If you don't, I'll shoot you down.
Bang bang.

(Girl explains, *"And then it comes down and you have to jump over it and you get over it..."*)

(JS) OK so, the rope is twirled high up when you say, "Helicopter." Then, on "bang bang," the rope is twirled at ground level? Is one person in the middle and turning the rope, and everybody jumping over it?

(Girl) Yeah, one is in the middle, and then, when we jump over it, we say, "Angel, devil, angel, devil," and if you miss on "angel," you don't have to take the end, but if you miss on "devil," then you have to.

(JS) You have to get in the middle?

(Girls) Right.

—St. Catherine of Siena Girl Scout troop, white girls, Metairie, La.

At Ursaline Academy in New Orleans, the white girls reported another variation of "Helicopter":

Helicopter helicopter please come down (*Rope is twirled high.*)
Helicopter helicopter spin me around (*Jumper spins.*)
Helicopter helicopter turn all around (*Rope twirler spins.*)
If you don't, I'll knock you down. (*Rope twirler lowers rope to ground.*)
Angels (*You jump, and if you miss on "angels," you get another turn.*)
Devils (*You jump, and if you miss on "devils" you are out.*)

—Ursaline Academy High School, white girls, New Orleans

One of the white Girl Scouts from St. Catherine of Siena reported, "There's a game called 'Queen Bee,' and you're a bee, and you're the queen, and you come over, and if they touch you while you're not in the rope, you're out, and you hafta take an end."

I asked, "So that's a combination of jump rope and tag, right?"

And the girl replied, "Yeah."

The Adolph Meyer Elementary group contributed a rhyme, which serves as a schoolyard chant, a counting-out formula, and a handclap:

2–4–6–8
Johnny had a rattlesnake
Snake died, Johnny cried
2–4–6–8.
—*Adolph Meyer Elementary, 5th-grade African American girls, Algiers, La.*

Other short, simple rhymes are:

O-N-E-1
T-W-O-2
T-H-R-E-E-3 (*and so on*).
—*Andrew Jackson Elementary, African American 3rd-grade girls; Desire Project Magrauder Center,*
5th-grade African American girls, New Orleans

Miss Louisa (*One girl turns the rope and jumps alone.*)
Alabama (*A friend jumps in with her.*)
Touchdown. (*Friend jumps out.*)

(As they jumped faster and faster, the turner said, "*That's right, your booty got tight!*")
—*Desire Project Magrauder Center, African American girls, New Orleans*

Oh-1–2–3–4 (*Jump standing straight.*)
Oh-1–2–3–4 (*Jump twisting from side to side.*)
Oh-1–2–3–4 (*Jump hunched over.*)
Oh-1–2–3–4. (*Jump hot peppers.*)
—*Andrew Jackson Elementary, African American 3rd-grade girls, New Orleans*

Johnny made a touchdown (*Touch hand to ground.*)
Be on time
Johnny made a touchdown (*Touch hand to ground.*)
Be on time
Johnny made three high 1–2–3. (*Jumper crouches and jumps with rope twirled above*
her head.)
—*Andrew Jackson Elementary, African American 3rd-grade girls, New Orleans*

1–2-Hallelujah
3–4-God bless ya'
5–6-I'll catch ya'
7–8-He caught ya'

9–10-He's ya boyfriend!
—*Andrew Jackson Elementary, African American 3rd-grade girls, New Orleans*

In Baton Rouge in 1974, middle-school girls from McKinley Junior High School jumped to the following:

Amos and Andy peppermint candy
I say stoop (*Jump crouching.*)
Amos and Andy peppermint candy
I say rise (*Jump standing up straight.*)
Amos and Andy peppermint candy
I say h-o-t spells HOT!
—*McKinley Junior High School, African American girls, Baton Rouge*

At Beechwood Elementary in Baker, Louisiana, kindergartners and first graders jumped to the following:

Amos and Andy peppermint candy
I say stoop
Amos and Andy peppermint candy
I say rise
Amos and Andy peppermint candy
I say run out
Amos and Andy peppermint candy
I say come in
Amos and Andy peppermint candy
I say do cold (*The rope is turned slowly so it is slack.*)
Amos and Andy peppermint candy
I say give HOT!
—*Beechwood Elementary, African American kindergarten and 1st-grade girls, Baker, La.*

There are longer jump-rope jingles, which are sometimes also played as handclaps:

Policeman policeman do your duty
Here comes Jane the American beauty
She can wiggle, she can wobble
She can do the twist
But I bet you five dollars

That she can't do this
Close your eyes and count to ten
And if you miss start over again
1–2–3–4–5–6–7–8–9–10[5]
—*Beauregard Junior High School, 7th-grade African American girls, New Orleans*

Following are two variants of "Went Downtown to See Mr. Brown," which are more often used as handclaps, but were given twice as jump rope. The first comes from Louise Day Care Center, New Orleans, chanted by four-year-olds:

I went downtown to see Miss Brown
She gave me a nickel
I bought me a pickle
The pickle was sour
She gave me a bed
The bed was hard
She gave me a card
On that card it said:
Teddy Bear Teddy Bear turn around
Teddy Bear Teddy Bear touch the ground
Teddy Bear Teddy Bear go upstairs
Teddy Bear Teddy Bear say your prayers
Lord have mercy on my soul
How many chickens how many tell
I'll go back and steal some more.
—*Louise Day Care Center, Angelique and Quintella (I promised to use their names)*
African American 3- and 4-year-old girls, New Orleans

At John Dibert Elementary the final lines to the jingle above were:

Lord have mercy on my soul
How many chickens have I stole?
Let me see I check for sure
I'll go back and steal some more.
—*John Dibert Elementary, African American 6th-grade girls, New Orleans*

The following rhyme was submitted in writing. The boy who slipped it into my hand as I was walking out the door was a member of a class of Beauregard Junior High School twelve and thirteen-year-olds:

We went uptown to see Mr. Brown
He gave us a nickel to buy a pickle
The pickle was sour, he gave us a flower
The flower was yellow, he gave us a fellow
The fellow was sick, he gave us a stick
The stick was hard, he gave us a card
And on that card it said
Ladybug Ladybug turn all around
Ladybug Ladybug turn off the light
Ladybug Ladybug say good night.
—*Beauregard Junior High School 13-year-old African American boy, New Orleans*

Two more variants of "Ladybug" and "Teddy Bear" came from John Dibert Elementary:

Variant 1.

Teddy Bear Teddy Bear turn around
Teddy Bear Teddy Bear touch the ground
Teddy Bear Teddy Bear show your shoes (*Jump on one foot.*)
Teddy Bear Teddy Bear be excused. (*Jump out.*)

Variant 2.

Teddy Bear Teddy Bear jump on one foot one foot one foot
Teddy Bear Teddy Bear jump on two feet two feet two feet
Teddy Bear Teddy Bear jump on three feet three feet three feet (*Jump and touch the ground with one hand.*)
Teddy Bear Teddy Bear jump on four feet four feet four feet (*Touch the ground with both hands.*)
Teddy Bear Teddy Bear gonna run run. (*Get hots.*)
—*John Dibert Elementary, 5th- and 6th-grade African American girls, New Orleans*

At McKinley Junior High in Baton Rouge, in 1974, the girls skipped to:

Teddy Bear Teddy Bear turn around (*Spin while jumping.*)
Teddy Bear Teddy Bear touch the ground (*Touch ground while jumping.*)
Teddy Bear Teddy Bear show your shoes (*Kick high while jumping.*)
Teddy Bear Teddy Bear be excuse (*Jump out.*)

Teddy Bear Teddy Bear come back in (*Jump back in*.)
Teddy Bear Teddy Bear come upstairs (*Jump with knees bent high*.)
Teddy Bear Teddy Bear say your prayers (*Hold hands in prayer*.)
Lord have mercy on my soul
How many chickens have I sold? (*Some girls said, "Stole."*)
One last night and two the night before
Now I'm going to sell (*steal*) some more
5–10–15–20–25–30–35–40 . . . and you miss![6]
—*McKinley Junior High African American girls, Baton Rouge*

The girls at Adolph Meyer (fifth graders), at John Dibert (sixth graders), and at St. Joan of Arc bingo (fifteen and sixteen-year-olds), as well as Day Campers at Camp Ruth Lee, played variants of a very old English game collected by nineteenth century folklorists, among them, Lady Alice B. Gomme.[7]

Variant 1.

There's a little girl on green grass grows
She sing so sweet as she knows
Along come a fellow and kiss her on the cheek
How many kisses did he give?
1–2–3–4-5 . . . (Jump until you miss.)
—*Adolph Meyer Elementary, African American 5th-grade girls, Algiers, La.*

Variant 2.

Down by the river
Where the green grass grows
There's a little girl who's as sweet as she knows
She jumps, she skips, she hops, she (*Mumbles.*)
Down came a boy and
Kiss her on the cheek
How many kisses did he give her?
—*John Dibert Elementary, African American 6th-grade girls, New Orleans*

Variant 3. Two sisters, aged fifteen and sixteen, performed the next chant. They were two of the babysitters at St. Joan of Arc bingo:

Down by the valley where the green grass grows
There was a little girl singing sweet as a rose
She sing she sing she sing so sweet
Along come a boy and kiss her on the cheek
How many kisses did he get that week?
Carol Carol you oughta be ashame
You let a boy kiss you and
You didn't know his name
How many kisses did you get from him?
1–2–3–4 'til you miss.
—*St. Joan of Arc bingo babysitting, 16- and 17-year-old African American girls, New Orleans*

The sixth-grade girls at John Dibert Elementary chanted the last part of the rhyme above thus:

Allegra Allegra you oughta be ashamed
You let a boy kiss you and you don't know his name
How many kisses did he give you?
(One girl explained," And then you count, and then, when you be out, you say, "He got chapped lips!")
—*John Dibert Elementary, African American 6th-grade girls, New Orleans*

Variant 4. White girls from middle school, who were campers at Camp Ruth Lee, chanted:

Down in the meadow where the green grass grows
There sat Suzy as sweet as a rose
Then came . . . Chuck (*Someone in the group squeaks, "No! Not him!"*)
And kissed her on the cheek
How many kisses did she get that week?
1–2–3–4 . . .
—*Camp Ruth Lee middle-school white girls, Norwood, La.*

Perhaps the reiteration of the idea of kissing led the Camp Ruth Lee girls to recall the following verse, often used in autograph books.

Mary and John sitting in a tree
K-I-S-S-I-N-G
First come love

Then come marriage
Then come John with a baby carriage

(Girls) We have another version.
(JS) OK go.

Mary and John sitting in a tree
K-i-s-s-i-n-g
First come love
Then come marriage
K-i-s-s-i-n-g
Mary fell off and broke her knee
John came down and save her life
Now I pronounce you man and wife
K-i-s-s-i-n-g

The same campers remembered:

Down by the ocean
Down by the sea
Johnny broke a bottle and blamed it on me
I told Ma
Ma told Pa
Johnny got a whipping and ha ha ha
1–2–3–4–5–6 . . .

They continued:

Apple on a stick
Makes me sick
Makes my heart go 2–4–6
Not because I'm dirty
Not because I'm clean
Just because I kissed a boy behind a magazine
Hey girl I bet you can't do this
Close your eyes and count to ten
If you can't you are a big fat hen
1–2–3–4–5–6–7–8–9–10–
Did not miss
So you are not a big fat hen.[8]

(Also given as a handclap from other recorded groups.)
—*Camp Ruth Lee, middle-school white campers, Norwood, La.*

A single African American girl standing with the camper group chanted the following, and the directions are her own:

Mary Mary when you gonna get married?
A-b-c-d-e-f-g-h-i-j-k-l-m-n-o-p . . .
(*Whatever letter she misses on, she names a boy's name.*)
Where you gonna get married?
Church, house, toilet hole
What kinda wedding dress will you have?
Silk, toilet paper, rags
What kinda house will you live in?
Stone, brick, mud
How many children will you have?
1–2–3–4–5–6–7–8–9–10
(*The number you miss on is the number you will have.*)
What kinda hair will your children have?
Nappy head, curly head, b-b-shot
What kinda car will you have?
Raggy, bumpy, brand new
What class family will you be in?
High class, middle class, low class
When you are old what will you be?
Rich, poor, middle class[9]
—*Camp Ruth Lee, African American middle-school girl, Norwood, La.*

Two tiny white campers arrived and asked to do something.

(JS) Where are you from?
(Girls) Uh, St. Aloysius in Baton Rouge. Can we do "Apple on a Stick?"
(JS) Sure.

(As noted earlier, "Apple on a Stick" was collected at different times, both as a jump rope rhyme and as a handclap. The one that follows is slightly different from the one given earlier by the older campers. The girls clapped in 4/4 time, and fit the words to the meter by added clapping.)

Apple on a stick (*Clap.*)
Makes me sick (*Clap.*)
Makes my heart go 2–4–6 (*Clap.*)
Not because the apple (*Clap.*)
Not because the stick (*Clap.*)
Just because my boyfriend makes me sick
Boys boys have some fun
Here comes Julie with a mini skirt on
She can wiggle (*Jump and wiggle.*)
She can wobble (*Jump and 'wobble'*)
She can do the twist (*Jump twisting at waist.*)
Bet you five dollars
She can't do this (*Jump, spreading legs.*)
And if you miss
You start over again
1–2–3–4–5–6 . . .
—*Camp Ruth Lee, white girls, St. Aloysius Elementary School, Baton Rouge. They must have been in 2nd or 3rd grade*

Visiting with friends in Chalmette, Louisiana, in 2007, I recorded a white high school senior handclapping to an alternate version of "Apple on a Stick":

Apple on a stick
Makes me sick
Makes my heart go 2–4–6
Not because I'm dirty
Not because I'm clean
Just because I kissed a boy
Behind the magazine
Ooooo girl look at this
I see Charlie
He can wobble
He can wiggle
He can do the split
But I bet you five dollars
He can't do this
Close your eyes and count to ten
If you miss you gotta kiss him once again.
(*Close eyes and continue clapping pattern.*)
1–2–3–4–5–6–7–8–9–10
—*White Chalmette High School senior, Chalmette, La.*

The girls at John Dibert played a game called "School." One of them explained:

> "When the rope starts turning, we call it "Kindergarten." Then everybody goes in once for first grade, and you go on to jump twice for second grade and three times for third, you know." I asked, "What do you do after High School?" (The girl) "You go to college." A boy interrupted, "You get hots! You get HOTS!" The girl continued, "The first one to get to college wins."
>
> —*John Dibert Elementary, white 5th-grade girl, New Orleans*

Variations of "School" could be elaborate. The following method of play was described by the girls at the St. Catherine of Siena Girl Scout meeting held in their troop mistress's elegant house in Old Metairie, a New Orleans suburb:

(Girl) You go "S-C-H-double-O-L for "school," with a period, question mark, comma, and don't be late for school," and then you go, "Kindergarten, first grade, second grade, and all like that, and then . . . with kindergarten you go right through, and with first grade you jump once, and second you do two, and then, when you get up to sixth grade, you have to jump backwards, back . . . um . . . the other way, and then, um, seventh grade you gotta close ya eyes. Eighth grade you gotta jump on one foot. For ninth grade you have to touch the ground and jump with one hand down. (*Demonstrates crouching down and ducking the head.*)

(JS) You have to do that with "low waters"? (*"Low waters"—the rope is twirled above the jumper's head, so the jumper has to crouch while jumping.*)

(Girls as a group) Um hummm.

(JS) So you touch the ground while the turners turn the rope above your head?

(Girls) Yeah, you have to touch the ground—touch the ground.

(JS) Oh, I didn't know that. You do that with "low waters"? You crouch down when you do "low waters"?

(Girls) Um hummm, and tenth grade you have to go "one-two-three-four" (*As she counts, she spins in a circle with each number.*) After you get to ten, for graduation, you have to pick up a rock, put it in your hand, and jump. And you have to jump and you can't let the rock fall from your hand.

(JS) Open hand?

(Girl) Yeah, like that (*She holds her hand open and flat.*) That's how it goes.

> —*St. Catherine of Siena Girl Scout Troop, middle-school white girl, Old Metairie, La.*

At Eisenhower Elementary School, a Vietnamese girl had a beautiful Chinese jump rope made of red and green rubber bands fastened together to make a large circle. A friend explained, "First you have to take some rubber bands and tie them together. And when it all done, there's a lot of different ways of playing."

(JS) Tell me some.
(Girl) Well, one game that we call in-out-side-side-on-in-out. In, you have to
  jump in the rope; then you have to jump out, then you have to go outside,
  then you have to go to the other side, then you have to jump on the rope,
  then you get out.
          —Eisenhower Elementary School, African American 5th-grade girl, New Orleans

The girls ran off before I could get them to demonstrate the method of play. But on another day, a group of third-grade girls at Andrew Jackson did demonstrate how to play Chinese jump rope. They stood, two girls facing one another, with a long elastic band stretched around their ankles. A third girl was the "jumper." They chanted:

Jump in (The jumper hops into the space between the bands.)
Jump out (Jumper jumps outside the bands.)
Jump side to side (Jumper hops from one side of the band to the other.)
Jump in
Jump out
Jump side to side
Jump on (Jumper steps on band.)
Jump in
Jump out
Jump side to side
Jump on
Jump out.
          —Andrew Jackson Elementary, 3rd-grade African American girl, New Orleans

At one point I asked, "What constitutes a "miss" when you play jump rope?" There were several different answers—"You miss when you jump on the rope." "When the rope hits your leg." "And when, like, the rope falls out of somebody's hand because of you, you hit the rope, and the rope goes flying out of somebody's hand." "Or when it's somebody's turn and you don't jump on time." A final description of "missing" came from the girls at Ursaline Academy, "And when you play 'Don't Skip a Link' like, 'Don't—skip—a—link'—and when you say 'link,'" the next person jumps in, and if she don't, she misses."

(JS) Wait, I did not get "Don't Skip a Link." How does that go?"

(Girl) Oh, what we were playing today was "Don't Skip a Link." Like, (*She hops up on each word.*) Don't—skip—a—link, and when you say "link" the next person jumps in. And when people miss, they have to stand outside. And if you miss in that game, and, uh, then you don't get to jump in on "link." You jump in on another "link" after that. You see, another time around. The next time around that is called the "link."

—*Ursaline Academy, teenage white girl, New Orleans*

Ursaline Academy is an all-girls private Catholic school. The collecting session, a transcript of which follows, took place in a classroom under the watchful gaze of two nuns. It took a while for the girls to loosen up under the piercing surveillance of their teachers.

(JS) Did *you* play jump rope? (*I turned to a second girl.*)

(Girl) We played, uh, Skip-a-Link, and uh, one person would jump in, and the rope would go around, and then another person would jump, and then, she would run out, and the rope would turn faster and faster, and the jumpers would have to jump faster and faster. And, of course, if you missed, you would have to step out. It was wild! I mean we used to spend our whole recess . . . we would run out there and jump as fast as we could for ten minutes. (*Girls in background saying, "Yes" and offering approval.*)

(JS) So it was your favorite?

(Girl) Yes!

(Person puts up her hand.) We used to play "High Water."

(JS) How do you play "High Water"?

(Girl) The rope starts out on the ground and everybody jumps over. Then they run around, and the rope is a little higher, and everybody jumps over. And it gets higher and higher, and you can't step on it.

(Another girl volunteers.) I don't know if it is a game, but "Snakes."

(JS) How does "Snakes" go?

(Volunteer) You wiggle the rope, and you jump in, and try not to miss.

(JS) How could you tell if anybody missed?

(Girl) You stepped on the rope.

(Girl) We used to say:

> Dumb dumb dodo, catch me if you can
> I can run faster than anybody can

And then they would have to run through the rope while the rope was turning, and

try not to miss or get caught. It was fast!
—*Ursaline Academy, teenage white girls, New Orleans*

Among the Beechwood Elementary, Baton Rouge, kindergartners there was a jump rope rhyme, which was coordinated by the leader of the rope-jumping crew. The lead girl signaled for each girl to take her turn by calling her by name:

Vote vote vote for little Jackie (*Leader points to Jackie to jump in.*)
She meets Lonnie at the door (Leader signals Lonnie to jump in.)
Lonnie is a lady and she knows how to vote
So she don't need Jackie any more (*Jackie jumps out.*)
Vote vote vote for little Lonnie
She meets Vivian at the door (*Leader signals Vivian to jump in.*)
Vivian is a lady and she knows how to vote
So she don't need Lonnie any more. (*Lonnie jumps out.*)

The Beechwood Elementary girls added two more rhymes where someone's name was utilized:

There go Veronica seeking round
See could your feet touch the ground
If you jump 'til twenty-one
You may have an extra turn.

And:

Baby Suzie think she cutesy
All she know is Baby Suzie
If she go to twenty-fo
She may have another go.
—*Beechwood Elementary, kindergarten African American girls, Baton Rouge*

At Camp Ruth Lee (1974), I met with girls from many small towns in Louisiana. The girls crowded around saying, "I know one! I know one!" Catherine from Sherwood Forest Elementary in Baton Rouge chanted:

Lincoln Lincoln you been drinkin' (*Lincoln rhymed with "drinkin".*)
Looks like coffee

Smells like wine
Tastes like rotten turpentine.

Then the girls shouted, "We got another."

Abraham Lincoln
What's that you been drinkin'
Tastes like water
Smells like wine
Oh, my gosh
It's turpentine.

The girls shouted, "And we got another one!"

Pretty little Dutch girl dressed in blue
These are the things I like to do
Curtsy to the captain (*Dip and hold hands out as if holding dress.*)
Bow to the queen (*Bow head and jump.*)
Turn my back on the yellow submarine. (*Turn around.*)[10]

(JS) All right? How about the other one you talked about? "Not Last Night"?
(Three girls)

Not last night but the night before
Twenty-four robbers came knockin' at my door
As I ran out, they ran in (*Jump out.*)
Hit me on the head with a rollin' pin (*Jump back in.*)
Asked them what they wanted and this is what they said
Spanish dancer turn around (*One girl does not turn. Two others turn around.*)
Spanish dancer do the high kick (*All kick.*)
Spanish dancer touch the ground (*All touch the ground with one hand.*)
Spanish dancer turn around (*One girl shouts, "We did that already!"*)
Spanish dancer get out of town. (*Jump out of the rope.*)

Later in the session, another camper added the lines:

Spanish dancer do the split.[11] (And she did!)
—*Camp Ruth Lee, 5th-grade white girls, Norwood, La.*

The same three girls hopped together in place and chanted:

> Peas in a pot
> They red hot
> Season 'em with all you got!

(Girl) Carla, do the blueberry one:

> Blueberry chocolate cherry easy I said over
> Here comes the teacher with the big fat stick
> You better get ready for arithmetic
> One and one is two
> Two and two is four
> Now it's time for spelling
> C-o-l-d for cold
> H-O-T for HOT!

(Girl) Now we gonna do what ya callit, run and chase somebody.
(JS) What?
(Girl) Ya turn the rope and say, "Run Carla, as fast as you can. I can run faster than Joyce can." And then you run and see can she run faster and not miss.
(Girl) We got:

> Teddy Bear Teddy Bear turn all around
> Teddy Bear Teddy Bear touch the ground
> Teddy Bear Teddy Bear show your shoes
> Teddy Bear Teddy Bear how old are you?
> Are you one?
> Are you two?
> Are you three?
> Are you four?

> (*"Five, six, seven, eight . . . until you miss."*)
> —*Camp Ruth Lee, 5th-grade white girls, Norwood La.*

Jump rope was especially popular at the elementary school I attended in Lafayette, Louisiana, in the late 1940s and early 1950s. Every morning and noon recess a girl named Linda raced everyone to the game closet so she could snag the jump rope before anybody else. Then she stationed herself in the well-worn jumping spot and lined her friends up just so. Everybody in her lineup was required to skip to the rhymes she dictated. Some of us balked at being bossed around and often chose to play "Jacks" instead of following her lead. Our school jacks were made of durable, heavy metal and had a bouncy, red, rubber ball. Our group played "Jacks" from the fourth grade to the eighth, while Linda and her friends carried on the jump rope tradition.

Interestingly, though jump rope jingles were among the most excitedly recounted schoolyard lore, not one child in the fifty years I collected in south Louisiana offered to share Jacks-playing memories with me.[12]

There is much more collecting to do in the field of jump rope. Only about half of the schools I surveyed from the early 1970s on, allowed children to play jump rope on the school grounds. While driving around the city of New Orleans, it was obvious that jump rope, tetherball, stickball, baseball, football, basketball, hopscotch, and wrestling were extremely popular. I saw these activities played on the sidewalks and in empty lots all over the city. I drove down Claiborne Avenue every day, going to and coming from work, and there was a continuing tetherball game played at the corner of Claiborne Avenue and Pauger Street. The girls attached a plastic one-gallon milk container by a rope to the street sign and played every afternoon. The same group of girls played "Double Dutch" jump rope many afternoons. This was played by turning two long lengths of rope, in an egg-beater fashion, while groups of girls jumped in, chanted something, and jumped out. I was always driving to work, or coming home tired when I saw them, and I regret that I never stopped to interview them.

JUST FOR FUN

I Googled "Double Dutch jump rope," January 30, 2020, and the first item that came up was a 4 minute, 54 second video of the "38th Annual Double Dutch World Championships—Sumter, S. C. June 17–18, 2011." The video featured young boys and girls jumping at amazing speeds. I read all the comments and enjoyed them—1, 324, 984 views. Web. Other videos featured at that site: "free style Double Dutch" where jumpers performed gymnastics and other nimble feats while jumping.

You could Google your favorite jump rope jingle and find out if it is featured on the Web. And, hey, you might want to video yourself and your friends skipping rope to a chant you would like to share.

CHAPTER 4

Hand Games

When I was collecting schoolyard games in south Louisiana, I seldom viewed children making a ring and shooting marbles, or spinning tops, games that were popular when I was a child in the 1950s. There were, however, certain amusements that ruled the recess time, and one of these was hand-clapping games.

I found that handclaps were extremely popular in New Orleans, Baton Rouge, Lafayette, and multiple towns in south Louisiana. At every school where I collected, girls, and on occasion, boys, played handclaps every day.[1]

Once, I visited Samuel J. Peters Junior High School on South Broad Street in New Orleans with a camera crew from WGNO television. We were working together filming children's games for summer three-minute "spots." The group of girls we met with was older, from twelve to fourteen, and they laughed and flirted while they lined up to be videotaped playing handclaps. There were boys dressed out for football practice across a field, and when they saw the cameramen and the microphones, some of the boys ran over to join in. For the next twenty minutes the boys and the girls performed handclaps. The teenage boys, fully dressed in bulky football gear, played with as much enthusiasm as the girls.

Under the heading "Hand Games," I have tried to include every game I gathered where the hands played a major part. This includes handclapping, hand and foot combination games, quiet parlor, and even baby finger games taught at home by mothers and siblings.

Handclaps generally involve two players who face each other and clap their hands in a pattern while they sing or chant a rhyme. The rhythms and clapping patterns of handclaps vary. They are predominantly in 4/4 time, but the performers used off-beat clapping, pauses, double claps to one beat, slaps to the body or head, and silent body motions in order to create a great variety of complex, syncopated clapping accompaniments to their rhymes.

The clapping pattern follows and accentuates the rhythm of the rhyme, and among African American children in particular, these clapping patterns become intricate. Black girls usually begin a handclap by clapping on the offbeat. While they continue this offbeat clapping, they often introduce intricate syncopation, hesitations for effect, body motions, and foot stomping. White girls who go to school with black girls pick up these mannerisms and intricacies, while white girls attending all-white schools, I observed, were more conservative in their handclap movements, using clapping on the beat, and more restrained rhythmical movements.

None of the special effects that accompany handclaps can be adequately conveyed in print. They have to be seen, and heard, to be fully appreciated. I perused YouTube for good examples of children playing handclaps, and was able to find a few that warrant viewing. "Rockin' Robin Hand Game 2017!" features four children, two boys, and two girls, from Costa Rica, Central America. They handclap to the recorded song in strict 4/4 time, but they do so with verve (30,203 views). "Hand Clapping Game "Slide" is performed by two white teenagers who produced several game tutorials on YouTube. Their "Slide" garnered 1,171,940 views as of December 31, 2018.

As stated above, handclaps usually involve two players, but I taped some where as many as twenty girls made a large circle, and all clapped and moved together. I never saw a boy voluntarily initiate a handclap, though several boys contributed in writing to this collection, and some played along when they saw the crowd form.

Many of the following rhymes were taped at Camp Ruth Lee, located in Norwood, Louisiana, with a large number of girls all talking and laughing at once. In some instances, I was not able to remember to ask for the informant's ages or schools. Where this happened, I will give the approximate age, and Camp Ruth Lee as the source.

> One-two-three-four
> One-two-three-four
> One-two-three-four
> One-two-three-four.
>
> —*This is the simplest handclap I recorded. Two 9-year-old white girls. Holden, La. Taped at Camp Ruth Lee*

In "One-two-three-four," the girls clapped their hands front-to-front, then back-to-back, then front-back, front-back, in time to the count. They went faster and faster until they became almost breathless. The first one not to follow the pattern missed.

The same two nine-year-olds continued with another version of 1–2–3–4:

(Although it is called "1–2–3–4," the clapping pattern resulted in ¾ time.)

    1 (*Clap clap.*) 2 (*Clap clap.*) 3 (*Clap clap.*) 4 (*Clap clap.*) (*Pause, then clap hands twice.*)

    1 (*Clap slap.*) 2 (*Clap slap.*) 3 (*Clap slap.*) 4 (*Clap slap.*) (*The rhythm is 1–2–3. The girls say, "One" and then follow with the "clap, clap." I note that on second line, they clapped on second beat and then slapped their hands on their torso for "slap." Repeat, inserting pauses to vary the beat. The partner has to follow all the changes or miss. The pattern goes faster and faster until one misses.*)

Other girls crowded forward, and soon there was a large circle all demanding to be heard. The boldest stepped closest to the microphone, and clapped to:

A-B-C

It's easy as 1–2–3

It's easy as do-re-mi

A-B-C

1–2–3, Baby

You and me Girl

(*Clap clap clap.*)

Yeah

(*Clap clap clap.*)

Come on Girl, show me what you can do.

Shake it, shake it Baby

Oooooh

Shake it, shake it, Baby

Oooooh

Do-re-mi 1–2–3

Do-re-mi 1–2–3

Out goes ME!

—Two African American girls, one from Mayfair Elementary, the other from Broadmoor Junior High. Baton Rouge. Taped at Camp Ruth Lee, Norwood, La.

The above is derived from the song "ABC" sung by the Jackson Five. I later taped an identical version of "ABC" at Baker Junior High School, Baker, Louisiana, with a mixed group of African American and white seventh-grade girls.

The following, "A Lang a Dang Dang," was a song sung on the school ground when I was a sixth grader in the 1950s. Here it is, still being sung in Baton Rouge in 1974:

A lang a dang dang
At my doorbell
I let it ring for a quarter to twelve
I looked out the window and guess who I saw
I saw my baby just a-lookin' at you.
I said, "A money Honey oo itchy Baby
A money Honey oo itchy Baby
A money Honey oo itchy Baby"
I let it ring for a quarter to twelve
I looked out the window and guess who I saw
I saw my Baby just a-lookin' at you.
I said, "A money Honey . . . (*Repeat the verses until tired, and stop.*)
—*Twelve-year-old African American girls, McKinley Junior High School, Baton Rouge*

The words "A money Honey oo itchy Baby" are from an old rock and roll song that was popular in the 1950s.[2]

"Apple on a Stick" reappears as a handclap, with slight variations, making it one of the most repeated chants held in my recordings:

Apple on a stick
Makes me sick
Makes my heart go 2–4–6
Not because I'm dirty
Not because I'm clean
Not because I kissed a boy
Behind a magazine.
Close your eyes and count to ten
If you miss you're a big, fat, hen.
1 (*Clap clap clap.*)
2 (*Clap clap clap.*)
3 (*Clap clap clap.*)
4 (*Clap clap clap.*)
. . . .
10 (*Clap clap clap.*)
Hey, hey, nobody is a big fat hen.
—*6th- and 7th-grade white girls, taped at Camp Ruth Lee, Norwood, La.*

A second version:

Apple on a stick
Makes me sick
Not because I'm dirty
Not because I'm clean
Not because I kissed a boy
Behind a magazine
Close your eyes and count to ten
If you miss you're a big, fat, hen. (*Count and clap as in the first rhyme.*)
—*Twelve-year-old white girl, St. Aloysius School, Baton Rouge. Taped at Camp Ruth Lee, Norwood, La.*

A third version:

Apple on a stick
Makes me sick
Makes my heart go 2–4–6
Not because the apple
Not because the stick
Just because the boys they make me sick.
Boys, boys, have some fun
Here comes Julie with the mini skirt on.
She can wiggle, she can waggle,
She can do most anything,
But I'll bet she can't clap like this (*Close eyes, continue clapping.*)
And if you miss you start over again
1–2–3–4–5–6–7–8–9–8–10.

(*Repeat until miss.*)[3]
—*Thirteen-year-old African American girl. Taped at Camp Ruth Lee, Norwood, La.*

Archie's here and Veronica, too.
Jughaid's here, now how 'bout you?
Now (I could not hear this line.)
Now let's get the rhythm of the hands (*Clap clap.*)
Now we got the rhythm of the hands (*Clap clap.*)
Now let's get the rhythm of the feet (*Stomp stomp.*)
Now we got the rhythm of the feet (*Stomp stomp.*)
Now let's get the rhythm of the (*Pause.*) Hot Dog!

Now we got the rhythm of the—Hot Dog!
Now let's get the rhythm of the—um um (*Swivel hips.*)
Now we got the rhythm of the—um um (*Swivel hips.*)
Now let's get the rhythm of the Jackson Five!
—*Thirteen-year-old African American girl, Valley Park Junior High, Baton Rouge. Taped at Camp Ruth Lee,*
Norwood, La.

In the rhyme above, and the one following, the girls used hesitation at the words "Hot Dog" and "um um." At "Hot Dog," they swung their hips back and forth after hesitating. At "um um," they rolled their eyes and swiveled in a circular motion.

The girls volunteered another "Archie and Veronica."

Archie's here, Veronica not
We need some money and we need it hot.
Now let's get the rhythm of the hands (*Clap clap.*)
Now we got the rhythm of the hands (*Clap clap.*)
Now let's get the rhythm of the foot (*Stomp stomp.*)
Now we got the rhythm of the foot (*Stomp stomp.*)
Now let's get the rhythm of the (*Pause.*) choo choo (*Raise hand as though blowing a*
whistle.)
Now we got the rhythm of the—choo choo
Now let's get the rhythm of the—hot dog
Now we got the rhythm of the—hot dog
Now let's get the rhythm of the um—um
Now we got the rhythm of the um—um
Now let's get the rhythm of the Jackson Five!
—*Thirteen-year-old African American girls, taped at Camp Ruth Lee, Norwood, La.*

The next series of handclaps begins with "A sailor went to sea sea sea." "A Sailor" incorporated pantomime gestures, as well as handclapping, body motions, and deep bowing. Variations on the "sailor" theme appeared in Baton Rouge, New Orleans, and at Camp Ruth Lee. The chant, and handclapping pattern, employs a 4/4 beat:

A sailor went to sea sea sea (*Put hand up to forehead as though peering into distance.*)
To see what he could see see see
But all that he could see see see
Was the bottom of the deep blue sea sea sea

A sailor went to chop chop chop (*Hack at inside of elbow with open hand.*)
To see what he could chop chop chop
But all that he could chop chop chop
Was the bottom of the deep blue chop chop chop

A sailor went to knee knee knee (*Touch knee with hand.*)
To see what he could knee knee knee
But all that he could knee knee knee
Was the bottom of the deep blue knee knee knee

A sailor went to oo-watch-i-cotch (*Shake hips vigorously.*)
To see what he could oo-watch-i-cotch
But all that he could oo-watch-i-cotch
Was the bottom of the deep blue oo-watch-i-cotch

A sailor went to sea sea sea, chop chop chop, knee knee knee, oo-watch-i-cotch.
(*Here go through all four movements.*)
—*African American 7th-grade girls, McKinley Junior High School. Baton Rouge, 1974; An identical variant was
recorded by African American girls, Zachary, La. Taped at Camp Ruth Lee, Norwood, La. 1974.*

A second group of girls at McKinley Junior High stepped forward and performed "A Sailor Went to Sea Sea Sea," using "My fellow" instead of "A sailor,"
and adding a new stanza:

My fellow went to Chi-na (*Put hands palm to palm and bow.*)
To see what he could Chi-na (*Put hands palm to palm, swivel hips, and bow.*)
But all that he could Chi-na (*Hands palm to palm, bow deeply.*)
Was the bottom of the deep blue Chi-na . . . (*Hands palm to palm, swivel whole body.*)
—*Camp Ruth Lee, Norwood, La.*

"A Sailor" was popular among both white and African American children
and was played at all venues, and across the years, I collected. Here are white
eight-year-olds from Valena C. Jones Elementary, New Orleans, 1979:

A sailor went to sea sea sea (*Hand to forehead.*)
To see what he could see see see
And all that he could see see see
Was the bottom of the deep blue sea sea sea
A sailor went to Chi-na (*Bend over in deep bow from the waist.*)

To see what he could Chi-na
But all that he could Chi-na
Was the bottom of the deep blue Chi-na.
A sailor went to oo-watch-i-cotch (*Shake hips vigorously.*)
To see what he could oo-watch-i-cotch
But all that he could oo-watch-i-cotch
Was the bottom of the deep blue oo-watch-i-cotch.
—*Valena C. Jones Elementary, 2nd-grade white girls, New Orleans*

The following next three variants were recorded in Lafayette Square, New Orleans, during the International Year of the Child celebration (1979). The participants were from different schools. I approached them while they were waiting in line to get their faces painted. When they heard the other children gathering around and playing for me, they joined together in a ragged circle of various ages, and chanted:

A sailor went to sea sea sea
To see what he could see see see
But all that he could see see see
Was the bottom of the ocean sea sea sea . . .
(*The players broke up in laughter; then one girl said, "Come on," and they began again.*)
A sailor went to chop chop chop (*Girls "chop" right hand on left arm.*)
To see what he could chop chop chop
But all that he could chop chop chop
Was the bottom of the ocean chop chop chop (*Mumble mumble . . .*)
(*Another, older, group of girls in the background stepped forward, broke in, and continued:*)
A sailor went to I I I (*Point to eye.*)
To see what he could I I I
But all that he could I I I
Was the bottom of the deep blue I I I
A sailor went to love love love (*Point to heart.*)
To see what he could love love love
But all that he could love love love
Was the bottom of the deep blue love love love
A sailor went to you you you (*Point to partner.*)
To see what he could you you you
But all that he could you you you
Was the bottom of the deep blue you you you

A sailor went to I love you (*On "I"– point to oneself; on "love"—cross arms across
breast like a hug; on "you"—point across to partner.*)
To see what he could I love you (*Repeat all actions.*)
But all that he could I love you (*Repeat all actions.*)
Was the bottom of the deep blue I love you. (*Repeat all actions.*)

The girls who chanted, "I love you" were white teenagers. They recalled they
had learned it at Valena C. Jones Elementary, New Orleans.

The next variant of "A Sailor" was handclapped by two white students at
Lusher Elementary School. The collecting group was half African American
and half white, and all the girls knew the rhyme, because everyone chanted
along with the two girls while they played:

A sailor went to sea sea sea
To see what he could see see see
But all that he could see see see
Was the bottom of the deep blue sea sea sea
A sailor went to Ha-wa-ii (*Do a "hula."*)
To see what he could Ha-wa-ii
But all that he could Ha-wa-ii
Was the bottom of the deep blue Ha-wa-ii
A sailor went to Hong Kong (*Put fingers up to eyes and stretch the eyelids "slanty."*)
To see what he could Hong Kong
But all that he could Hong Kong
Was the bottom of the deep blue Hong Kong
A sailor went to Chi-na (*Bow deep from the waist.*)
To see what he could Chi-na
But all that he could Chi-na
Was the bottom of the deep blue Chi-na.
—*Lusher Elementary, 3rd-grade white girls, New Orleans*

At Beechwood Elementary, Baker, Louisiana (1975), four kindergartners
clapped their version of "A Sailor":

A sailor went to sea sea sea
To see what he could see see see (*Put hand to brow as though looking.*)
· · · · · · · · · · ·
A sailor went to chop chop chop (*Make chopping motion inside elbow.*)
To see what he could chop chop chop

. . . .
A sailor went to knee knee knee (*Tap knee.*)
To see what he could knee knee knee

. . . .
A sailor went to Chi-na (*Swivel hips on "Chi-na."*)
To see what he could Chi-na

. . . .
A sailor went to oo-watch-i-cotch (*Shimmy whole body.*)
To see what he could oo-watch-i-cotch

. . . .
A sailor went to sea chop knee oo-watch-i-cotch (*Do all motions.*)
To see if he could see chop knee oo-watch-i-cotch
But all that he could see chop knee oo-watch-i-cotch
Was the bottom of the ocean
See chop knee OO-WATCH-I-COTCH!

—*Beechwood Elementary kindergarten white girls, Baker, La., 1975 (Identical to version played by African American girls at McKinley Junior High School, Baton Rouge, 1974.)*

Campers at Camp Ruth Lee (1974) gathered in a group, one African American and three white girls, all in the eighth grade. Their version of "A Sailor" reflects the fact that by the eighth-grade girls were beginning to forget certain phrases of earlier chants. Note the deletion of key ideas:

A sailor went to sea sea sea (*No accompanying motions, handclapped extremely fast.*)
When all he did was see see see
Was the bottom of the deep blue sea sea sea
When a sailor went to chop chop chop
When all he did was chop chop chop
Was the bottom of the deep blue chop chop chop
When a sailor went to knee knee knee
Was all he did was knee knee knee
Was the bottom of the deep blue knee knee knee
When a sailor went to oo watch-i-cotch
Was all he did was oo watch-i-cotch
Was the bottom of the deep blue oo watch-i-cotch
When the sailor went to sea chop knee OO WATCH I COTCH!

There was a lull, and a little squabbling, and then one of the white girls said, "I have a favorite one." She faced the girl she had just been arguing with and began:

My sailor went to dis dis dis (*Clap hands across left to right.*)
To see what he could dis dis dis
But all that he could dis dis dis
Was the bottom of the ocean dis dis dis

My sailor went to knee knee knee (*Slap the knee 3 times.*)
To see what he could knee knee knee
But all that he could knee knee knee
Was the bottom of the ocean knee knee knee

My sailor went to land land land (*Hands up together with opposite player.*)
To see what he could land land land
But all that he could land land land
Was the bottom of the ocean land land land

My sailor went to Dis-ney-land (*On "Dis," clap; on "ney," slap knees; on "land," slap hands together with partner.*)
To see what he could Dis-ney-land
But all that he could Dis-ney-land
Was the bottom of the ocean Dis-ney-land.
—*Camp Ruth Lee, 8th-grade white girls, Norwood, La.*

The high school girls at Ursaline Academy in New Orleans struggled to remember a variant of "A Sailor." The white girls began:

(Girl) I know one. My father went to sea sea sea . . . (Then all the girls in the class joined in and chanted.)

My father went to sea sea sea
To see what he could see see see
And all that he could see see see
Was the bottom of the deep blue sea sea sea . . .

The crowd broke up with "My father . . ." and "A sailor . . ." and then dwindled to a ragged mumble.

(JS) And then what?

(Group shouted) We go on to "oo watch-ee-watch!"

An African American girl who had listened while the other girls struggled to remember "A Sailor," stepped forward, chose a partner, and handclapped to this version, done without accompanying gestures:

> When a sailor went to sea sea sea
> Was all he did was sea sea sea
> Was the bottom of the deep blue sea sea sea
> When a sailor went to chop chop chop
> Was all he did was chop chop chop
> Was the bottom of the deep blue chop chop chop
> When the sailor went to knee knee knee
> Was all he did was knee knee knee
> Was the bottom of the deep blue knee knee knee
> When the sailor went to oo-watch-i-cotch
> Was all he did was oo-watch-i-cotch
> Was the bottom of the deep blue oo-watch-i-cotch.
> —*Twelve-year-old African American girl, Ursaline Academy, New Orleans*

"A Sailor" is nonsensical from the get go, but some versions strip the words to the very bone. The child did not seem to see the lack of sense of the last verse as it is stated, even though those around her had recited it differently. As with many nonsense formulas, the performer was saying the ritualized verbal pattern that sounded right to her, and she did not question the logic of it.[4]

At Lusher Elementary in New Orleans, the African American girls chanted the next game. I place it here because it has the word "sailor" in it as well:

> Have you ever ever ever in your long-legged life (*Stretch tall each time "long-legged"*
> *is said.*)
> Seen a long-legged sailor
> With his long-legged wife
> No, I never never never in my long-legged life
> Seen a long-legged sailor
> With his long-legged wife
>
> Have you ever ever ever
> In your pigeon-toed life

> Seen a pigeon-toed sailor with his pigeon-toed wife
> No, I never . . .

Another child interrupted, "Bow-legged!" Her partner responded, "Not me!" The second child shouted, "Oh yeah?" And the game ended in an argument, the last line of which was, "I wasn't talkin' about you!"[5]

I recorded a number of chants that included the word "China." The teen-agers at Ursaline Academy, New Orleans, contributed one:

> My father was from China
> My mother was from France
> My sister's in the hospital
> But taught me how to dance
> My father gave me a nickel
> My mother gave me a dime
> My sister gave me . . . something . . .

(The group consulted a bit and had trouble coming up with the next line.)

(Original girl) Then my father took my nickel, and my mother took something, and my sister gave me a dime, or something like that. Yeah. Then my sister took the dancing lessons, or whatever it was, and something like that, and then, they threw me out the house, and then . . . an alligator purse . . . (Laughter erupted from the group.)

The Ursaline ninth-grade girls continued with another reference to China:

> Chinese checkerboard sittin' on a fence
> Tryin' to make a dollar out of fifteen cents.
> He missed, he missed, he missed like this.

(*The handclap rhyme is repeated over and over, and each time the last line is accompa-nied by a changing, complicated footwork pattern. Whoever makes a misstep is out.*)
—*Also recorded by McKinley Junior High School 7th-grade African American girls, Baton Rouge*

The same Ursaline Academy girls then paired off and performed this next handclap with lightning speed. They called it "Concentration":

—Are you ready?
If so, let's go.
Can you get it?
Can you get it?
Can you get it?
Can you get it?

(On and on, faster and faster, until someone misses or until everybody gets bored and breaks up laughing.)
—*Ursaline Academy, teenage white girls, New Orleans*

"Concentration" was earlier taped twice at Camp Ruth Lee; first exactly as above, by white girls; then, as below, by African American girls:

Concentration (First girl.)
Are you ready? (First girl.)

I is (Second girl.)
Let's go! (First girl.)
1–2 (Second girl.)
2–3 (First girl.)
3–4 (Second girl.)
4–5
5–6
6–7
7–8
8–9
9–10
10–1

(The girls clap faster and faster until one forgets which number she is on, and then the onlookers and the winner shout, "You miss! You miss!)

At Camp Ruth Lee word got around that I was recording games and volunteers arrived; sometimes in groups, and sometimes alone. A single African American girl stepped forward, reached out, chose a partner, and began:

Dr. Hippy, Dr. Hoppy
Dr. Lemon-Lime

He surely got drunk off a bottle a' wine.
He went to the Doctor and the Doctor said
Now let's get the rhythm of the (*Clap clap.*)
Now I got the rhythm of the (*Clap clap.*)
Now let's get the rhythm of the (*Stomp stomp.*)
Now I got the rhythm of the (*Stomp stomp.*)
Now let's get the rhythm of the—hot dog (*Shake hips.*)
Now I got the rhythm of the—hot dog (*Shake hips.*)
Now let's get the rhythm of the clap clap, stomp stomp, hot dog!
—*Thirteen-year-old African American girl, Valley Park Junior High, Baton Rouge.*
Taped at Camp Ruth Lee, Norwood, La.

Sometimes the child voiced "clap clap" and "stomp stomp" aloud while she performed the actions. Sometimes she let the actions speak for themselves. Her hand-clapping partner was silent, possibly because she did not know the words.

Engine engine number nine
Going down Chicago line
If that train should jump the track
Do you want your money back?
—*7th-grade white girls, Baker Junior High, Baker, La. Taped at Camp Ruth Lee, Norwood, La.*

I jumped rope to "Engine Engine" in Lafayette, Louisiana, in the 1950s. We added the line "Yes, no, maybe so, certainly" until we missed. (Cited earlier in jump-rope chapter.)

Two white campers stepped up to the tape recorder and clapped and chanted:

Have you ever ever ever
In your long-legged life (*Stretch up tall.*)
Seen a long-legged spider (*Stretch.*)
With a long-legged wife? (*Stretch.*)
No, I never never never
In my long-legged life (*Stretch.*)
Seen a long-legged spider (*Stretch.*)
With his long-legged wife. (*Stretch.*)

Have you ever ever ever
In your short-legged life (*Squat.*)
Seen a short-legged spider (*Squat.*)
With a short-legged wife? (*Squat.*)
No, I never never never
In my short-legged life (*Squat.*)
Seen a short-legged spider (*Squat.*)
With a short-legged wife. (*Squat.*)

Have you ever ever ever
In your angel life (*Make a halo.*)
Seen an angel spider (*Make a halo.*)
With an angel wife? (*Make a halo.*)
No, I never never never
In my angel life (*Make a halo.*)
Seen an angel spider (*Make a halo.*)
With an angel wife. (*Make a halo.*)

Have you ever ever ever
In your devil life (*Hold fingers up like horns.*)
Seen a devil spider (*Hold fingers up like horns.*)
With a devil wife? (*Hold fingers up like horns.*)
No, I never never never
In my devil life (*Hold fingers up like horns.*)
Seen a devil spider (*Hold fingers up like horns.*)
With a devil wife. (*Hold fingers up like horns.*)

Have you ever ever ever
In your pigeon-toed life (*Walk pigeon-toed.*)
Seen a pigeon-toed spider (*Walk pigeon-toed.*)
With a pigeon-toed wife? (*Walk pigeon-toed.*)
No, I never never never
In my pigeon-toed life (*Walk pigeon-toed.*)
Seen a pigeon-toed spider (*Walk pigeon-toed.*)
With a pigeon-toed wife. (*Walk pigeon-toed.*)

Have you ever ever ever
In your bow-legged life (*Walk bow-legged.*)
Seen a bow-legged spider (*Walk bow-legged.*)

With a bow-legged wife? (*Walk bow-legged.*)
No, I never never never
In my bow-legged life (*Walk bow-legged.*)
Seen a bow-legged spider (*Walk bow-legged.*)
And his bow-legged wife. (*Walk bow-legged.*)

Have you ever ever ever
In your smoking life (*Imitate smoking.*)
Seen a smoking spider (*Imitate smoking.*)
With a smoking wife? (*Imitate smoking.*)
No, I've never never never
In my smoking life (*Imitate smoking.*)
Seen a smoking spider (*Imitate smoking.*)
With a smoking wife. (*Imitate smoking.*)

—*Sung by two nine-year-old white campers from Holden, La. Taped at Camp Ruth Lee, Norwood, La.*

"Have You Ever" was also collected as part of the Janice Pierce written collection (1974):

Have you ever ever ever in your long-legged life
Seen a long-legged sailor with a long-legged wife?
No, I've never never never in my long-legged life
Seen a long-legged sailor with a long-legged wife.

Have you ever ever ever in your pint-toed life (pigeon-toed?)
Seen a pint-toed sailor with a pint-toed wife?
No, I've never never never in my pint-toed life
Seen a pint-toed sailor with a pint-toed wife.

Have you ever ever ever in your short-legged life
Seen a short-legged sailor with a short-legged wife?
No, I've never never never in my short-legged life
Seen a short-legged sailor with a short-legged wife.

—*Thirteen-year-old African American girl, McKinley Junior High, Baton Rouge. Submitted in writing.*

Following are seven handclaps related to the jingle beginning "I am a pretty little Dutch girl." "Pretty Little Dutch Girl" is a perennial favorite. Wikipedia. org "Pretty Little Dutch Girl" (October 30, 2018) traces the rhyme to the nineteen forties and provides twelve variations, some quite long and involved.

I am a pretty little Dutch girl
As funny as funny can be
And all the boys behind my back
Come following me to see.
My fellow's name is Jello
He comes from Alabamo
With a cherry on his nose
And a pickle on his toes
Saying e-i-e-i-o-o-o

—*Two nine-year-old white campers from Holden, La. Taped at Camp Ruth Lee, Norwood, La.*

I am a funny little Dutch girl
As funny as funny can be
With all those boys behind my back
Is calling me to see.
My fellow name is Bab-o
He come from Al-a-bam-o
With a hicky on his nose
And a big fat toes
Singing e-i-e-i-o Bab-o.

—*6th-grade African American girl, University Terrace Elementary, Baton Rouge 1974*

The girl who sang the song above told me that her mother had taught it to her. The girl was about eleven or twelve. I remember singing and handclapping to a similar "Little Dutch Girl" when I was the same age, in 1952. Note how close are the 1974 variant, and the one we sang in 1952:

I am a pretty little Dutch girl
As pretty as pretty can be
And all the boys behind my back
All follow me to see.
My fellow's name is Bab-o
He comes from Al-a-bam-o
With a pickle on his nose
And a cherry on his toes
Singing e-i-e-i-o Bab-o.

—*St. Genevieve School, Lafayette, La., 1950s*

The real wonder is that I can remember this jingle verbatim all these years later.

> I am a pretty little schoolgirl
> As pretty as pretty can be
> And all the boys around my back
> Go crazy over me.
> I have a boyfriend Fatty
> Who comes from Cincinnati
> With forty-eight toes
> And a pickle on his nose
> And that's the way the story goes.
> One day when I was walking
> I heard my boyfriend talking
> To a pretty little girl
> With a strawberry curl
> And this is what he said to her:
> I l-o-v-e love you
> I k-i-s-s kiss you
> I k-i-s-s kiss you on your
> F-a-c-e- face face face.
> —*Twelve-year-old white girl, Camp Ruth Lee, Norwood, La.*

Listeners on the sidelines contributed another rhyme related to "Little Dutch Girl."

> My boyfriend's name is Tommy
> He looks just like his mommy
> With a cherry on his nose
> And a pickle on his toes
> And this is how my story goes
> One day as I was walking
> I heard my boyfriend talking
> To a sweet little girl with the strawberry curls
> And this is what he said to her
> I l-o-v-e love you
> I k-i-s-s kiss you
> I'll meet you in the d-a-r-k p-a-r-k
> Tonight!
> —*Twelve-year-old white girls, Camp Ruth Lee, Norwood, La.*

The following variant comes from Philadelphia, Pennsylvania. My office mate from Louisiana State University (1974) heard me chanting and recalled it:

> I am a pretty little Dutch girl
> As pretty as pretty can be
> And all the boys around my way
> Go wicky wacky over me.
> My boyfriend's name is Kevin
> He comes from jolly old Devon
> With a cherry on his nose
> And ten fat toes
> That is the way my story goes.
> —*Philadelphia, Pa., public school 1960s*

The final version of "Dutch Girl" is slightly altered:

> I know a little hoola girl
> The prettiest prettiest hoola girl
> All the boys around her waist
> Are crazy about the hoola girl.
> One day when I was walking
> I heard my boyfriend talking
> To the pretty little hoola girl
> In her temple shorter curls
> And this is what he said
> I l-o-v-e love you
> I k-i-s-s kiss you
> Jump in the lake, swallow a snake
> Come back out with a tummy ache.
> —*7th-grade African American boy, McKinley Junior High School, Baton Rouge. Submitted in writing*

Since the above was submitted in a sheaf of writings, I did not get a chance to ask the boy who wrote it what he meant by "temple shorter curls." The words seem to be a heard, but unseen, version of "Shirley Temple curls." Shirley Temple has often been referenced in children's schoolyard lore, and the words "temple shorter" and Shirley Temple are close in sound.

A closing comment on "Pretty Little Dutch Girl." The final lines ending the last variation—"Jump in the lake swallow a snake / Come back out with a tummy ache"—were frequently used as a taunt on the playgrounds where

I went to school. We shouted it whenever we could not think of anything better to say, but wanted to taunt someone.[6]

I don't wanna go back no more more more
The (ears? Pigs?) are listening at the door door door
Catch you by the collar
Make you pay a dollar
I don't wanna go back no more more more
Fish in the haystack fish fish
Who you gonna marry? Tommy.
What you gonna feed him? Leg bones.
What you gonna kiss with? With a stick.
What you gonna kill with? Ice pick.
Ice pick ice pick ICE PICK!
—Two African American girls, Mayfair Elementary School, Baton Rouge.
Taped at Camp Ruth Lee, Norwood, La.

Here are five variations on the theme of "Somebody had a steamboat":

Mary had a steamboat
The steamboat had a bell
Mary went to Heaven
The steamboat went to—
Hello operator
Give me number nine
And if you don't
I'll kick you in the—
Behind the refrigerator
Lies a piece of glass
And if you don't
Pick it up
I'll kick you in the—
As I was saying
Mary had a steamboat . . .
—White Louisiana State University student in her twenties. Learned at Mandeville High School, Mandeville, La.,
1960s. Submitted in writing

Miss Mary had a kettle
The kettle had a bell

Miss Mary went to heaven
The kettle went to—
Hello operator
Give me number nine
If that number's busy
I'll kick you in the—
Behind the refrigerator
There laid a piece of glass
Miss Mary fell upon it
And cut her little—
Ask me no more questions
I'll tell you no more lies
This is what she told us
Before she shut her eyes eyes eyes

—White eighteen-year-old Istrouma High School girl, Baton Rouge. Submitted in writing

Miss Mary had a steamboat
The steamboat had a bell
Miss Mary went to heaven
The steamboat went to
Hello operator
Give me number nine
And if you disconnect me
I'll kick your little
Behind the refrigerator
There was a piece of glass
Miss Mary sat upon it
And cut her little
Ask me no more questions
I'll tell you no more lies
Miss Mary went to heaven
To get above her class.

—7th and 8th-grade African American girls. Some from Delmont Elementary, and some from Istrouma Junior High School, Baton Rouge. Taped at Camp Ruth Lee, Norwood, La.

The following "Hello Operator" is a fragment written down for me by a freshman English student at Louisiana State University in 1974. She apologized for having forgotten most of the jingle:

Hello Operator, give me number nine
And if you don't I'll kick you in the
Behind the refrigerator lies a piece of glass
And if you don't pick it up I'll kick you in the
As I was saying
Mary had a steamboat . . .[7]

—Twenty-year-old white Louisiana State University Student. She learned it at Mandeville High School, Mandeville, La., 1960s. Submitted in writing

The following, "Mary and John" handclaps are adaptations of autograph book rhymes:

Mary and John sitting in a tree
K-i-s-s-i-n-g
First comes love
Then comes marriage
Then comes John
With a baby carriage.

—Twelve-year-old white girl. Taped at Camp Ruth Lee, Norwood, La.

Mary and John
Sitting in a tree
K-i-s-s-i-n-g
First comes love
Then comes marriage
K-i-s-s-i-n-g
John and Mary sitting in a tree
K-i-s-s-i-n-g
Mary fall off
And break her knee
John come down
And save her life
Now I pronounce you man and wife
K-i-s-s-i-n-g.

—Eleven-year-old African American girl. Delmont Elementary School, Baton Rouge, Taped at Camp Ruth Lee, Norwood, La.

Mary and John sitting in a tree
Mary fell down and broke her knee

John came down to save her life
Now I pronounce you man and wife.

—6th-grade white girls. St. Anthony School, Baton Rouge. Taped at Camp Ruth Lee, Norwood, La.

Mary and John
Sitting in a tree
K-i-s-s-i-n-g
First comes love
Then comes marriage
Then comes a baby
In a baby carriage.[8]

—6th-grade white girls, St. Anthony School, Baton Rouge. Taped at Camp Ruth Lee, Norwood, La.

The St. Anthony girls used "Mary and John" to tease their friends. They had first supplied real names in the place of "Mary" and "John," and there was a lot of "Aw, quit it!" and "Don't you dare!" going on while I taped. The girls being teased then insisted that I substitute "Mary" and "John" in place of the real names in the typed copy.

May Sue, May Sue, May Sue
From Alabama
Hey little girl with the dippity doo (*Make circular motion at temple with finger.*)
Your mama's got the measles and your papa too
You take a a-b-c-d-e-f-g (*Shake hips to the left.*)
You take a h-i-j-k-l-m-n-o-p (*Shake hips to the right.*)
You take a booster shot (*Make motion like giving a shot in the hip, three times.*)
You take a booster shot
You take a booster shot
And FREEZE! (*Girls freeze.*)

—7th-grade white girls, Sherwood Forest Elementary. Taped Camp Ruth Lee, Norwood, La.

The girls paired off in twos and clapped "May Sue," first to a chant and then again to a tune that one girl remembered. All the girls were white, and about twelve years old. Their rhythm featured a strict 4/4 pattern.

Several African American girls sauntered up and joined the white girls. The new arrivals described themselves as being from Zachary, Holden, Baker, and Baton Rouge. They contributed a slightly modified version of "May Sue" where the clapping pattern displayed syncopation:

May Zoo (*Clap stomp clap.*)
May Zoo (*Clap stomp clap.*)
May Zoo from Alabama (*Clap stomp clap stomp clap stomp clap.*)
Hey little girl with the zippity do (*Twirl finger near temple.*)
Your mama's got the measles and your papa's got the flu
You take a a-b-c-d-e-f-g (*Shake hips to left.*)
You take a h-i-j-k-l-m-n-o-p (*Shake hips to right.*)
You take a booster shot (*Mime shot in the hip.*)
You take a booster shot
You take a booster shot.
And FREEZE! (*Freeze for a few seconds.*)

Later, I collected the identical chant, complete with off-beat clapping pattern, from African American girls at Baker Junior High and Bakerfield Elementary, both in Baker and at University Terrace Elementary in Baton Rouge (1974). After I moved to New Orleans in 1975, I recorded "Miss Sue" and "May Zoo" again. Every group of African American children utilized the syncopated form. At the St. Joan of Arc bingo babysitting group, teenagers ended "May Zoo" with a shout of, "Don't show your TEETH!" At the taping session at Gates of Prayer Hebrew Synagogue (1979), the white girls shouted at the end, "Aha!—You moved!" To which one of the players complained, "I didn't never do it before!" I asked, "OK. So if she unfreezes, what happens? I was told, "She got to take my arm and hit it while she says the rhyme again."

In all performances, the verbal differences in versions were minimal. The gestures remained universal. On the line "Hey, little girl with the dippity doo," there was a pause in which the players made a circular motion with their index finger at their temple; then at a-b-c-d-e-f-g / h-i-j-k-l-m-n-o-p, all players, both African American and white, shook their hips to one side, then the other. These motions were all precisely alike, no matter what school the girls attended.

Mary May May May
All dressed in black black black
She had some buttons buttons buttons
All down her back back back
She asked her mother mother mother
For fifteen cents cents cents
To see the elephant elephant elephant
Jump over the fence fence fence

She jumped so high high high
She touched the sky sky sky
She never came back back back
'Til the Fourth of July ly ly
She fell out of bed bed bed
And hit her head head head
On a piece of corn bread bread bread
The doctor said said said
That's what you get get get
For fartin' in bed bed bed.

—*1st- and 2nd-grade white girls, Dalton Elementary School, Baton Rouge*

"Mary May May May" was the first hand game I ever recorded. My informants were three diminutive neighbor girls I heard playing out in the front yard of a home down the block. I ran outside, asked if I could record them, and their mother said I could. The players were two seven-year-olds, and an eight-year-old, all students at Dalton Elementary. All were white. A few weeks later, I taped the following at McKinley Junior High, where all seven girls playing the hand game were African American:

Miss Mary Mack Mack Mack
All dressed in black black black
With twenty-four buttons buttons buttons
All down her back back back
She asked her mother for fifteen cents cents cents
To see the elephant elephant elephant
Jump over the fence fence fence
He jumped so high high high
'Til he touched the sky sky sky
And he never came back back back
'Til the Fourth of July ly ly
July can't walk walk walk
July can't talk talk talk
July can't eat eat eat
With a knife and a fork fork fork.

—*7th-grade African American girls, McKinley Junior High, Baton Rouge*

"Mary Mack" has been around for a long time. My mother remembered a version chanted as a jump rope rhyme in New Orleans during the 1920s:

Mary Mack
Dressed in black
Three gold buttons
Down her back
I love coffee
I love tea
I love the boys
And the boys love me.

—Mrs. W. W. Pitre, learned at Crossman School, New Orleans, 1920s

The next four variations of "Mary Mack" were all submitted in writing. I record them exactly as they were written. The popularity of "Mary Mack" is evidenced by the fact that versions came from University Terrace Elementary, McKinley Junior High, Dalton Elementary, and Prescott Junior High (Janice Pierce collection), in Baton Rouge; and Bakersfield Elementary in Baker, Louisiana, and the version from my mother's memory from New Orleans. Those below exist in my collection in the handwriting of the children themselves. They were replies sent in as a class assignment by their teacher, Janice Pierce:

Mrs. Mary Mac Mac Mac
All dressed in black black black
With twenty four buttons
On her back back back
She asked her mother mother mother
For fifteen cents cents cents
To see the heaven heaven heaven
She jumped so high high high
She touched the sky sky sky
And never came back back back
Before july ly ly
She fell on the bed bed bed
And hit her head head head
On a piece of cornbread cornbread cornbread
The doctor said said said
That's what you get get get
For falling in bed bed bed.

—Prescott Junior High School twelve-year-old white boy. He interviewed his second-grade sister, Baton Rouge.
Janice Pierce Collection

Miss Mary Lou Lou Lou
All dressed in blue blue blue
With twenty-four buttons buttons buttons
Straight down her back back back
She asked her mother mother mother
For fifteen cent cent cent
To see the elephant elephant elephant
Jump over the fence fence fence
He jumped so high high high
He touched the sky sky sky
And he never came back back back
'Til the fourth of July ly ly.

—Thirteen-year-old African American girl, McKinley Junior High, Baton Rouge. Submitted in writing.
Janice Pierce Collection

Miss Mary Mac Mac Mac
All dressed in black black black
With twenty four buttons buttons buttons
Right down her back back back
She ate ten muffins muffins muffins
For fifteen cents cents cents

. . . .

—Incomplete version submitted in writing. 7th-grade African American boy, McKinley Junior High School,
Baton Rouge. Janice Peirce collection

The change in the line "She ate ten muffins muffins muffins / For fifteen cents cents cents" instead of the usual "She asked her mother mother mother / For fifteen cents cents cents," is an excellent example of the way changes occur in oral transmission of schoolyard lore. The next example starts out close to the conventional lines, but by line five, the words change, and make a droll and unexpected difference:

Mrs. Mary Mack Mack Mack
All dressed in black black black
With twenty four buttons buttons buttons
Right down her back back back
She ate some mother mother mother
For fifteen cents cents cents

To see the elephants elephants elephants
Jump the fence . . . [9]

—Incomplete version. McKinley Junior High School, 7th-grade girl, Baton Rouge. Janice Pierce Collection

Miss Suzie had a baby
She named him Tiny Tim
She put him in the bathtub
To see if he could swim
He drank up all the water
He ate up all the soap
He tried to eat the bathtub
But it wouldn't go down his throat.
Miss Suzie called the doctor
Miss Suzie called the nurse
Miss Suzie called the lady with the alligator purse.
In came the doctor
In came the nurse
In came the lady with the alligator purse
Out came the doctor
Out came the nurse
Out came the lady with the alligator purse
The doctor said mumps
The nurse said measles
The lady with the alligator purse said sneezles.

—Twelve-year-old white girl, St. Anthony School, Baton Rouge

An alternate ending to the above:

In came the doctor
In came the nurse
In came the lady with the alligator purse.
"Mumps," said the doctor
"Measles," said the nurse
"Nothing," said the lady with the alligator purse.
Out walked the doctor
Out walked the nurse
Out walked the lady with the alligator purse.

—Eighteen-year-old white girl, Istrouma High School, Baton Rouge

Another alternate ending:

> Miss Lucy called the doctor
> The doctor called the nurse
> The nurse called the lady with the alligator purse
> I don't need no doctor
> I don't need no nurse
> I don't need no lady with the alligator purse
> Bang! Went the doctor
> Bang! Went the nurse
> Bang! Bang! Went the lady with the alligator purse.
> —*7th-grade African American girls, McKinley Junior High School, Baton Rouge*

I asked the girls what the "Bang!" meant, and they said it was the door slamming behind the people when they "left out."

Another alternate ending:

> A penny to the doctor
> A penny to the nurse
> A dollar to the lady with the alligator purse.
> —*1st-grade white girl, LaSalle Elementary School, Baton Rouge*

> I had a little teddy bear
> His name was Tiny Tim
> I put him in the bathtub
> To see if he could swim
> He drank up all the water
> He drank up all the soap (?)
> He tried to eat the bathtub
> But it wouldn't go down his throat throat throat
> In came the doctor
> In came the nurse
> In came the lady with the alligator purse purse purse
> Out came the doctor
> Out came the nurse
> Out came the lady with the alligator purse purse purse.
> —*Twelve-year-old white girl, Prescott Junior High School, Baton Rouge. Interviewed her sister in the 5th grade.*
> *Submitted in writing. Janice Pierce Collection*

The following variant was collected from a male friend in his late fifties. He lived in New Orleans but had learned "Lulu" in a Worthington, Minnesota, public school during the 1920s:

> Lulu had a baby
> She named him Bobbie Jim
> She took him to the pisspot
> To learn him how to swim.
> He floated to the bottom
> He floated to the top
> Lulu got excited
> And grabbed him by the cock.
> *—Male friend in his fifties, New Orleans*

The St. Joan of Arc bingo babysitters sang the ending:

> . . . .
> In walked the doctor
> In walked the nurse
> In walked the lady with the alligator purse
> Measles said the doctor
> Mumps said the nurse
> Nothing said the lady with the alligator purse
> Out walked the doctor
> Out walked the nurse
> Out walked the lady with the alligator purse.
> *—Same ending: John Dibert Elementary; Ursaline Academy, New Orleans (1977);*
> *Gates of Prayer Hebrew Synagogue, Metairie, La. (1979)*

"Miss Suzie," sometimes "Miss Lucy," sometimes "Miss Sally," was played at every recording venue I visited in New Orleans, Baton Rouge, and Lafayette. When there was a hesitation in recalling it, the crowd of children prompted each other.

Here is a transcription of sixth graders at John Dibert Elementary in New Orleans (1981) as they urged one another along:

> *(White girl begins.)*
> Miss Suzie had a baby . . . uh
> *(Group of white and African American girls joins in.)*

She named him Tiny Tim
She put him in the bathtub
To see if he could swim
He drank up all the water
He ate up all the soap
He tried to eat the bathtub
But it wouldn't go down his throat . . . (*Pause.*)
(*Another white child says:*)
And then it goes . . .
(*An African American girl says:*)
And there's something about a doctor . . .
(*Several children in chorus:*)
A doctor called the nurse
The nurse called the lady with
The alligator purse
(*An African American boy shouts:*)
Y'all drunk!
(*Original white girl:*)
The doctor gave him a nickel
I mean a penny . . . or somethin'
No, it goes "Mumps" said the doctor
"Measles" said the nurse
"Nothin'" said the lady with the alligator purse
(*Group shouts.*) Oh WOW! We said it all!

The various voices heard in this group rendition of "Miss Suzie" demonstrate well how children teach each other. One child begins a familiar chant, but forgets certain lines. At points where there is a lapse of memory, or a loss of the thread, other children supply the next line, and the flow remains smooth. Learning takes place with immediacy, and without pain.[10]

The following five entries feature slightly varied versions of "Rubber Dolly," a handclap popular since the nineteen forties:

My mama told me
If I was goody
That she would buy me
A rubber dolly
My auntie told her

I kissed a soldier
Now she want [sic] buy me
A rubber dolly.
Ohhh! 3–6–9 the goose drunk wine
The monkey took the back of the 3–6–9
The line broke
The monkey got choke
And we all went to heaven
In a little row boat.
Amen.

—Submitted in writing by a 7th-grade African American boy. McKinley Junior High School, Baton Rouge.
Spelling and grammar his own. Janice Pierce Collection

My mama told me
When I was teenie
That she would buy me
A new bikini.
But someone told her
I kissed a fella
Now she won't buy me
A new bikini.

—Submitted in writing by a twenty-year-old white Louisiana State University student. Her note: "This was popular
from the second to fourth grades at Mandeville High School, Mandeville, La. I didn't know what a bikini was."

Say say say and arithmetic
My mama told me
If I was goodie
That she would buy me
A rubber dolly.
My auntie told her
I kissed a soldier
Now she won't buy me
A rubber dolly.
Ohhh! 3–6–9 the goose drank wine
The monkey chewed tobacco
On the streetcar line
The line broke
The monkey got choked
And they all went to heaven

In a little row boat
Bam! Bam!
—*African American twelve-year-old girls, McKinley Junior High, Baton Rouge*

The handclapping motions to "Rubber Dolly" were complex. The girls at McKinley Junior High made a circle containing six, sometimes eight, players. There had to be an even number. After a false start or two, where some players had to be dropped because they could not do the motions, four girls remained and performed the handclap. They started out putting their hands, palms together, to say "Say say say and arithmetic." Then, for the rest of the song, they clapped hands, first side to side and then across, with the girl facing them. The girls had to alternate clapping across from above and then below the hands of the girls to their right. So—two girls clapped at face level and then at waist level, while the others clapped at waist level and then at face level. (I know the explanation I provide is confusing. Go to "YouTube Rubber Dolly Song Shirley Ellis" for a spirited rendition of the song—with *equally* confusing clapping directions.)

A slightly different version of "Rubber Dolly" echoes the last one or two words of each line. The clapping pattern, with the repeat included, creates an 8/8 pattern:

My mama told me (told me)
If I was goodie (goodie)
That she would buy me (buy me)
A rubber dolly (dolly)
My auntie told her (told her)
I kissed a soldier (soldier)
Now she won't buy me (buy me)
A rubber dolly (dolly)
. . . .
—*University Terrace Elementary, 6th-grade African American girls, Baton Rouge*

At Camp Ruth Lee a little girl began and ended her song this way:

A A A and a Z Z Z
Like a ooo ma da ma
Like a 1–2–3
My mama told me
. . . .

3–6–9 the goose drank wine
The monkey played the fiddle
On the sweet potato vine
The vine broke
The monkey got choked
And they all went to heaven
In a little motorboat
Chop! Chop!

—6th-grade African American girl, Mayfair Elementary, Baton Rouge. Taped at Camp Ruth Lee, Norwood, La.

I sang the phrase "3–6–9 the goose drank wine / the monkey played the fiddle / On the streetcar line" when I was a child in Lafayette, Louisiana, in the 1940s. Something preceded the "3–6–9," but I cannot remember what it was.[11]

In one session at Camp Ruth Lee, one of the girls from Holden, Louisiana, stepped forward with a friend and handclapped and sang:

Oh Baby, when I get so lonely
And I dream about you
Can't live without you
That's why I dream about you.
And when I put my arms around you
I want to be free free free-a-
Free free free-a
Free free free a—gain!
If this world should come to an end
Then I'd be free free free—a
Free free free—a
Free free free a—gain![12]

—Like the handclaps derived from "ABC" and "Rockin' Robin," this song is taken from a popular song. Ten-year-old white girls. Taped at Camp Ruth Lee, Norwood, La.

Two new white girls then sang:

Our spades are two lips together
Twilight and daylight
Singing a song for you.
What is the mea-e-ning
Of flowers grow-oo-ing?

That tells a sto-oo-ry
About cha cha ca boo choo
Cha cha ca boo choo
Cha cha ca boo choo
(*Turn around three times.*)
Cha cha cha!
—*Seven-year-old white girls, Northside Elementary School, Denham Springs, La.*
Taped at Camp Ruth Lee, Norwood, La.

"Our spades" is a strange little song. Since the singers were first graders, I was not sure I got a complete or reliable version; certainly, the words were very unusual. The rhythm was a sharp "one two and three four," tango rhythm. The girls clapped loudly on "one two," then more softly on the rest of each line. I then came across it in another variant, cited below. Among the campers listening to the seven-year-olds sing was a white girl who said she was in the fifth grade at La Salle Elementary in East Baton Rouge Parish (1974). The girl sang and handclapped the following song, certainly a variation of "Our Spades," with a friend:

The face (?) space (?) are two lips together
Twilight in Heaven
Proving my love to you
What is the mee- e- ning
Of flowers grow-oo-ing
They tell the sto-oo-ry
Of there's some
Cha cha cha cha boom one
Cha cha cha cha boom two
Cha cha cha cha boom three
(*Clap clap, clap clap, clap clap, clap clap.*)
Cha cha cha.

The song "Twilight Forever," continued in favor, and in 1979, at Ursaline Academy, the white teenagers sang:

Our spades are two lips together
Twilight forever (Some said "in heaven")
Sending my love to you
What is the me-e-ning

Of flowers grow-o-ing
They tell the sto-o-ry
About my love of (Others said "Of true love's glory")
(Here laughter interrupts the flow)
. . . .
In summer's rain
In gay Paree
For you and me
Chop chop

(Girl from the back of the group) We sing another one that is the opposite of
that.
(JS) Step forward and sing.
(Girl)

They say that two lips are parted
Twilight in hell
Saving my hate for you
What is the mee-e-ning
Of flowers dy-i-ing
They tell of li-i-ies
Of my hate in a trash can
Rain in Spain
In gay Paree . . .

(Girl) We have an alternate ending of it that goes, "Our hearts go dump tiddy
ump ump ump / And our eyes go tink tink tink," and then we go back, and
say it all backwards, like, "They say our two lips are parted . . ." So we say it for-
wards, then we say it backwards."[13]
—*Ursaline Academy, white teenagers New Orleans*

Back a bit in time to Camp Ruth Lee, where more campers had arrived to
be recorded.

(JS) Where are you from?
(Girl) I live in Baton Rouge, and I go to St. Aloysius.
(Second girl) I'm in the third grade, and next year . . . Zachary Elementary is
where I went last year, but I don't know where I will go next year.

Then they sang and clapped to an extended song where "China" was featured:

My mama told me to open the door
Gee I don't wanna
I opened the door
He fell on the floor
That crazy old man from China
My mother told me to
Take off his hat
Gee I don't wanna
I took off his hat
He knocked me down flat
That crazy old man from China
My mama told me to take off his shirt
Gee I don't wanna
I took off his shirt
He fell in the dirt
That crazy old man from China
My mama told me to fry him some fish
Gee I don't wanna
I fried him some fish
He ate up the dish
That crazy old man from China
My mama told me to put him to bed
Gee I don't wanna
I put him to bed
He stood on his head
That crazy old man from China
My mama told me to turn off the light
Gee I don't wanna
I turned off the light
He kissed me good night
That crazy old man from China
My mama told me to wake him up
I woke him up with one big gulp
That crazy old man from China
My mama told me to bring him a smoke

Gee I don't wanna
I brought him a smoke
He let out a choke
That crazy old man from China
My mama told me to bring him home
Gee I don't wanna
I brought him home
He ate up the phone
That crazy old man from China.[14]

—*White campers, St. Aloysius School in Baton Rouge, and Zachary Elementary School in Zachary, La.*
Taped at Camp Ruth Lee, Norwood, La.

More campers joined the crowd, and they identified their schools as Mayfair Elementary, St. Joseph's Academy, and Sherwood Forest Elementary, all in Baton Rouge. After playing variants of "Apple on a Stick," and "Under the Bamboo Tree," two African American girls suddenly took a stance, hands crossed over their chests, and this handclap began:

Cross down (*Hands crossed over chest, then hands slap thighs.*)
When Billy was one (*Hands cross chest, thigh slap, then clap.*)
He loved to suck his thumb (*Repeat motions.*)
One Billy One Billy
Half past one
Cross down
When Billy was two
He loved to tie his shoe
Shoe Billy shoe Billy
Half past two
Cross down
When Billy was three
He learned to climb a tree
Tree little tree little
Half past tree
Cross down
When Billy was four
He learned to shut the door
Four little four little
Half past four
Cross down

When Billy was five
He learned to swim and dive
Dive little dive little
Half past five
Cross down
When Billy was six
He learned to take a fix
Fix little fix little
Half past six
Cross down
When Billy was seven
He learned to go to heaven
Heaven little heaven little
Half past heaven
Cross down
When Billy was eight
He learned to shut the gate
Gate little gate little
Half past eight
Cross down
When Billy was nine
He learned to drink up wine
Wine little wine little
Half past nine
Cross down
When Billy was ten
He learned to say the end!

(JS) Good! Wow!
(Girls) You know how to do like this? (*They hold their hands palm up and slap hands.*)
(JS) Let's see.

(Girls) A-b-c
It's easy as 1–2–3
I see it's just do-re-mi
A-b-C 1–2–3 baby you and me girl
(*Clap clap clap.*)
I think I love you (Sung in a high voice by one girl.)

(Girls) Come on, Girl, show me what you can do
Shake it shake it Baby
Shake it shake it Baby
Oh now shake it shake it Baby
Oh do-re-mi
Oh now with me
1–2–3
Baby—You and ME!

(Girls, excitedly) We know more! We're from Istrouma High![15]
One girl begins the next chant, but hesitatingly:

I don't wanna go to bed no more more more
There's a big fat policeman at the door door door
He catch me by the collar
He really make me holler . . . I forget . . . [16]

(Second girl) Go ahead, say it!
(Girl) You were gonna do it with me!
They begin clapping to the rhyme again:

I don't wanna go to bed no more more more
There's a big fat policeman at the door door door
Catch me by the collar
Make me pay a dollar
I don't wanna go to bed no more more more
Fish in a haystack
Fish fish
Who you gonna marry?
Tomm-y
What you gonna feed him?
Horse pee
What you gonna kill with
Ice pick
Ice pick, ice pick
Ice pick!

The two girls hurry into a variant of "Rubber Dolly":

A-B-C and a zee zee zee
And a oo ah ma la
And a 1–2–3
My mama told me
If I was goody
That she would buy me a rubber dolly
My Auntie told her I kissed a soldier
Now she won't buy me a rubber dolly
3–6–9 the goose drank wine
The monkey played the fiddle (*The second girl said, "The monkey chewed tobacco.*)
On the sweet potato vine (*The second girl said "Street car line."*)
The vine (*line*) broke
The monkey got choked
And they all went to heaven in a little rowboat (*motorboat*)
Clap clap.

They segued into:

Now let's get the rhythm of the hands
Clap clap
Now we got the rhythm of the hands
Clap clap
Now let's get the rhythm of the feet
Stomp stomp
Now we got the rhythm of the feet
Stomp stomp
Now let's get the rhythm of the (*Pause.*) hot dog (*Shake hips.*)
Now we got the rhythm of the (*Pause.*) hot dog (*Shake hips.*)
Now let's get the rhythm of the (*Pause.*) unh unh
(*Swivel hips sexily.*)
Now we got the rhythm of the (*Pause.*) unh unh
(*Swivel hips sexily.*)
Now let's get the rhythm of the Jackson Five!

(Girl) Mine goes:

Doctor Hickey Doctor Hockey Doctor Number Nine
He surely got drunk off a bottle of wine
He went to the doctor and the doctor said

Let's get the rhythm of the—unh unh (*Swivel hips.*)
Now I got the rhythm of the—unh unh (*Swivel hips.*)
Now let's get the rhythm of the stomp stomp (*Stomp stomp.*)
Now we got the rhythm of the stomp stomp (*Stomp stomp.*)
Now let's get the rhythm of the—hot dog (*Shake hips.*)
Now we got the rhythm of the—hot dog (*Shake hips.*)
Unh unh, stomp stomp, HOT DOG! (*Swivel, stomp, shake.*)

(Two new white girls) I'm Julie. I'm Gretchen.
(JS) Where do you go to school?
(Girls) Istrouma!
(JS) What are ya'll gonna do?
(Girls) Ronald McDonald!
(JS) OK, go.

Ronald McDonald
A biscuit (*Swivel hips on each "A biscuit."*)
Oooo gotcha mama
A biscuit
I got a boyfriend
A biscuit
He so sweet
A biscuit
Like a cherry tree
A biscuit
Ice cream soda with a cherry on top
Down down baby
Down by the roller coaster
Shoo shoo baby
I will never let you go
Shimmy shimmy co co pop
Shimmy shimmy rock
Shimmy shimmy co co pop
Shimmy shimmy rock.

The words "Ronald McDonald" led into the next handclap:
(Same two girls)

McDonald's is your kinda place
They serve you rattlesnakes
French fries from your toes
Drinks run from outa your nose
The last time I went there
They stole my underwear
McDonald's is your kinda place
Your kinda place![17]

(Girls) This is just numbers:

One two (*Clap clap.*) (*Clap across twice, clap own hands twice. Repeat faster and faster.*)
Three four (*Clap clap.*)
Five six (*Clap clap.*)
Seven eight (*Clap clap.*)
Nine ten. (*Clap clap.*)
—*Taped at Camp Ruth Lee, Norwood, La.*

In 1984, in Chalmette, Louisiana, at Happy Face Nursery School, I interviewed white first and second graders who were in after-school care. One second grader told me, "We don't sing anything on the school ground. We make up things. We learn a lot of stuff at bingo."

(JS) Y'all do handclaps at bingo?
(Girl) No, we make it all up.
(JS) OK. Y'all do something.

Two girls squared off and put their hands up, and began to handclap:

Big Mac, Filet of fish, Quarter Pounder, French fries (*Clap in 4/4 time on the beat.*)
Iced Coke, thick shakes sundaes and apple pies
(*Repeat four times, then gradually stop.*)
Have you got a break today, at McDonald's? (*Shouted after clapping stopped.*)

The same two girls then signaled with their hands up to begin another handclap:

A golden bowl (*Clap in 4/4 beat.*)
Diddy ump diddy ump

I'm feeling fine
Diddy ump diddy ump
Goes cross my mind
Diddy ump diddy ump
Oh golden bowl . . .

(JS) Oh, that's a good one. Where did you learn that?
(Girls shout) At the bingo!

The two girls then launched into:

I wish I had a nickel
I wish I had a dime
I wish I had a boyfriend
That kissed me all the time
My mama gave me a nickel
My father gave me a dime
My sister gave me a boyfriend
That kissed me all the time
My mama took my nickel
My father took my dime
My sister took her boyfriend
That kissed me all the time
She gave me Frankenstein
He made me do the dishes
He made me do the floors
He made me eat a cock-a-roach
And I kicked him out the door
Whoooo![18]

The two girls then thought for a moment and gave me their version of "Rockin' Robin," the song by the Jackson Five that inspired numerous handclap
variants from 1972 to the turn of the century:

Tweedle tweedle dee
Tweedle tweedle dee
A tweet a tweet
A bumblebee
He rocks in the treetops all the day long

A rockin and a boppin and a singin this song
All the little girls on Bourbon Street
Like to hear the robin go tweet tweet tweet
Rockin' Robin
Rock rock tonight
Rockin' Robin
Rock rock tonight
Next thing you know I was doin' the funky chicken
Rockin' Robin rock rock tonight
Rockin' Robin rock rock tonight
Went upstairs to take my bath
Next thing you know I was sayin' my prayers
Rockin' Robin rock rock tonight
Rockin' Robin rock rock tonight
Went to town meet my pal around
Next thing you know I was boogieing on down
Rockin' Robin rock rock tonight
Rockin' Robin rock rock tonight
I went to the store to get me some more
The next thing you know I was sittin' at the bar
Rockin' Robin rock rock tonight
Rockin' Robin rock rock tonight
We went to school to learn the golden rule
Next thing you know I had broken all the rules
Rockin' Robin rock rock tonight
Rockin' Robin rock rock tonight.[19]

The chant faded at the end as the girls seemed to have utilized all the verses they had at hand. There was a lull, then, a first-grade girl leaned in and shared:

Sittin' in the clover
Easy eisy over
She bought me ice cream
She bought me cake
She brought me home with a belly ache
Mama Mama I feel sick
Call the doctor quick quick
Doctor Doctor will I die?
One two three four five
I'm alive!

The second-grade girl thought a bit, then said, "I remember one. It's about the little old man from China."

This was the second time a child had offered a rhyme song about "a little old man from China."

(JS) All right. Do it.
(Girl) Come on, we can do it together.

The two girls softly practiced together, thinking the chant through. Then they began a variation of the handclap cited earlier featuring "That crazy old man from China."

My mama told me to open the door
Gee, I didn't wanna
I opened the door
And he fell on the floor
That crazy old man from China

My mama told me to put on his pants
Gee, I didn't wanna
I put on his pants
He gave me a slap
That crazy old man from China
My mama told me to put him to bed

Gee, I didn't wanna
I put him to bed
He kissed me on the head
That crazy old man from China

My mama told me to take him to the show
Gee, I didn't wanna
I took him to the show
I lost my toe
That crazy old man from China

My mama told me to wave goodbye
Gee, I didn't wanna
I waved goodbye

He punched me in the eye
That crazy old man from China . . .
—*White first and second graders, Happy Face Nursery School, Chalmette, La.*

(JS) Did you learn that at school?
(Second grader) We don't sing *anything* on the school ground. We make things
    up. We learn lots of stuff at bingo.
(JS) Y'all do those handclaps at bingo?
(Girl) No, we make it all up.

This insistence that "we make it all up," is a common thread among children who share lore with one another. Sometimes the statement is "My sister
makes all this up." Or "We make it up on the bus." The fact that "The Crazy
Old Man from China" was shared by children in summer camp near Baton
Rouge, and by second graders in Chalmette, Louisiana, is no surprise. Some
of the same child lore, almost word for word, was chanted by schoolchildren
in England, Scotland, Ireland, and New Zealand.[20]

The following chant, "Shake Shake Shake," was recorded by a white seven-
year-old girl from Crocker Elementary, New Orleans (1979).

Shake shake shake
Eenie meenie jipsakeenie
Oo a domileenie
Otchie kotchie liverotchie
I love you
L-O-V-E stands for love
Take a peach take a plum
Take a piece of bubblegum
Hey boy, what's your name?
John Wayne
Watcha got?
Hot dog
Gimme some. (*Clap clap.*)

The same seven-year-old from Crocker Elementary chanted the following. It
can be used as a group cheer, everyone standing facing front and doing the
actions together, or it can be a handclap. The "3–6–9" beginning occurred
repeatedly in games I collected:

3–6–9 the goose drank wine
The monkey chewed tobacco on the streetcar line
The line broke
The monkey got choked
And they all went to heaven in a little motorboat
Chop chop
Now let's get the rhythm of the hands (*Clap clap.*)
We got the rhythm of the hands (*Clap clap.*)
Now let's get the rhythm of the feet (*Clap clap.*)
Now we got the rhythm of the feet (*Stomp stomp.*)
Now let's get the rhythm of the count by fives
5–10–15–20– . . . . 100[21]

The seven-year-old said, "The one 100 lands on is the next one . . ." and before I could ask her what she meant by that, another child tapped me on the arm. I asked the tapper, "Did you know it a different way?" She nodded, "Some of it goes, "Now let's get the rhythm of the hip—and you raise your hip like that." I asked, "Where did you learn it?" She replied, "I went to Crocker, too."

The session continued, and I asked, "Who knows more of those?" An African American girl said, "I know one that goes like this":

Jack be nimble, Jack be quick
Jack jump over the candlestick
Jack jump high, Jack jump low
Jack fell down and broke his toe.

She added, "But you do that with your hands." So I asked, "Oh, you do a hand-clap to that? Does it have any motions to it?" And the girl volunteered further:

"Yeah, you do like—
Jack be nimble (*Jumps up a bit.*)
Jack be quick (*Jumps to side.*)
Jack jump over the candlestick (*Jumps with legs wide apart.*)
Jack fell down and broke his crown (*A chorus of "NO!" from group.*)
Jack jump high (*Leaps up.*)
Jack jump low (*Crouches.*)
Jack fell down and broke his toe. (*Pained expression.*)[22]
—*African American and white girls, Crocker Elementary, New Orleans*

This next handclap comes from Lacoste Elementary School in Chalmette, Louisiana. The white girls identified themselves as fourth graders, but the tiny size of the players and their piping voices led me to think they were more like second or third graders (1977).

My father is a trash man a trash man a trash man
My father is a trash man and this is what he says
Poo-ooo (*Hold nose.*)
My mother is a baker a baker a baker
My mother is a baker and this is what she says
Poo-ooo yum-yum (*Hold nose, then rub belly.*)
My sister is a hula a hula a hula
My sister is a hula and this is what she says
Poo-ooo yum-yum hula hula (*Hold nose, rub belly, hula dance.*)
My brother is a cowboy cowboy cowboy
My brother is a cowboy and this is what he says
Poo-ooo yum-yum hula hula bang bang (*Shoot finger like a gun.*)
My sister is a baby a baby a baby
My sister is a baby and this is what she says
Poo-ooo yum-yum hula hula bang bang MOMMY! (*Hold both hands out.*)
—*Lacoste Elementary, Chalmette, La.*

Across town, also in Chalmette (1977), three small white girls at Happy Face Nursery School had a slightly different variant:

(JS) Do you do any games like this? (*Clap hands together.*) What grade are you in?
(Girls) Second.
(Girls) Yeah!

The girls struggle to put their hands in the correct position, and break into laughter when they "miss."

My Father is a garbage man a garbage man a garbage man
My father is a garbage man (*Begin giggling.*)
And he stinks poo ooo (*Hold nose.*)
My mother is a baker lady a baker lady a baker lady
My mother is a baker lady
And she smells just like this poo ooo yum yum (*Hold nose, rub tummy.*)
My sister is a hula girl a hula girl a hula girl

My sister is a hula girl
And she moves like this poo ooo yum yum hula hula (*Hold nose, rub tummy, hula dance.*)
My brother is a cowboy a cowboy a cowboy
My brother is a cowboy
And this is how he goes all day
Poo ooo yum yum hula hula bang bang waa waa (*Hold nose, rub tummy, hula dance, shoot finger like gun, make kissing motion.*)
My boyfriend is a kisser a kisser a kisser
My boyfriend is a kisser
And this is how he goes all day
Poo ooo yum yum hula hula bang bang waa waa. (*Make all motions.*)[23]
—*Happy Face Nursery School, Chalmette, La.*

The next handclap was recorded by three white six-year-olds and one African American six-year-old. They were playing games in Lafayette Square during the International Year of the Child Festival in New Orleans (1979). They said they were first graders at "St. 'Enild School from across the river." St. Benilde School is in Metairie, Louisiana, across the Seventeenth Street canal from New Orleans. Their handclap is one of the few traditional parent-child games in this collection.

Patty cake patty cake baker's man
Make me a cake just as fast as you can
Roll it and pat it and mark it with a B
And put it in the oven for Baby and me.
—*International Year of the Child Festival, New Orleans*

At the St. Catherine of Siena Girl Scout meeting in Old Metairie one of the white girls volunteered, "I know one."

(JS) You know one? OK—go.
(Girl) We need four hands. Like that. So!

One time they see a little ship
One time they see a boat
Hip! Hop! Wanna go and shop
Not too sweet
Wanna piece of meat

Meat too tough
Wanna ride a bus
Bus too full
Wanna ride a bull
Bull too fat
Wanna ride a cat
Cat too mean
Wanna jelly bean
Bean too red
Wanna go to bed
Close your eyes and count to ten
If you miss start over again
1–2–3–4–5–6–7–8–9–10.
—*St. Catherine of Siena Girl Scout, Old Metairie, La.*

In 1998, I collected for almost one hour from a small group of kindergarten girls and three rowdy third-grade boys, at Myrtle Place Elementary School in Lafayette, Louisiana. The recording session was held in an echoing cafeteria where the noise reached ear-splitting levels, and the boys made every effort to dominate by howling, screeching, knocking the girls about, and grabbing the microphone out of my hand. From this frenetic session I managed to transcribe a handclap that incorporated elements of several other, well-known, threads:

(Group of girls shout) I—I—I know "A Bumblebee."
(JS) Shhhh, boys. (*Boys scream and gabble.*)
(Girls)

A bee a bee a bumblebee
She rocks in the treetops all day long
Hoppin' and a-hoppin' and a-singin' this song
All the little birds on Jaybird Street
Like to hear the robin go tweet, tweet, tweet
Rockin' Robin (sayin') rock rock tonight
Rockin' Robin (sayin') rock rock tonight
Awwww—I went downtown to see Charlie Brown
He gave me a nickel
I bought me a pickle
Pickle was sour

I bought me a flower
The flower was dead
I bought me a bed
The bed was hard
I bought me a card
The card was broken
Teddy Bear Teddy Bear turn around
Teddy Bear Teddy Bear touch the ground
Teddy Bear Teddy Bear tie your shoes
Teddy Bear Teddy Bear sing the blues.
—*White kindergartners, Myrtle Place Elementary, Lafayette, La.*

"A Bee a Bee a Bumblebee," begins with several lines from "Rockin' Robin," Michael Jackson's hit song of 1972. "Rockin' Robin" appeared in various iterations repeatedly from 1972 to 2018. The children then segued into "I went downtown to see Charlie Brown," by inserting the transitional word "Awwww." And, finally, the chant ended with lines from the jump-rope rhyme "Teddy Bear."[24]

Earlier in time, seventh-grade campers at Camp Ruth Lee had handclapped their version of "Rockin' Robin":

Tweedly tweedly dee
Tweedly tweedly dee
Tweet tweet a rock beat
Rocks in the treetops all day long
Rockin' and a boppin' an'
A-singin' this song
All the little birds on Jaybird Street
Love to hear the robin go tweet tweet tweet
Rockin' robin rock rock rock
Rockin' robin rock rock rock
Go Rockin' robin you really gonna rock tonight
Hey every little bird and his chickadee
Every little bird on top his tree
The chick turn to him
(Unintelligible line.)
Every little bird say go man go.
—*7th-grade African American and white girls, Baker Junior High School, Baker, La. One of the girls said,*
"I got that record at home." Taped at Camp Ruth Lee, Norwood, La.

Ronald McDonald—a biscuit
Ooo foxy mama—a biscuit
I got a boyfriend—a biscuit
He's so sweet—a biscuit
Like a cherry tree—a biscuit
Ice cream soda with a cherry on top
Down by baby down by the roller coaster
Choo choo baby
I don't wanna let you go
Shimmy shimmy co co pop
Shimmy shimmy rock
Shimmy shimmy co co pop
Shimmy shimmy rock.

—Two African American girls, Delmont Elementary and Istrouma Junior High, Baton Rouge.
Taped at Camp Ruth Lee, Norwood, La.

Two teenage African American girls at St. Joan of Arc bingo, who were enthusiastic participants in this collection, worked hard to recall the words to "Shimmy Shimmy Coke-a-Pop":

Down down baby, down by the roller coaster
Sweet sweet baby, I don't want to let you go
Shimmy shimmy coke-a-pop
Shimmy shimmy coke-a-pop
Shimmy shimmy rock
Shimmy shimmy lollipop
You missed!

One girl said, "There's more, but I can't remember."[25]

The following song, "Playmate," is, like "Rubber Dolly," a children's adaptation of a popular song. Wikipedia, 1/5/2018, tells us "Playmate" was, "ostensibly written by Saxie Dowell. The main theme was note-for-note plagiarized from the 1904 intermezzo "Lola" by Charles L. Johnson, for which Johnson sued, settling out of court for an undisclosed sum."

Say say say playmate
Come out and play with me
And bring your dollies three
Climb up my apple tree

Slide down my rain barrel
Into my cellar door
And we'll be jolly friends forevermore.

So sorry, Playmate
I cannot play with you
My dollies have the flu
And mumps and measles too
I got no rain barrel
I got no cellar door
But we'll be jolly friends
Forever more, more more.

—*Twelve-year-old white girl, Northwestern Middle School, Zachary, La.*

"Say Say Say Playmate" was all the rage in Lafayette, Louisiana, in the 1950s, when I attended St. Genevieve School. We sang it on the school ground, but I never saw it implemented as a handclap until I recorded it in East Baton Rouge Parish. The following parody, "Say Say Say Hippie," sung for me by the same twelve-year-old white girl who sang the above, is of interest, not only because it is a good parody, but because the girl insisted that she had made it up herself. Later, I collected identical versions of "Say Say Say Hippie" from a graduate of Tara High School, and from the sixth graders at University Terrace in Baton Rouge:

Say say say Hippie
Come out and smoke with me
And bring your LSD
Climb up my hashish tree
Slide down my pot barrel
Into the cellar door—KA-POW!
And we'll be jolly friends
Forever more more more

So sorry Hippie
I cannot play with you
My LSD turned blue
And pink and purple too
I got no rain barrel
I got no cellar door

> But we'll be Hippie friends
> Forever more more more.
> *—Twelve-year-old white girl, Northwestern Middle School, Zachary, La.*

After I had encountered "Say Say Say Hippie" a second time, I asked the source, a graduate from Tara High School, if she had made it up herself. She answered, "Oh no! Everybody knows that song." Janice Pierce, who was involved in collecting with me, reported "Playmate" in two separate segments at Walnut Hills Elementary School, Baton Rouge:

> Shim shim my playmate
> Come out and play with me
> And bring your dolly three
> Climb up my apple tree.
> Slide down my rain barrel
> Into my cellar door
> And we'll be jolly friends
> Forever more more more!
>
> (*Submitted in writing.*)

And later on a tape, after several other entries:

> Say my playmate
> I cannot play with you
> My dolly's got the flu
> Boo hoo boo hoo boo hoo
> I have no rain barrel
> I have no cellar door
> But we'll be jolly friends
> Forever more more more more more![26]
> *—African American and white 3rd-grade girls, Walnut Hills Elementary School, Baton Rouge. Janice Pierce collection*

> Take me out to the ball game
> Take me out to the crowd
> Buy me some peanuts and cracker jacks
> I don't care if I never come back
> For it's root toot toot
> For the home team

If they don't win it's a shame
For it's one two three strikes you're out
At the old ball game
Game game game game.[27]
—*Twelve-year-old white girls. Taped at Camp Ruth Lee, Norwood, La.*

S O S sail my ship
Every night they have a fight
And this is what they said to me
Boys are rotten made of cotton
Girls are dandy made of candy
Oka boca oka boca I win you
I love coffee I love tea
I love Mark and he loves me
I married coffee I married tea
I married Mark and he married me.
—*Prescott Junior High School, twelve-year-old African American girl. Baton Rouge.*
Submitted in writing. Janice Pierce Collection

And here is "Under the Bamboo Tree," a song with a history:

Under the bamboo
Under the bamboo tree
True love for you my darling
True love for me
Bam bam bam
Under we'll marry
Happy we'll always be
Under the bamboo tree
Cha cha cha—ole!
—*Ten-year-old white girls. Camp Ruth Lee, Norwood, La.*

"Under the Bamboo" was collected three times in the early 1970s, once as above, then twice more, with slight variations. All variants come from the Camp Ruth Lee collection:

Under the bamboo
Under the bamboo tree
True love for you my darling

True love for me
After we marry
Happy we'll always be
Under the bamboo tree
Cha cha cha 3–5–4 ole!

—*Ten and thirteen-year-old African American Girls, Broadmoor Junior High and Mayfair Elementary, Baton Rouge.*
Taped at Camp Ruth Lee, Norwood, La.

Under the bamboo
Under the bamboo tree
True love for you my darling
True love for me (*Pause pause pause.*)
After we're married
Happily we'll be
Under the bamboo tree
(*Clap clap, slap slap, snap snap.*)
Ole!
Bump tiddy ump ump
Bump yay!

—*Seven-year-old African American girl, Northside Elementary, Denham Springs, La.*
Taped at Camp Ruth Lee, Norwood, La.

The clapping in "Under the Bamboo Tree," started on the second syllable, un-DER, and continued in a 4/4 rhythm giving the handclap a jaunty syncopation. On the line "clap clap, slap slap, snap snap," the singer clapped, slapped her thighs, and snapped her fingers.[28]

Winston taste good like a cigarette should
Winston taste good like a P—I—want a piece of pie
Pie too sweet, wanta piece of meat
Meat too tough, wanta ride a bus
Bus too full wanta ride a bull
Bull too fast, want my money back.

—*7th-grade white girl, Prescott Junior High, Baton Rouge. Submitted in writing. Janice Pierce collection*

Crackdown, when Billy was one
He loved to suck his thumb.
Thumb little thumb little
Half past one

Crackdown, when Billy was two
He loved to tie his shoe
Shoe little shoe little
Half past two
Crackdown, when Billy was three
He loved to climb a tree
Tree little tree little
Half past three
Crackdown, when Billy was four
He loved to shut the door
Four little four little
Half past four
Crackdown, when Billy was five
He loved to swim and dive
Dive little dive little
Half past five
Crackdown, when Billy was six
He learned to pick up sticks
Sticks little sticks little
Half past six
Crackdown, when Billy was seven
He learned to went to heaven
Heaven little heaven little
Half past seven
Crackdown, when Billy was eight
He learned to shut the gate
Gate little gate little
Half past eight
Crackdown, when Billy was nine
He learned to drink some wine
Wine little wine little
Half past nine
Crackdown, when Billy was ten
He learned to say THE END!

—Twelve-year-old African American girls, Valley Park Junior High, Baton Rouge.
Taped at Camp Ruth Lee, Norwood, La.

On "Crackdown," the players crossed their arms over their chests, tapped their shoulders, then slapped their thighs. The rest of the chant was done by clapping hands together and across to a partner in increasingly complex ways. As soon as the first group of chanters finished "Crackdown," more campers stepped forward saying, "I know one! I know one!

Crossdown (*Same crossed arm, tapped shoulder, then slap thigh motion.*)
When Billy Boy was one
He learned to suck his thumb
Thumb Billy thumb Billy
Half past one
Crossdown
When Billy Boy was two
He learned to tie his shoe
Shoe Billy shoe Billy
Half past shoe
Crossdown
When Billy Boy was three
He liked to climb a tree
Tree Billy tree Billy
Half past tree
Crossdown
When Billy Boy was four
He learned to shut the door
Door Billy door Billy
Half past door
Crossdown
When Billy Boy was five
He learned to swim and dive
Dive Billy dive Billy
Half past five
Crossdown
When Billy Boy was six
He learned to pick up sticks
Sticks Billy sticks Billy
Half past sticks
Crossdown
When Billy Boy was seven
He liked to go to heaven
Heaven Billy heaven Billy
Half past heaven

Crossdown
When Billy Boy was eight
He liked to shut the gate
Gate Billy gate Billy
Half past gate
Crossdown
When Billy Boy was nine
He liked to plant some signs
Signs Billy signs Billy
Half past sign
Crossdown
When Billy Boy was ten
He liked to say the hen
Hen Billy hen Billy
Half past hen
Crossdown
When Billy Boy was eleven
He liked to play with (*Pause.*) fellows
(*Here everybody breaks into laughter.*)
Fellows Billy fellows Billy.

(The laughter got louder, and the game ended.)
—*African American girls ranging in age from ten to thirteen, Istrouma Junior High School and Delmont Elementary, Baton Rouge. Taped at Camp Ruth Lee, Norwood, La.*

Janice Pierce collected "Billy Boy" at Walnut Hills Elementary School when she was taping games. She said it was regularly sung on the bus and was one of the few songs that did not also serve as a jump rope game. The Walnut Hills version was almost identical to the one above, so I give here only those stanzas that differed:

. . . .
When little Billy was seven
He learned to count to eleven
Eleven Billy eleven Billy
Half past seven
. . . .
When little Billy was eight
He learned to roller skate

Skate Billy skate Billy
Half past eight
. . . .
When little Billy was ten
He learned to write with a pen
Pen Billy pen Billy
Half past ten
Cross down THE END![29]

—African American and white 3rd-grade girls, Walnut Hills Elementary, Baton Rouge. Janice Pierce Collection

The next handclap has antecedents in England and is quite old. The wording and the directions for play in the nineteenth-century versions reflect a seemingly more refined time.[30]

The modern children have leached the elegance from the English versions, kept the heartbreak, and wear no nineteenth-century pinafores. Instead, they have imbued their variants with a vivid, earthier, liveliness:

Variation 1:

When I was a baby baby baby
When I was a baby baby baby
I said Unh! Unh! Unh! Unh! Unh! (*Thumb in mouth and sway side to side.*)
All day long, all day long.

When I was a child child child
When I was a child child child
I said Jump! Jump! Jump! Jump! Jump! (*Jump.*)
All day long, all day long.

When I was a teenager teenager teenager
When I was a teenager teenager teenager
This is what I did
I went Unh! Unh! Unh! Unh! Unh! (*Swing hips side to side.*)
All day long, all day long.

When I got married married married
When I got married married married
This is what I did
I went Unh! Unh! Unh! Unh! Unh! (*Kiss air from side to side.*)
All day long, all day long.

When the baby died died died
When the baby died died died
This is what I did
I went Unh! Unh! Unh! Unh! Unh! (*Cover eyes and mimic crying.*)
All day long, all day long.

When my husband died died died
When my husband died died died
This is what I did
I said Hurray! Hurray! Hurray! Hurray! Hurray! (*Jump and wave arms
while shouting.*)
All day long, all day long.

When I died died died
When I died died died
This is what I did
I went Unh! Unh! Unh! Unh! Unh! (*Hold stomach and slowly sink down.*)
All day long, all day long.
—*1st- and 2nd-grade white girls, Dalton Elementary School, Baton Rouge*

The handclap above is one of the first games I can remember recording in
1974. Two of the girls were in second grade, and one was a first grader.

Later, in December 1975, I recorded the game again, when a large group
of fourth, fifth, and sixth graders at University Terrace Elementary School,
all African American, made a ring consisting of fifteen or more players, and
performed their variation of the rhyme. Their version was more energetic and
included a topical allusion to "Kung fu," at that time the dance and movie rage:

When I was a baby baby baby
When I was a baby
This what I do
I say a um a um a um a um a um (*Thumb in mouth.*)
All day long, all day long.

When I was a girl girl girl
When I was a girl
This what I do
I say a jump a jump a jump a jump a jump (*Girls jump.*)
All day long, all day long.

When I was a teenager a teenager a teenager
When I was a teenager
This what I do
I say a woomp a woomp a woomp woomp woomp
(*Swing hips from side to side.*)
All day long, all day long.

When I was a lady a lady a lady
When I was a lady
This what I do
I say a umph a umph a umph umph umph
(*Hand on hip and sway side to side flirtingly.*)
All day long, all day long.

When I got married married married
When I got married
This what I do
I say a smack a smack a smack smack smack
(*Kiss from side to side.*)
All day long, all day long.

When I had a baby a baby a baby
When I had a baby
This what I do
I went Unh a Unh a Unh Unh Unh
(*Crouch with legs spread apart and a pained expression. Grunting, and much laughter.*)
All day long, all day long.

When my husband beat me beat me beat me
When my husband beat me
This what I do
I say, "Get out! "Get out!" "Get out my house."
(*Left fist on hip, right arm raised, finger jabbing forcefully.*)
All day long, all day long.

When my baby died died died
When my baby died
This what I do
I say Why? Why? Why she die?

(*Arms raised in supplication*.)
All day long, all day long

When my husband died died died
When my husband died
This what I do
I say Hurray! Hurray! Hurray! Hurray! Hurray!
(*Jump, and fling arms in the air*.)
All day long all day long.

When I done Kung Fu Kung Fu Kung Fu
When I done Kung Fu
This what I do
I do a humph a humph a humph humph humph
(*Girls lunge forward, delivering blows with fists left and right, as they say "humph."*)
All day long, all day long.

When I had a fight fight fight
When I had a fight
This what I do
I say I gotcha I gotcha I gotcha in the stomach
(*Girls kick and punch*.)
All day long, all day long.

When I took a bath a bath a bath
When I took a bath (*Much clowning and laughter here*.)
This what I do
I say a scrub a scrub a scrub scrub scrub
(*Raise arm and "scrub" under armpit*.)
All day long, all day long.

When I was old old old
When I was old old old
This what I do
I say a cripple a cripple a cripple cripple cripple
(*Walk bent over, with walker, or holding a cane*.)
All day long, all day long,

When I died died died
When I died

> This what I do
> I say I'm dead I'm dead
> Dead Dead DEAD!

> (Here several girls fell to the ground, twitched, and lay still.)
> —*African American girls, University Terrace Elementary School, Baton Rouge*

This is one of those games the girls can expand if a leader comes up with a satisfactory new stanza. The "Kung fu" reference attests to this adaptability. By next year, there might be a new addition to the stanzas, or, perhaps, the Kung fu allusion will be dropped as faddish and forgotten.

Both the white group and the African American students played this handclap with great enthusiasm. The white girls were more reserved, their movements somewhat restrained, except for the lines "When my husband died died died / I said Hurray! Hurray! Hurray! Hurray! Hurray!" where they jumped up and down and waved their arms.

The African American girls threw themselves totally into the actions of the song and vied with each other in their performances. Some would step forward when it came time to jump, or walk "a woomp, a woomp," or cry, or die. When they acted out "When I had a baby," they spread their legs apart, put on pained expressions, and grunted, and broke up laughing for a minute. At "When I was old old old / I say a cripple a cripple a cripple . . ." two or three girls bent their bodies, shriveled their faces, and mimicked an old person with a cane, to perfection.[31]

In 2008, I did one of my final taping sessions at J. W. Faulk Elementary School in Lafayette, Louisiana. It was a supremely noisy recording session, with boys shouting throughout and girls yelling louder and louder, attempting to be heard over the din generated by the boys. All players were African American third graders:

(Girls) We can do a handclap. We go:

> Scooby Doo where are you?
> If a boy had a toy and a girl had a child
> Wrap it up in toilet paper
> Put it down the elevator
> First base means stop (*Pause.*)
> Second base means stop (*Pause.*)

Third base means better not stop
'Cause a S-T-O-P
Means STOP![32]

(Girls) We know another one:

Down by the riverside hanky panky
Where the bullfrogs jump from bank to banky
I said a-e-i-o-u
Pledge allegiance to the flag
Michael Jackson is a fag
Michael Jackson is a fag
Coca Cola burned his butt
Now he's drinkin' Seven-Up
Seven-Up has no caffeine
Now he's drinkin' gasoline
Gasoline has made him mad
Now he said I'M BAD![33]

The noise level got wilder. The boys were jumping around and screaming in the back of the room. The coach blew a whistle and shouted, "Hey! Be quiet." The noise momentarily abated.

(Girls)

See see see
I don't wanna go to college
Any more more more
There's a big fat patayta
At the door door door
He pulled me by the collar
He made me pay a dollar
You see what I mean
You big jelly bean
Wash your face with gasoline.[34]

Boys started a tussle. Shouts of "Get off! Get off!" Taunting yells of "Blah, Blah, Blah!" The coach rounded up the boys and led them out the door to the baseball field.

(Girls)

Chili chili baby (*Clap.*)
I know karate (*Clap.*)
Chili chili baby (*Clap.*)
I can move my body (*Clap.*)
Chili chili baby
OOPS! I'm sorry (*Hold hands wide apart.*)
You missed (*Jump and put feet wide apart.*)
You missed (*Jump and cross feet.*)
You missed like this! (*Jump—and lead player either puts feet apart, crosses feet, or puts one foot in front of the other. Whoever does not follow the pattern, misses.*)

(Girls) Ah hah! You missed! (*Then the girls put their hands together and began to clap.*)
(JS) OK good—what's this?
(Girls)

Slide—
Slide oh (*Slide hands against one another, palms together.*)
Slide one flip flap (*Clap on "one," hit hands back to back, then front to front, on "flip flap."*)
One two one two flip flap (*Clap on "One two," hands back to back on "flip," and palm to palm on "flap."*)
One X two X three X (*X means clap.*)
One XX two XX three XX (*XX means flip flap.*)
One X two X three X four X
One XX two XX three XX four XX
One X two X three X four X five X six X seven X eight X.

(One girl misses) Girl! What you doin'?
(Leader) So you missed on that one . . .
(Girl) I got one! I got my play . . .
(Girls began again)

Slide—one X one X open up open up (*Put hands wide apart on "open up."*)
One X two X three X (X means clap.)
One X two X three X
One X two X three X four X

Open up X open up X open up X open up X
One X two X three X four X five X
One X two X three X four X five X (*Open up hands at end of this line five times.*)
One X two X three X four X five X six X
One X two X three X four X five X six X (*Open hands six times.*)
Open up X open up X open up X open up X
Open up X Open up X (*Girls begin to slow down. They are getting tired but so far have
not missed a beat.*)
One X two X—no—One X two X. (*Girls stop.*)[35]

(Girl) I can make one of that up.
(JS) OK how does it go?
(Girl) Sunset Park . . . Sunset Park, that's the neighborhood . . .
(JS) Show me how it goes
(Girl) Oh—um—I just do it? Wait—hold on—(*Giggles.*) I got it . . .

It's time (*Clap stomp.*) to get live (*Clap stomp.*)
It's time (*Clap stomp.*) to represent (*Clap stomp.*)

(Come on y'all, say it with me.)
(Whole group)

It's time (*Clap stomp.*) to get live (*Clap stomp.*)
It's time (*Clap stomp.*) to represent (*Clap stomp.*)
Sunset Park (*Clap stomp.*) what time (*Clap stomp.*) is it? (*Clap stomp.*)
Yeah! (*Laughter and hands over mouths to suppress giggles.*)

(JS) That was very good. What was that—cheers? You know any more cheers?
(Girls) I do! I do! I know. I know!
(Girl)

Clap clap stomp clap clap clap stomp. (*Tries to do it slowly, loses beat, then does clap
and stomp very fast and gets it right.*)
Stomp clap clap stomp clap clap stomp clap
Stomp clap clap stomp clap clap stomp clap
Stomp clap clap stomp clap clap stomp clap
Opp opp!

(JS) Yes? (I laughed.)

(Another girl) Can I do one like that?

(JS) You can do one, too.

(Girl) Oh (*She does the stomp and clap routine again with a slight difference in the rhythm.*)

> Stomp clap clap clap stomp clap (*Pause.*)
> Stomp clap clap clap stomp clap (*Pause.*)
> Stomp clap stomp clap stomp clap (*Pause.*)
> Stomp.

(JS) OK so there's no words to that?

(Girl) I know one—

> We are the girls from Lafayette High Uh UH!
> So you know we can do our best Uh UH!
> So otherwise take your shot Uh UH!
> So let them see that stuff you got Uh UH!
> Stomp and clap stomp stomp and clap[36]

(JS) OK do you play any other handclap games?

(Girl) Me? Mmmmmmm . . . we need four people—me—me—uh—come on, you go up first.

(Girl) I can be in it too, Megan? (*Girls jostle for a spot. There are supposed to be four, but six or seven line up.*)

(JS) Leave some space, children.

Ashley pushes her way in, making the number of the group eight players.

(Megan) OK. Four white horses—y'all supposed to go up for yours—oh—ready—set—go!

> Four white horses go up the river
> Four white horses up the river—
> (Look—y'all supposed to go *up* for yours—oh, ready—set—go.)

(JS) Can you just give me the words to that one?

(Megan)

> Four white horses
> Up the river

> Hey hey hey
> Up tomorrow
> Up tomorrow is a rainy day
> Come on and join your own shadow play
> Shadow play is a ripe banana
> Up tomorrow is a rainy day.[37]

(JS) All right—do you have another one? You? All right—you.

(Girl) Me? Mmmmmmm . . . we need four people—me—me—uh—come on, you go up first.

(Girl)

> Oo la la (She speaks in a rush.)
> Who think they bad
> I slip my horses
> (Mumble.)
> She think she bad but—uh
> She think she fine.

(JS) Wait wait wait—I want you to give me that again because I'm not sure I understood everything you said. So start slowly—give it to me.

(Girl)

> Oo la la
> Who think they bad
> I do
> Slip it up my portion
> Fightin' is my motion UH!
> UH! She think she bad
> Baby, don't make me mad UH!
> She think she fine
> I'm enough to blow your mind!

(Girl interrupts.) Let's say "A tee a tee a bumblebee . . .

> A tee a tee a bumblebee
> She rocks in the treetops
> All day long
> Huffin' and a puffin' and
> A singin' that song . . .

(The group gets larger as the girls play—more girls join in from the back of the room.)

All the little birds . . .
(The group breaks into two, and the two groups contest one another's clapping patterns.) They begin again:

A tee a tee a bumblebee
She rocks in the treetops all day long
Huffin' and a puffin and (That's not how . . . Do this . . . Another set of girls interrupts the clapping pattern.)

(JS) OK. Could two people do this so I can get the whole game?
(Girls) Me! Me!
(JS) Just you two.
(Two girls)

A tee a tee a bumblebee
She rocks on the treetops
All day long
Huffin' and puffin' and
Singin' that song
All the little birdies on Jaymar Street
Like to hear the robin go
Tweet Tweet tweet
Rockin' Robin say rock rock tonight
Rockin' Robin say rock rock tonight
I went downtown
To see James Brown
I gave me a nickel
To buy me a pickle
The pickle was sour
I bought me a flower
The flower was dead
I bought me a bed
The bed was hard
I bought me a card
The card said
Teddy Bear Teddy Bear turn around
Teddy Bear Teddy Bear touch the ground

> Teddy Bear Teddy Bear show your shoes
> Teddy Bear Teddy Bear be excused
> (Someone shouts, "I Love You!")
> Teddy Bear Teddy Bear go upstairs
> Teddy Bear Teddy Bear say your prayers
> Teddy Bear Teddy Bear switch off the light
> Teddy Bear Teddy Bear say good night.[38]

I watched the crowd as the two girls played out the handclap, and I could see that if I had asked others in the group to chant the rhyme, I would have gotten different variations on the theme. I could see heads shaking, mouths working, alternate lines being muttered. So many variants of one game existed in one play event!

(Girl rushes into.) My name is Dinah, rock my boat . . .
(JS) Wait wait . . .
(Girl begins again.)

> My name is Dinah
> My boat rock rock my boat
> I wanna slide and dive
> And punch you in the eye
> I want to slip and dip
> And punch you in the lip
> I want you and you to rock my boat too . . . (*Pause.*)

(JS) Who knows something else?
(Girl) Ask the song—ask them all about the—yeah—
(General hubbub—shouting—noise . . . then)
About six third-grade girls gather, and sway side to side, and sing:

> It's about seven o'clock
> I'm in my drop top
> Cruisin' the streets (*Clap.*) (*Girls giggle.*)
> I got a real pretty pretty little thing
> That's waitin' for me
> I pull up an-ti-ci-pa-tin'
> Your love so easily rated (*Clap.*) (*One girl begins to do a seductive dance.*) I got plans
> to put my hands in places

I never seen girl
You know what I mean girl
Let me take you to a place nice and quiet
There ain't no one there to interrupt
Ain't gotta rush
I just want to take you nice and slow
And do what you want to do to me
See I been waitin' for this so long
I'll be makin' love until the sun comes up
Baby—I just wanna take it nice and slow
I tell you what I wanna do
Now here we are drivin' around town
Contemplatin' where I want to lay you down
Girl you got me sayin'
(Three lines are inaudible.)
My my my wish that I will pull over
And get things started right now
'Cause I wanna do something funky to you girl
Baby—I wanna do something funky to you Babe . . . (Girls are shouting, "Call out my name, and call me USHER RAYMOND!" And then they begin shouting out lines independently causing confusion. Girls scream and laugh.)[39]

(JS) OK. OK. You have to keep your voices a little lower.
(Girls) OK. (Then they start shouting again.)
(Ashley) Wait . . . You gotta get in line . . . You gotta . . .
(JS) What's happening here?
(Ashley) It could go on . . . whatever y'all saying go on there . . . (She points to the microphone.) Get in line—you—you—and you . . . (Ashley organizes the singers.)

Third-grade girls sing:
Hey little mama why you dance so funky?
Hey little mama you so funky y-2-c
Hey little mama why you dressed so funky?
Get on the floor and shake it like a monkey
Shake it to the right
Shake it to the left
Do the funky dance
Shake it all night

Shake that thing
Now look at me and do what I do
Shake that stuff both up and down
Shake it down to the ground
Shake it shake it shake it shake it
Do that funky monkey break
Girl that's all you do today
You look so funky you drive me crazy
Hey little mama why you look so funky?
Now look at me and shake your big butt
Make that butt go out and in
You look so funky I want to say
Hey little mama why you dressed so funky
Hey little mama you so funky y-2-c![40]

Same group of third-grade girls:

Bang bang choo choo train
Come on girl now do your thang
Yeah yeah—why not
Yeah yeah—why not
My back is achin' my skirt too tight
My booty shakin' from left to right
To the left
To the right
To the left to the right
To the left to the right
To the left to the right
Now get it get it RIGHT ON![41]

The third-grade girls segue into:

Please hey hey
Please hey hey
Please hey hey
Let me ride that donkey donkey
Let me ride that donkey donkey . . .[42]
—*African American third grade, J. W. Faulk Elementary, Lafayette, La.*

The girls are singing and dancing along to this when the coach enters and blows his whistle, putting a stop to the dancing and the recording session.

Some handclaps have few or no words, only extremely complicated clapping rhythms, which require great dexterity. Following are three handclaps from Andrew Jackson Elementary:

In "Hot Hands," the third-grade girls started at medium speed but sped up at the second or third number and continued to increase speed until one "messed up." Two girls said the numbers and the word "clap" aloud:

One (*clap*) clap (*front*) clap (*back*)
Two (*clap*) clap clap (*front back*) clap clap (*front back*)
Three (*clap*) clap clap clap (*front back front*) clap clap clap (*front back* front). (*Continue adding on and going faster and faster until one misses.*)

The next game, "bingo," had two variants that I collected from Andrew Jackson Elementary School, New Orleans. The third-grade girls played it one way, and the sixth-grade girls played it another:

The third-grade girls counted out loud and crossed their hands over when they clapped their hands together with their partner's.

One (*clap*) clap (*left across*) clap (*clap own*) clap (*right across*)
Two (*clap*) clap (*left across*) clap (*clap own*) clap (*right across*)
Three (*clap*) clap (*left across*) clap (*clap own*) clap (*right across*)
Four (*clap*) clap (*left across*) clap (*clap own*) clap (*right across*)
B (*clap own*) I (*left across*) N (*right across*) G (*left across*)
O (*right across*)
I (*clap own*) N N N N (*Slap palms together with partner four times.*)
Bingo! (*Shout and clap own hands.*)

The sixth graders said:

One (*clap*) clap (*front*) clap (*back*)
Two (*clap*) clap (*front*) clap (*back*)
Three (*clap*) clap (*front*) clap (*back*)
Four (*clap*) clap (*front*) clap (*back*)
(*Double time*) Oh 1 (*clap*) clap (*front*)
2 (*clap*) clap (*back*)
3–4 (*clap clap*) front)
Oh B (*clap*) I (*cross right*) IN (*clap own*) IN (*cross left*) IN (*clap*) IN (*cross right*) IN (*clap*)

G (*cross left*) G (*clap*) G (*clap*) G (*cross right*) Bingo! (*clap twice*)[43]
—*Andrew Jackson Elementary, African American 3rd- and 6th-grade girls, New Orleans*

In 2007 I revisited some of my old collecting venues. At a birthday party for the children of girls I had collected from in the 1980s, I asked *their* children if they knew any handclapping games. Two young girls, Kaysey, aged 11, and Kayten, aged 14, stepped up to be recorded. They had lived in a number of cities in Mississippi and Arkansas following their displacement after Hurricane Katrina. After their wanderings, the two girls were back in Chalmette, where they were attending Chalmette High School. The schoolyard lore they recorded in this session mirrored much of the lore I had been collecting for the past thirty years:

Tic tac toe (*Clap clap clap.*)
Give me an X (*On X cross arms.*)
Give me an O (*On O make circle with arms.*)
Give me three in a row (*Clap clap clap.*)
Rock, paper, scissors (*Form "rock," "paper," "scissors."*)
Sheet (*Hands held out flat.*)
I win
You lose
Now you get a big fat bruise (Kayten punches her sister's bicep.)
I win
You lose
Now *you* get a big fat bruise. ("And you pop 'em in the arm.")

(Sister)
No, you go
Splish splash
Now you got a big FROG! (And Kaysey punches her sister on the bicep.)

The girls stood around rubbing their arms and wincing. I had never before seen a handclap end in a forceful punch.

(JS) I never heard that one before. Any more?
(Kaysey) I got one—Lemonade . . .
(JS) How does it go?

Lemonade (*Clap clap.*)
Crunchy ice (*Clap clap.*)
Sip it once (*Clap clap.*)
Sip it twice (*Clap clap.*)
Lemonade (*Clap clap.*)
Crunchy ice (*Clap clap.*)
Sip it once (*Clap clap.*)
Sip it twice (*Clap clap.*)
Turn around touch the ground
Kick your boyfriend out of town
Freeze!

Kaysey says, "Then if somebody moves, the one who stands still wins."

(Kaysey) Wait . . . wait . . . watch (*Claps hands.*)

I went to a Chinese restaurant
To buy a yak a mein
They asked what my name was
And this is what I said said said
My name is Kaysey
The boys said oh oh oh
And I said ahhhh
Mess with me
And I'll mess you up!

Kayten and Kaysey then put their hands up and clapped to:

D-i-s-c-o-
That's the way my disco goes
D-i-s-c-o-
That's the way my disco goes
My name is Katie
All the boys are sweet on me
I know I'm sexy
I know I'm fine
You mess with me
I'll blow your mind.

Then:

> Down by the riverside
> Down by the sea
> Johnny broke a bottle
> And blamed it on me
> Ma told Pa
> Pa told Ma
> Johnny got a whippin'
> So ha ha ha.

The girls continued to slap hands, and tried to smack each other around. We all giggled. One of the girls reached out, and slapped her sister, and shouted, "Hey!"

(JS) All right. What was the one y'all used to sing? . . ."Little Suzy?"
(Kayten) Oh, yeah . . . I know the one you talkin' about.
(And then they chanted a variant of "When I Was a Baby" that I had not heard before.)
(Kaysey)

> Little Suzy had a . . . nooo . . .
> When Suzy was a baby a baby a baby
> When Suzy was a baby
> This is what she said
> Wah wah (*Her sister says, "Snorkle snorkle."*)
> When Miss Suzy was a toddler a toddler a toddler
> When Miss Suzy was a toddler
> This is what she said
> Wah wah scribble scratch
> When Miss Suzy was a kid a kid a kid
> When Miss Suzy was a kid
> This is what she said
> Wah wah scribble scratch
> I want this and I want that
> When Miss Suzy was a teenager a teenager a teenager
> When Miss Suzy was a teenager
> This is what she said
> Wah wah scribble scratch
> I want this and I want that

OOO AAAH I lost my bra
I lost it in my boyfriend's car
When Miss Suzy was a doc . . . wait . . . Was a mom a mom
When Miss Suzy was a mom
This is what she said
Wah wah scribble scratch
I want this and I want that
OOO AHH I lost my bra
I lost it in my boyfriend's car
Wait . . . Clean my teeth and scratch my back—or something like that.

(*Kaysey takes over . . . Kaysey has been chanting softly along as her older sister says the handclap words—she says hurriedly . . .*)

When Miss Suzy was dead dead dead
When Miss Suzy was dead dead dead
This is what she said
Wah wah scribble scratch
I want this and I want that
OOOO AHHH I lost my bra
I lost it in my boyfriend's car
Get my teeth and scratch my back.

(Kayten) And I don't know what . . . And . . . leave me all to lie in peace? . . . Right?
   Yeah, I think that's it.
(JS) You mean after she was dead?
(Kayten) Yeah.
(JS) Very good.
(Kaysey) Um . . . there's one more—Isn't it a shame . . .
(Kayten) I don't know that one . . .
(Kaysey)

Shame shame shame
I don't want to go to Mexico no more more more
There's a big fat cop at the door door door
He grabbed me by the collar
He made me pay a dollar
I don't want to go to Mexico no more more more
Shame!
—*White girls, Chalmette, La.*

Kayten and Kaysey represent a second generation of children I recorded from the same family in Chalmette. Their fund of schoolyard lore had been broadened by their displacement and wanderings due to Hurricane Katrina. The girls had moved in the first three months to Tylertown, Mississippi, then to Jonesboro, Arkansas. Finally, they had attended school for two years in Little Rock, Arkansas, before moving back to their hometown of Chalmette. Everywhere they had lived, they had learned new versions of handclaps and jump-rope rhymes.

There are some games that involve handclapping and hand play that might not be technically identified as "handclaps." These include the following game, submitted in writing, a variation of "Concentration:"

Girls sit in a row. Girl on right hand is leader. Clapping goes like this:

Hands together twice. Hands on lap twice. Hands on your right leg, and right-handed neighbor's left leg twice. Hands on your left leg and left-handed neighbor's right leg twice.

Chant in time: "Rhy-thm" (Say while clapping hands together, do the rest in silence. All words spoken only on handclaps.) "Name of" "Ani—mals" (Topic chosen by leader.) "Pi-ig" (By second girl.), etc, to end, then begins again at leader and continues until someone cannot think of a word or messes up clapping pattern. This person goes to the end of the line. (Very popular game, 3–6-grade.)

—*As written by twenty-year-old white student at Louisiana State University.*
Learned at Mandeville High School, Mandeville, La.

The next two examples are dexterity hand games boys played for me. Lusher Elementary fourth graders played "Slap Hands."

One boy put his hands out, palms up. The second boy rested his hands, palms down, on the first boys open hands. The first boy tried to slap one or both of the second boy's hands with his own hands before the first boy could retract his.[44]

The same two boys demonstrated "Thumb Wrestling." In this game, the boys put their hands together, thumbs locked. Then they went "1-2-3" and tried to pull the opponent's thumb down on the table for a count of three.

Some other games involving the hands other than clapping games:

"Scissors, Paper, Rock"

Usually two players, sometimes more, face each other and ball up one fist. The players raise fist three times. On the third motion, the raised hand comes down in one of three positions—palm flat (paper); fist balled up (rock); or index and middle finger held out like a pair of scissors (scissors). Scissors "cuts" paper, so if the hands come down, one "scissors," the other "paper," the one who loses (paper) must either pay a forfeit, or get hit, whatever the agreed rules state. Rock breaks scissors, and paper covers rock.

In Ville Platte, Louisiana, where I saw the game played, the youngsters used to have to get a "six-inch hit" as a penalty for losing. This "six-inch hit" was measured off by the winner.[45]

—Sissors, Paper, Rock described by twelve-year-old white boy. Ville Platte, La.

"Things Fly"

(played in Lafayette, La. when I was a child): The players sat in a circle, usually around a table. The leader raised her hand and said, "Birds fly" (or any other accurate animal that flies.) All players had to quickly raise their hand. A hesitation was as good as a miss. The leader proceeds: "Bees fly," "Wasps fly"; then throws in "Butter flies," or "Cows fly," etc. If a player raises her hand on any inaccurate call, she gets hit on the forehead with a thimble-covered finger. Ouch!

—Jeanne Soileau, memory

"Cache cache la bague," or "Hide the Ring"

This game was played on rainy days when I was a child. The children sat in a circle. One child was chosen to hold the thimble, or button, or ring (bague). This child held the ring between her hands so that it could not be seen. Then everybody held their hands out palms together, and she slid her hands between the out-held hands. As she walked around the group, she said, "Cache cache la bague," and without being obvious, deposited it in someone's hand. Then another child was chosen to guess who had the ring. If the guess was right, she got to hide the ring next time. If the guess was wrong, the child who held the ring got to hide it next.

—Lafayette, La. 1950s, Jeanne Soileau

Two little games my aunt Susan Bassett Lirette played with me and my brother in the 1940s, and then played with her great-nieces and nephews in the 1970s:

> This is the stream where the birdies come to drink
> (*Hold child's hand palm up. Tap child's palm.*)
> This one saw it.
> (*Pinch little finger.*)
> This one shot it.
> (*Pinch ring finger.*)
> This one cleaned it.
> (*Pinch middle finger.*)
> This one cooked it.
> (*Pinch index finger.*)
> The little fat one ate it all up!
> (*Pinch thumb.*)
> And didn't leave any for _____
> (*Tickle child on stomach and say his name.*)

This next game is performed by an adult while a child watches. Again, it was one taught me by my aunt Susan Bassett Lirette. But once I learned it, I passed it on to my friends at St. Genevieve School in Lafayette, Louisiana in the 1950s:

> These are my mother's knives and forks,
> (*Hands held so interlaced fingers stick up.*)
> This is my mother's table.
> (*Hands turned over, fingers interlaced, so they make a flat "table."*)
> This is my sister's looking glass.
> (*Raise two pinkie fingers, ends together.*)
> And this is the baby's cradle.
> (*Raise two index fingers as well as pinkie fingers, making hands cradle-like. Let the child rock the cradle.*)
> This is the church house.
> (*Lower pinkie fingers, leaving index fingers pointed up, tips together.*)
> Open the door, and see all the people.
> (*Turn hands over again so fingers stick up. Wiggle fingers.*)
> —*Lafayette, La. Jeanne Soileau*

As noted earlier, New Orleans schools being integrated, it was difficult to make a clear distinction between white handclaps and African American ones. But there was a clear-cut difference in style of play and delivery. Handclaps are intimately concentrated play, where the players coordinate the rhymes, the rhythms, the touching and slapping of hands, and all other body motions involved. All classes of African American girls and boys who recorded games got quickly caught up in the performance role. There was seldom any urging needed to secure performers. Middle- and upper-class white children, however, were often extremely self-conscious and would sometimes refuse to perform, even if they knew the games well. This happened at Metairie Park Country Day School in Old Metairie, a suburb of New Orleans, in 1981. I visited two classrooms and taped the children as they recited many games in the company of their schoolmates. When called upon to individually step forward and play a game for the tape recorder, however, the children visibly wilted at the thought of performing. This problem had yet to occur with African American children, in large measure because their culture is performance oriented.

White boys routinely refused to join in playing handclaps, except to make fun of them. They knew the words, and I saw them mouth along while the girls played, but the standard answer to "Do you play handclaps?" was a re-sounding shout of "No!" This was not true of African American boys. They sometimes knew more games than the girls. In a John Dibert Elementary fourth-grade class, one African American boy led all the handclaps and per-formed "A-B-C" and "Tweedle dee" with a girl partner. It was mentioned in the introduction that at Samuel J. Peters Junior High School, several football players aged fourteen and fifteen performed handclaps on videotape for WGNO television. Again, this is an outgrowth of the performance-oriented culture—he who moves best, speaks best, is best.[46]

Sometimes it is possible, simply by recording the game, to judge the age of the children. "Patty Cake," and "My Father Is a Trash Man," were usually kindergarten, first-, second-, or third-grade handclap games. This does not mean that very small children did not know more "sophisticated," longer rhymes. The two girls at Louise Day Care Center were only three and four years old, yet they knew variants of "I Went Downtown to See Mr. Brown," and "Tweedle Dee." Their versions reflected the fact that they did not always hear accurately. Two of their instances of approximated learning were the lines "Lord have mercy go my soul / How many chickens how many tell," and "A rock in the treetops goes tweet tweet tweet," but preschoolers Quintella and Angelique were already well indoctrinated into children's folklore at their tender age.

Why do older children and adults fail to recall their childhood folk games? In several instances, the teenage boys and girls at St. Joan of Arc bingo started a game, then faded out, or broke up into giggles. White teenagers were usually even more forgetful than African American teenagers. Forgetfulness is, in part, a form of blocking out. Most teenagers and young adults begin to feel, around the age of thirteen or so, that their children's folklore should be set aside along with toys and dolls and that grown-up things should take their place. For them, joke telling, joining in cheers at organized games, and engaging in teases and taunts take the place of schoolyard lore. The dynamics of memory, though, are complex—some adults, with a little prompting, can bring their childhood games to memory all their lives.

JUST FOR FUN

Google "Handclapping Game "Slide"—YouTube." Uploaded Jun 10, 2009 (1,313,409 views as of Feb. 1, 2020.) On YouTube.com, two white girls play "Slide" and then demonstrate how it is played.

JUST FOR FUN

YouTube has a video entitled "Anne and Virginia playing "Say Say My Playmate." At https: / / www.YouTube.com / watch?v=RxxDZQ.Qnk. Anne and Virginia handclap to an extended variant of "Say Say Say Playmate," which includes additions I had never heard.

CHAPTER 5

Rhymes and Songs

One thing I learned while collecting over the years is that most children love to sing. Boys and girls sing at camp, on the school ground, at home, on the school bus, everywhere. This chapter has sections of all kinds of songs and rhymes. The first set contains rhymes and nursery rhymes, which are usually chanted, rather than sung. The second section is schoolyard songs, mostly parodies of well-known tunes like "Battle Hymn of the Republic," "On Top of Old Smoky," and "Row Row Row Your Boat." The third section features camp songs and includes popular songs and song parodies sung by the kids on the playground or in class "when the teacher leaves."

RHYMES

The youngest of my interviewees were from three to six years old. These children often recited nursery rhymes when asked to supply a schoolyard speech.

One six-year-old at the St. Joan of Arc bingo babysitting crowd told me:

> 1–2 buckle my shoe
> 3–4 shut the door
> 5–6 pick up sticks
> 7–8 lay them straight
> 9–10 a big fat hen.[1]
> —*St. Joan of Arc 6-year-old African American child, New Orleans*

Many five- and six-year-olds have the basic idea of the schoolyard rhymes but are perfectly happy just making it up to fit the main idea. For example:

> I ate some peanut butter
> I saw a . . . When I opened the box of peanut butter

I was sick. I saw a roach.
I called my mother and I told her and then she got the swat.
I scooped the peanut butter up and then I . . . and then . . .
I slided up, and then I played outside.
—*St. Joan of Arc bingo 6-year-old African American boy, New Orleans*

A large number of children recited nursery rhymes. Some of these were exactly like those learned in school or at home, a few were parodies, and a smaller number were misread, or mislearned. The following variant of "Little Bo Peep" is a gem and a good example of how a rhyme or song changes in oral tradition. The small girl who recited it for me had stepped forward out of the crowd at St. Joan of Arc bingo:

Little Bo Peep has lost her sheep
Couldn't know where to find them
Leave them alone and they will come home
Leaving their trails behind them.
—*St. Joan of Arc bingo 4-year-old African American girl, New Orleans*

The little girl at St. Joan of Arc bingo went on to explain that she knew the rhyme "Because I got a puzzle. I got a puzzle about it." A friend of hers came up and asked me to record her rhyme:

Hey diddle diddle the cat and the fiddle
The cow jumped over the moon
The little dog laughed to see what had passed
And the dish ran away with the spoon.

She continued:

Humpty Dumpty sat on the wall
Humpty Dumpty had a great fall
All the king's horses and all the king's men
Couldn't put Humpty together again.

The two girls, and their preschool friends then went on to record "Little Miss Muffett" and "Jack and Jill." At their age, they could not see any difference between traditional nursery rhymes and schoolyard folklore.
—*St. Joan of Arc bingo babysitting venue, New Orleans*

Older students sometimes used the childlike games to elicit hoots and laughter. A tall sixth grader at John Dibert Elementary delighted his audience by ticking off his fingers to:

> This little piggy went shoppin'
> This little piggy stayed home
> This little piggy had roast beef
> This little piggy had none
> This little piggy said "Wee wee wee" all the way home.
> —*John Dibert Elementary, 6th-grade African American boy, New Orleans*

The same children at John Dibert then sang several versions of "On Top of Old Smoky." Everyone sang along in this equally mixed African American and white class:

> On top of old Smoky all covered with cheese
> I shot my poor teacher when somebody sneezed
> I went to his funeral
> I went to his grave
> Instead of throwing flowers I threw hand grenades.
> —*John Dibert Elementary, African American and white 6th graders, New Orleans*

This was greeted by loud laughter, and glances in the teacher's direction. The teacher laughed along with the students and encouraged them to continue.

A white girl sang this version:

> On top of Old Smoky all covered with cheese
> I lost my poor meatball when somebody sneezed
> It rolled off the table and onto the floor
> And then my poor meatball rolled out of the door.
> It rolled in the garden and under a bush
> And then my poor meatball was nothing but mush
> Early next summer it grew into a tree
> It grew little meatballs all ready for me.[2]

Her friends fell all over themselves and slapped each other on the back, so the girl continued:

> Glory glory hallelujah
> The teacher hit me with a ruler

Met her at the door with a level .44
And she ain't my teacher no more
I went to her funeral
I went to her grave
Instead of throwing flowers I threw hand grenades.

Another student followed with:

Glory glory how peculiar
My teacher hit me with a ruler
I met her in the attic with a loaded automatic
An' my teacher ain't gonna teach no more.

He thought a second, then sang:

We have tortured every teacher
And we've broken every rule
We've marched into the office
And we shot the principal
And the brats go marching on.[3]
—*John Dibert Elementary 6th-grade African American and white classmates, New Orleans*

An African American boy in the same John Dibert group supplied an alternate version of a song included earlier on in the chapter on handclaps:

Miss Suzie had a steamboat
The steamboat had a bell
Suzie went to heaven
The steamboat went to hell—
Oh operator, give me number nine
And if you don't connect me
I'll kick you in the be—
Hind the refrigerator
There was a piece of glass . . . I'm not . . .
Johnny heard a . . . no
Ask me no more questions
Tell me no more lies
And . . . I'm not sure about the rest.
—*John Dibert Elementary, 6th-grade African American boy, New Orleans*

The student might have been embarrassed to sing the rest, but I have gotten one version of the ending from other children in other locations:

> Behind the refrigerator
> There lay a piece of glass
> And if you do not help me I'll kick you in the
> Ask me no more questions, tell me no more lies,
> This is what she told us, before she shut her eyes.

An alternate ending goes:

> The boys are in the bathroom zipping up their flies.

I heard another alternate ending from a kindergartner in Lafayette, Louisiana, who sang:

> The boys are in the barnyard eating apple pies.[4]

The kindergartner was part of a group taped in 1998, at an after-school care venue held in the cafeteria at Myrtle Place Elementary School. The after-school group was comprised of kindergartners, first graders, and third graders, and was supervised by two teachers. The entire taping session was dominated by a large, loud, African American, third-grade boy named Michael. Michael out-shouted the rest of the assemblage, wrested the microphone from my hand repeatedly, and finally had to be isolated for a period of time on the other side of the room. When he settled down, Michael contributed rhymes, but in his own way. Here is part of the transcription:

(Michael) **Hoot** jam **hoot** jam hee na **hoot** dam . . .

(JS) Can you do me a game?

(Michael) **Hoot** jammy **hoot** jammy HOOT JAM!

(Teacher) Michael! Michael! You'll have to go to the . . .

(Michael sings.) I hate you, you hate me . . .

(JS) How does that go?

(Michael) That's the (Mumble.) song. I hate that . . .

(JS) Oh, that's the song? Well, you don't play that on the playground, do you?

(Michael) It's about. (Michael grabs the microphone out of my hand, and tries to yank it toward himself.)

(JS) Watch out for the microphone! Wait—wait—watch out for the microphone!
  (I laugh nervously.)
(Michael) I HATE it!
(Children are giggling hysterically now.)
(Teacher) Go ahead.
(Michael speaks in a rush, and unintelligibly. He puts his mouth directly against
  the microphone and babbles. I pull away, and Michael lunges forward, and
  grabs the microphone, babbling as fast as he can.) Mumble, mumble . . . GI
  Joe! . . .
(JS) I can't hear you! You can't . . . wait! Wait! Wait! WAIT! You can't have the micro-
  phone. Do it again slowly.
(Children are laughing and pummeling each other. Michael calms down a bit.)
(Michael)

> Tic tac toe
> Three in a row
> Barney got shot by G I Joe
> Mama called the doctor and the Doctor said
> There it is—Barney's dead.

(JS) OK. That's good. Got another one? Gimme another one.
(Michael)

> I hate you you hate me
> Let's get together and kill Barney
> With a two by four up Barney's butt
> No more purple dinosaur.[5]

Michael has no more to contribute, but he continues to hum and cackle and
screech throughout the rest of the recording. This behavior was not unusual
for boys. In a number of my recordings the sound of raucous boys vying for
attention made recording, and subsequent transcription, sometimes difficult,
sometimes impossible.

The next transcription, done earlier in time, demonstrates how smoothly a
session can take place when all contributors behave well and feel comfortable
with one another.

Three white girls at Camp Ruth Lee sang, danced, and demonstrated handclaps and jump rope rhymes for over an hour one Sunday afternoon in 1974.
When they finished, they asked me if I was interested in some of the "little

rhymes" they said for fun during recess time. Of course, I said I would love it if they would share, and this is what followed:

(JS) Do you want to give your names?
(Girls) Jennifer. Lisa. Katherine.

> How dry I am
> How wet I'll be
> If I don't find the bathroom key.
> I found the key
> Now where's the door?
> Oh, it's too late
> I've wet the floor. (Girls giggle.)[6]

(JS) You have another one?
(Girls)

> Fatty fatty two by four
> Can't get through the bathroom door
> So he did it on the floor
> Licked it up and did some more.[7]
> —*White campers, Camp Ruth Lee, Norwood, La.*

I laughed when the girls sang these two rhymes above because they are the exact rhymes, word for word, my schoolmates and I shared with one another. Giggling and feeling guilty, we teased others on the school ground at St. Genevieve School when I was in elementary school in the late 1940s.

(Girl campers continue) We have more:

> Coca Cola went to town
> Pepsi Cola shot him down
> Dr. Pepper fixed him up
> Now they call him Seven-Up.

(Katherine) Now we have a political jingle:

> Nixon Nixon he's our man
> Wallace belongs in a frying pan

> Nixon Nixon he's our man
> Humphrey belongs in the garbage can
> Nixon Nixon he's our man
> If he can't do it nobody can.[8]

(Lisa) Oh! I want . . . Popeye the sailor man jingle . . .

> I'm Popeye the sailor man toot toot
> He lives in the garbage can toot toot
> He eats all the worms
> And licks up the germs
> I'm Popeye the sailor man toot toot.

(Lisa) And I have another one:

> I'm Popeye the sailor man toot toot
> I live in a frying pan toot toot
> Turn on the heater
> And burn off my wiener
> I'm Popeye the sailor man toot toot.

(The girls confer.) Oh! Oh! Noooo! (They laugh.)
(Katherine)

> I'm Popeye the sailor man toot toot
> I live in a frying pan toot toot
> Turn on the gas
> And burn off my ass
> I'm Popeye the sailor man toot toot. (The girls hide their faces and giggle.)[9]

Then all three girls join in and sing:

> Hi ho hi ho we're off to school we go
> With hand grenades and razor blades
> Hi ho hi ho hi ho hi ho
> Hi ho I bit my teacher's toe
> She bit me back that dirty rat
> Hi ho hi ho hi ho hi ho
> Hi ho it's off to school we go

The water tastes like turpentine
The principal looks like Frankenstein
Hi ho hi ho hi ho hi ho
Hi ho . . . and it goes on like that . . .[10]

Then they sing:

Mine eyes have seen the glory of the burning of the school
We have tortured all the teachers
We have broken all the rules
We are going to hang the principal tomorrow afternoon
We kids are marching on.

(JS) You all said there was a second version. What school is it from?
(Girls) Ours is from Sherwood Forest.
(Girl) And mine is from Northwestern Middle School.
(JS) OK. Let's go.
(Girls)

Our eyes have seen the glory of the burning of the school
We have tortured all the teachers
We have broken all the rules (Girls beat loudly on tables.)
We are marching to the office to attack the principal (Bang bang bang.)
Our school is burning down down down down . . . (Bam bam bam bam.)[11]

Another girl joins in, "I know one from St. Joseph's Academy."

On top of old Smoky
All covered with sand
I hit my poor teacher with a green rubber band
I couldn't have missed her . . .

(No . . . wait . . .)

I hit her with pleasure
I hit her with pride
I couldn't have missed her
She's a hundred feet wide
I went to her funeral

I went to her grave
Some people threw flowers
I threw hand grenades.

(Lisa) Uh . . . wait:

Glory glory hallelujah
Teacher hit me with a ruler
Met her at the door
With a loaded .44
And she ain't my teacher no more more more more.
—*Taped at Camp Ruth Lee, white girls, Norwood, La.*

Later in the day, I interviewed a camp counselor who had graduated in 1973 from Tara High School in Baton Rouge. She sang:

Suffocation we love suffocation
Suffocation the game we love to play
First you take a plastic bag
Then you put it on your head
Go to bed
Wake up dead
Oh oh oh oh suffocation
We love suffocation
Suffocation it's the game we play.[12]

Then Mary and Tascha, campers who were also graduates of Tara High, joined the camp counselor, and sang:

I was a virgin in my freshman year
I was a virgin with my conscience clear
I never smoked or drank or stayed out late
Until a Tara boy asked me for a date

He taught me how to smoke a pack a day
He taught me how to drink and run away
He taught me fun new ways to use the floor
And now I ain't a little virgin
I ain't a little virgin

I ain't a little virgin
No more!
I ain't kiddin'
I ain't a little virgin
No more!

(Girls) Let's sing the "Comet" one.

Comet, it makes your teeth turn green
Comet, it tastes like gasoline
Comet, it makes you vomit
So get some Comet
And vomit
Today![13]

(Girls continue)
If you do see a hearse go by
You will be the next to die
They wrap you up in a big white sheet
And bury you about six feet deep.
The worms crawl
The worms crawl out
The worms play pinochle on your snout
Your stomach turns a slimy green
And pus comes out like Score hair cream.[14]

(One girl)

I'm looking over my dead dog Rover
That I ran over with the mower
One leg is shattered
The other one's torn
The third leg is scattered all over the lawn
No need explaining the leg remaining
Is hanging from the bathroom door
Oh, I'm looking over my dead dog Rover
That I ran over with the mower.[15]

Another girl begins, "I hear you knockin,'" and the two other girls say, "I can't sing that one!"

(JS) Go ahead.
(Girl)

> I hear you knockin' but you can't come in
> Do doot do doot
> I'm in my nightie and it's kinda thin
> Do doot do doot
> I'd let you in but I know it's a sin
> Do doot do doot
> Hi, Honey, come on in![16]

After putting their heads together, the girls asked, "Can we do two more songs? The first one is called "Scab sandwiches." You want us to do it?"

(JS) Yeah!
(Girls)

> Scab sandwiches pus on top
> Mayonnaise, mustard, monkey snot
> Cat guts, eyeball tea
> Scab sandwiches for you and me
> I forgot my spoon
> But I have my straw!

(JS) OK!

Squeals of laughter, followed by:

> Come up come up come up raw meat come up come up
> Come up come up come up raw meat come up
> I'm coming, I'm coming I hear you calling
> Hasten Jason get the basin
> Urp, flop, get the mop.[17]

The girls ended their session with:

Mama mia Papa pia
Baby's got the diarrhea!
—*White teenage graduates from Tara High School, Baton Rouge. Transcript from tape Camp Ruth Lee, 1974*

The songs "Suffocation," and "I Was a Virgin in my Freshman Year," were new to me. However, "Comet," "If You Do See a Hearse Go By," "I'm Looking Over my Dead Dog Rover," "I Hear You Knocking," and "How Dry I Am" were all current when I was in high school in the late 1950s. We sang one when I was in the third grade that I have not yet come across in south Louisiana. It was to the tune of "Jealousy."

Leprosy it's crawling all over me
There goes my eyeball right into your high ball
It's only my leprosy
It keeps on itching me
There goes my right ear right into your Regal beer.[18]

There was more, but being an adult now, I can't recall it.

A new group of campers walked up. There were two white and three African American girls, and all were talking excitedly. They were in their early teens. The girls milled around, trying to think of something different to say, and finally asked, "Can we do some cheers?"

(JS) Sure, go 'head. Oh, where are you all from?
(Girls) Tara High! Valley Park!

Valley Park got soooooul
Valley Park got soooooul
Valley Park got soooooul
Oh ooh oh s-o-u-l
Hey hey
What does that say?
Hey hey
Soooooul.

(Girls) We got another one.
(JS) OK.
(Girl) (Starts softly.) We gonna do Humpty Dumpty—

Valley Park's got the hump ty dump dump dump
Valley Park's got the hump ty dump dump dump
Oh oh oh Humpty Dumpty sat on the wall
Humpty Dumpty had a great fall
Hump ty dump dump dump.

One girl says, "And, uh, I say, uh, what did I say?

(Lead girl) I had a little rooster . . .
(Girls)

I had a little rooster (*Each line is echoed. I had a little rooster.*)
I sat him on the fence (*I sat him on the fence.*)
He yelled for the Hawks (*He yelled for the Hawks.*)
'Cause he had no sense. (*'Cause he had no sense.*)
(All) A root a root a rooty toot toot
A root a root a rooty toot toot.

(Lead girl)

I bought another rooster (*I bought another rooster.*)
I sat him on the fence (*I sat him on the fence.*)
He yelled for the Wildcats (*He yelled for the Wildcats.*)
'Cause he had some sense ('*Cause he had some sense.*)
A root a root a rooty toot toot
A root a root a rooty toot toot.

(Girls) Let's do another one!

Down by the green grass information
We got a little team gonna beat dictation
We know it
We got it
(Indecipherable.)
Soul sister number nine
Sock it to me one more time.

Then:

R BB R BB
Walkin' down the street
Ten times a week
You know it
I said it
I get it
I meant it
I mean to recommend it
I'm cool
I'm calm
I'm Soul Sister number nine
Sock it to me one more time
Um um um UM UM.

(White girls) We know some from other schools too.
(JS) OK.
(Girls)

I'm a raindrop
I'm a raindrop
I'm a raindrop from the sky.
But I'd rather be a raindrop
Than a dip-shit from Broadmoor High

(African American girl) Do you really want that?
(JS) I do.
(African American girl) Well . . . I don't know who this is . . . she's three years old,
dumb, blind, and dark skinned. Can anybody . . . ?

Then she begins:

Born in the backwoods raised like a bear
Double coat of back teeth
Double coat of hair
Cast iron belly
And a twenty-foot rod
I'm a mean motherfucker
I'm a Trojan by God![19]

(JS) Thanks.
(Girls)

> Oh we the Jaguars
> Don't take no mess
> Tsk tsk tsk
> No matter many
> Don't take no chance
> 2–3–4
> Go Jaguars go
> Hey hey hey
> Keep on doin' that stuff
> Hey hey hey
> Go Jaguars go
> Hey hey hey
> Keep on doin' that stuff
> Hey hey hey
> Bam! (*Clap.*) Unh unh unh!
> Stomp! (*Clap.*) Unh unh unh!
> Go Jaguars go! Unh unh!

(JS) I don't know yours. Is it a different school? What school is the Jaguars?
(Girls) Mayfair.
(JS) Mayfair? And you got a different school?
(Girls) We got Eden Park.
(JS) Eden Park? Let's hear yours.

> We are the Rams
> Don't take no stuff
> In 'bout a minute
> We jump in your chest
> Go Rams go
> Hey hey hey
> Keep on doin' your stuff
> Hey hey
> (And we go)
> Go Rams go
> Hey hey hey
> Keep on doin' your stuff

Angela! (*Leap forward arms above head.*)
Carla![20]
—*White and African American campers, Camp Ruth Lee, Norwood, La.*

Here the girls all broke up in laughter. At the end of the session, two white camp counselors began to sing their favorite camp song:

Little Rabbit Foo Foo (*Make hopping motions with hand.*)
Hoppin' through the forest
Pickin' up the bluebirds and boppin' them on the head. (*Pick up "bluebirds" and bop their heads.*)
Down came the big fat fairy (*Arms raised, then come down.*)
And she said
Little Rabbit Foo Foo (*Shake finger.*)
I don't want to see you (*Shake head.*)
Pickin' up the bluebirds and (*Pick up "bluebirds" and bop.*)
Boppin' them on the head.
If you don't stop it
I'll punish you
And turn you into a counselor!
—*Taped at Camp Ruth Lee, white camp counselors, Norwood, La.*

Looking through the penciled scribblings I have kept in a box, I found this cheer dictated to me from an unidentified source:

To the left to the right
To the left to the right
To the left oh oh oh
My back is achin' my pants too tight
My booty shakin' from left to right
My socks is high, my afro comb
Get it together right on right on
UNH—are we got the spirit
What you say now
UNH—are we got the spirit
1–2–3–4–5
The Mighty Eagles gonna skin 'em alive
UNH—are we got the spirit
What you say now

UNH—are we got the spirit
6–7–8–9–10
The Mighty Eagles gonna do it again
UNH—are we got the spirit?

MORE CAMP SONGS

The first part of what follows is a direct transcription of part of the tape made at the St. Joan of Arc bingo babysitting in New Orleans. This selected few pages contains many day-camp, and overnight-camp songs. The children were all African American, and ranged in age from three to eighteen. The transcript is a wonderful example of the liveliness that results from an unsupervised taping. With the absence of adults, the children laughed, joked, and teased each other freely. The people in charge of babysitting were all teenagers. Carol, her sister, and a young man named Gregory organized play, and struggled to minimize chaos.

(Tape on)
(General confusion)
(Carol) Did any of you went to day camp?
(Boy) Not me!
(Carol) I went to NORD (New Orleans Recreation Department) Day Camp.
(Another boy sings) At day camp one day!
(Carol) What time?
(Boy) On Robert E. Lee.
(Carol sings) I had a peanut, I had a peanut, I had a peanut last night . . .
(Somebody) SHHHH!
(Carol) Hey ya'll . . . !
(Boys interrupt and say the song is wrong.)
(JS) If you guys want to, you can sing with us, and then you won't want to dance and sing over there.
(Carol) They gonna help.
(Boys) You sing this song.
(Carol) You went to NORD day camp, huh?
(Boy) Yeah.
(Carol) You know "Found a Peanut"?
(Boy) Yeah.
(Carol) NORD day camp?

(Boy) Yeah.

(Carol) For true?

(Boy) Yeah.

(Carol) But you probably din't listen, you know. Did they ever tell you a song, "I Had a Peanut"? Did they ever teach you "Hands on Myself What Have I Here"? That's more fun anyway (sings):

> Hands on myself what have I here?
> This is my hand right over here . . .

(Boy) Oh yeah, I remember that.

(Carol continues)

> This is my right foot, stamp stamp stamp
> That's what I learned at day camp (*Clap clap.*)
> Hands on myself what have I here?
> I have this is my eyes peering right over here
> I feel my hands over here, stamp stamp stamp
> That's what I learned at day camp.[1]

(Boy) I know how to do it.

(Eight-year-old child) I know one. I wanna sing.

(JS) OK sing.

(Child) a-b-c-d-e-f-g-8 by . . . oh . . . a-b-c-d-e-f-g-8-j-k-l-m-n-o-p-q-r-s-t-u-v-x- and now I go to my 1–2–3 . . . 1–2–3–4–5–6–7–8–9–10.

(JS) Very good. How old are you?

(Child) Eight.

(JS) Eight? That's very good. (To another child) Sing me something.

(Child) Popeye the sailor man . . . oh, wait . . .

(Another child)

> I'm Popeye the sailor man poop poop
> I live in the garbage can poop poop
> I like to go swimmin' with baldheaded wimmin
> I'm Popeye the sailor man poop poop.

(Same child) I know how to say another one.

> I'm Popeye the sailor man poop poop
> I live in the garbage can poop poop
> He never go swimmin' with baldheaded wimmin
> I'm Popeye the sailor man poop poop.

(JS to Carol) Do you know "Popeye the sailor man"?
(Carol) Yeah.

> I'm Popeye the sailor man
> I live in the . . . (Carol breaks up laughing)

(JS) Garbage can?
(Carol) No!
(JS) Say it in my ear.
(Carol) I swear you wouldn't want to hear this one.
(Child) I know one. I know one!
(JS) You tell me later, Carol, because I want to write that one down.
(Loud confusion.)
(Carol) You write that one down!
(Child)

> I'm Popeye the sailor man
> He live in a garbage can
> He sat on a hot stove and burned his toes . . .

(Another child) No, that's not it! (Then he repeats the one about "baldheaded
    wimmin" but says "redheaded wimmin.")
(Child) I know one.

> I'm Popeye the sailor man poop poop
> He live in the garbage can poop poop
> He turned on the gas and burned his ass
> He Popeye the sailor man poop poop.[2]

(Little girl) I know . . . What you SAID!
(Child sidles up.) Are you my friend?
(JS) Yes.
(Child) I gonna tell you this.
(JS) OK.

(Child) Are you my friend?

(JS) Yes.

(Child) Then don't put your boogie in the garbage can.

(JS) Oh, how awful!

(Child repeats gleefully.) You turn on the gas, and burn off his . . . ooop!

(JS) All right, have you got another one?

(Carol) Yeah, it's about the lady and the crocodile . . .

> Oh she sailed away on a happy summer day
> On the back of a crocodile,
> Said she, "It's plain as it can be, I'm riding down the Nile."
> Oh, the croc winked his eye as she waved her friends goodbye
> Wearing a happy smile
> At the end of the ride, the lady was inside of the back of the crocodile![3]

(Child) I know one! I know a Christmas song.

(Carol) Wait! You sing it like this next. You go—you do motions—you go

> Oh, she sailed away on a happy summer day *(Make a circle like the sun.)*
> On the *(Make a wavy motion.)* of a *(Flap hands together like the mouth of the crocodile.)*
> Said she, "It's *(Make straight lines with hand.)* as it can be
> I'm riding down the *(Wavy motions like water.)*
> So the *(Clap hands.)* winked his eye *(Point to eye.)* as he *(Wave.)* his friends goodbye
> Wearing a happy *(Smile big.)*
> At the end of the *(Wavy motion.)*, the lady was *(Circle motion.)* of the *(Clap clap clap.)*.

(Carol) That's a camp song.

(Chorus of voices) We wanna say a Popeye song!

(JS) Say a Popeye.

(Boy repeats previous "Popeye" song)

> I'm Popeye the sailor man
> I live in a garbage can
> I'm Popeye the sailor man
> Turn on the gas and burn off his ass
> I'm Popeye the sailor man.

(A chorus of embarrassed screeches and giggles from the small children.)

(JS) How old are you?

(Child) Six.

(JS) What's your name?

(Child) Michael.

(Another child) I know one!

(JS) What's your one?

(Child) Lemme say a Christmas song.

(JS) Yeah?

(Child) I wanna say a Christmas song.

(Another child) Wait! You and my friend stop . . .

(JS) Stop what?

(Child) You and my friend stop eating boogers out of the garbage can.

(JS) Oooooh! How horrible!

(Child puts her hands over her mouth and giggles.)

(Carol) Sing Lollipop . . . (She begins)

> L-o-double-l-i-p-o-p spells lollipop lollipop
> It's the only decent kind of candy candy
> The guy who make it must have been a dandy
> L-o-double-l-i-p-o-p you see
> It's a lick on a stick guaranteed to make you sick
> Lollipop for me.

> (Carol continues) And then we Dunbar camp—
> D-U-N-B-A-R Camp spells Dunbar camp Dunbar camp
> It's the only decent kind of day camp
> The guy who made it must have been a real champ.
> D-u-n-b-a-r C-a-m-p you see
> It's the camp for a champ guaranteed to make you champ
> Dunbar Camp (*Clap.*) for me. (*Clap.*)

(JS) Was that like a cheer?

(Carol) I love it, yes. Yeah, there's a NORD cheer like this—

> All the boys and girls of NORD
> That you hear so much about
> Whenever we go marching
> You hear the people shout
> We're noted for our thoughtfulness

And pleasant things we do
Most everybody likes us
And we hope you like us too.

(Little kid again) Oh, I know. I know. I know a Christmas song.
(Carol) Wait, wait, wait just a minute, c'mon. We gonna do "Rise and Shine." Rise
   and shine—Oh, I don't know. Let him do it. Let him go.
(Little boy)

Dashing through the snow
On a one-horse open sleigh . . . (Giggle giggle.)

(Another child interrupts) I know one! I know one!

I'm Popeye the sailor man
He live in a garbage can
He like to go swimmin' with bow-legged wimmin
He Popeye the sailor man.

(JS) OK.
(Carol) Lolli lolli pop. That one go lolli pop—three lollipops in a row.

L-o-double l-i-p-o-p spells lollipop
It's the only decent kind of candy.

(Another teenager breaks in.) That don't sound right. Where did you learn that
   one?
(Carol's sister) Day camp. I learned all these things at day camp. Carol, come
   here. Lordy, she hear 'em all day. Come here, sing lollipop.
(A group of girls quickly start to vie with one another.) They sing:

As we go marching and the band begins to play p-l-a-y
You will hear us shouting
The boys and girls of NORD Hooray!

(Girl) We used to love that one.
(Girl in the background shouts.)

Down down Baby down by the roller coaster—

(Group joins in.)

> Down down Baby down by the roller coaster
> Sweet sweet Baby I don't want to let you go
> Shimmy shimmy co co pop
> Shimmy shimmy rock
> Shimmy shimmy co co pop
> Shimmy shimmy lollipop
> You missed![4]

(Carol interrupts by chanting louder than the other girls.)

> Rise and shine and you got the glory glory
> Rise and shine and you got the glory glory
> Rise and shine and you got the glory glory, children of the Lord
> The Lord told Noah to build an arky arky
> The Lord told Noah to build an arky arky
> Build it out of hickory barky barky, children of the Lord
> The animals they came by twosie twosie twosie
> The animals they came by twosie twosie twosie
> Elephants and kangaroosie roosie roosie, children of the Lord
> (We used to love this!)
> So rise and shine and give Lord the glory glory
> *(I messed up, it was after "The animals came by twosie twosie.")*
> It rained and rained for forty daysie daysies
> It rained and rained for forty daysie daysies
> Nearly drove those animals crazy crazy crazy
> Children of the Lord
> The sun came out and showed its glory glory
> The sun came out and showed its glory glory
> Everything was hunky dory dory
> Children of the Lord.[5]

(Carol continues) I like "Hands on Myself"...
(Girl breaks in.) I found a peanut!
(JS) Who knows a cheer?
(People start shouting.) I was down by the ...
(Another person) No, I doesn't ...

(Somebody) Who knows "Down by the Graveyard"? Something about the graveyard . . . You know "Down by the Graveyard"? You know a cheer?

(Someone else) Down burying . . .

(Older boy) Oh yeah!

(Carol) I can't remember that cheer.

(Someone shouts) Conrad!

(JS) Conrad is a playground at NORD?

(Kids) Yeah!

(Boy) He gonna kill him!

(Carol) Harrell playground. H-a-r-r-e-l-l.

(JS) OK where's that?

(Kids) Leonidas and Claiborne!

(Boy interrupts.) Conrad is Hamilton Street and _____, and they play
against the Lions Center. It's neighborhood NORD football teams. And they
cheer up against each other. And they go:

> V-i-c-t-o-r-y Victory victory that's our cry
> Victory victory that's our cry
> Down the road there's an old cemetery
> That's the corral for the _____
> We've buried . . .

(Girls interrupt) We know one! We know one!

(JS) Wait.

(Little boy) It names everything last night. (?)

> Hey! Old King Cole was a merry old soul
> He married the woman in the shoe
> Was he? Was he? . . .

(JS) OK, you forgot?

(Little boy) He had so many children that he cried!

(JS) OK. What's the other one?

(Carol) He . . . Hey! Wanna do "Did You Feed my Cow"?

> Did you feed my cow? (Group echoes) Yes, m'am.
> Oh, did you feed my cow? Yes, m'am.
> Did my cow get sick? Yes, m'am.
> Did she get sick full of ticks? Yes, m'am.

(No, we got all messed up. It's . . .)

Did you feed my cow? Yes, m'am.
Did you feed my cow? Yes, m'am.
What did you feed him? Corn and hay.
What did you feed him? Corn and hay.
Did my cow get sick? Yes, m'am.
Did my cow get sick? Yes, m'am.
Did he get sick from a tick? Yes, m'am.
Did he get sick from a tick? Yes, m'am.
Did you milk my cow? Yes, m'am.
Did you milk my cow? Yes, m'am.[6]

(Followed by loud confusion.)
(JS) Where did you get that one?
(Carol) Day camp.
(Little boy) I know one!
(Teenage boy) That's a camp song! You went to Benjamin. No wonder you know
    any. ("Benjamin" is Benjamin Franklin High, the elite public school in New
    Orleans.)
(Carol) Doodly day . . .
(Chaos ensues.)
(Six-year-old girl sidles up.)

Little Miss Muffett
Sat on a tuffett
Eating her curds and whey
Along came a spider and
Sat down beside her
And frightened Miss Muffett away.

(JS) You know any more?
(Six-year-old girl) Old King Cole . . .
(Another child) I know one! I know one!
(Six-year-old girl) Old King Cole . . . (She is interrupted again.)
(Carol) I found a peanut—I had a peanut, I had a peanut just now—
OK. Wait . . .

I had a peanut, I had a peanut, I had a peanut last night.
Oh last night had a peanut, had a peanut last night

> I cracked it open, I cracked it open, I cracked it open last night . . .
> You can't record the whole song, it takes forever.

(JS) That's all right, go ahead.
(Carol)

> I cracked it open, I cracked it open, I cracked it open last night.
> Oh last night cracked it open, cracked it open last night.
> It was rotten, it was rotten, it was rotten last night.
> Oh last night it was rotten, it was rotten last night
> I ate it anyway, I ate it anyway, I ate it anyway last night.
> Oh last night ate it anyway, ate it anyway last night
> I got sick, I got sick, I got sick last night.
> Oh last night got sick, got sick last night
> I called the doctor (repeat)
> He didn't come . . .
> I died anyway . . .
> I went to heaven . . .
> The gate was closed . . .
> I called St. Peter . . .
> He didn't answer . . .
> I went the other way . . .
> The devil was waiting . . .
> I went to hell . . .
> I guess![7]

(Carol) I don't remember. Natalie made that up.
(Group of small kids.) We know one! We know one!
(JS) Wait! This little boy wants to say one.
(Boy) I know a joke.
(Carol sings loudly, outshouting the boy.) We goin' on a bear hunt . . .
(Teenage boy) I know that one!
(JS) Do you really know one? (To another small boy who has been repeatedly tapping me on the arm.) OK tell me.
(Boy)

> My name is Michael
> I live in the jungle
> My girlfriend Judy . . . (Hesitates, forgets the rest.)

(JS) All right, you know one?

(Girl) I never say that!

(Carol's sister to Carol.) You remember this one? You remember this one? "You got Fifteen Bottles of Pop on the Wall?"

(Carol) Yeah.

(Carol's sister) But Carol knows . . . She knows "The Other Day I Met a Bear."Wait. "We goin' on a bear hunt."

(Carol) Wait . . ."The other day . . ." (The rest of her friends echo each line.)

The other day (*The other day*)

I met a bear (*I met a bear*)

Deep in the woods (*Deep in the woods*)

Away out there (*Away out there*)

The other day I met a bear, deep in the woods, away out there. (*All together*)

I looked at him (*I looked at him*)

He looked at me (*He looked at me*)

I sized him up (*I sized him up*)

He sized up me (*He sized up me*)

I looked at him, he looked at me, I sized him up, he sized up me. (*All together*)

He said I think (*He said I think*)

You better run (*You better run*)

Because you ain't (*Because you ain't*)

Got any gun (*Got any gun*)

He said I think you better run, because you ain't got any gun (*All together*)

And so I ran (*And so I ran*)

To the nearest street (*To the nearest street*)

But that old bear (*But that old bear*)

Was after me (*Was after me*)

And so I ran to the nearest street, but that old bear was after me. (*All together*)

I reached a tree (*I reached a tree*)

The nearest branch (*The nearest branch*)

Was ten feet up (*Was ten feet up*)

To reach that branch I'd have to jump (*To reach that branch I'd have to jump*)

The nearest branch was ten feet up, to reach that branch, I'd have to jump. (*All together*)

I reached that branch (*I reached that branch*)

On the way back down (*On the way back down*)

And that old bear (*And that old bear*)

Was not around (*Was not around*)

I reached that branch on the way down, and that old bear was not around. (*All together*)

That's all there is (*That's all there is*)

There ain't no more (*There ain't no more*)

Until we meet that bear once more (*Until we meet that bear once more*)

That's all there is, there ain't no more, until we meet that bear once more. (*All together*)

(Carol) I love it! "I'm goin' on a bear hunt!"

(JS) I know that one. (I was afraid of running out of tape.) OK give me a tongue twister.

(Child)

Peter Piper picked a peck of pickled peppers.

If Peter Piper picked a peck of pickled peppers,

Where's the peck of pickled peppers Peter Piper picked?

(Carol) I can say that better than her. (Repeats the tongue twister faster.)

(JS) That's very good. I think I'll have to quit on that 'cause the TV just went on. (*Pause on tape.*)

(Tape back on. Loud noise for a while.)

(Child)

Rubber baby buggy bumpers.

Rubber baby buggy bumpers.

(Same child) But I still can't say, "Strange strategic statistics."

(JS) What?

(Child) Strange strategic statistics.

(Another child) I know one. Rub a dub dub, three men in a tub, rub a dub dub, three men in a tub. (Repeats it several times, faster and faster.)

(JS) How old are you?

(Child) Six.

(Carol) That one's easy. Ummm, how much wood would a woodchuck chuck if a woodchuck could chuck wood? He'd chuck as much as a woodchuck could chuck wood. Right? A proper cuppa coffee in a copper coffee pot. (Repeats several times.)

(JS) Do you know any more? (Negative response.) OK.

(End of tape.)

Everything on the preceding tape confirms that children who go to day camps memorize and share the camp songs they learn there with their siblings and friends. When I worked as assistant camp counselor for only one summer at Camp Ruth Lee, in Norwood, Louisiana, we sang camp songs from a set of typewritten notebooks. The notebooks remained in the camp library at the end of sessions. The children sang songs every night around the campfire. They then, like Carol, carried their memorized songs out into the play world and shared them with friends.

In the transcript of the St. Joan of Arc bingo babysitting session, I included material from one of the choicest tapes I have. There were others, where everyone shouted at once, airplanes flew over, trucks rumbled by, air conditioners hummed loudly, and children argued for five minutes at a time over nitpicky things. These were torture to try to transcribe into usable material.

There were other camp songs I heard on the playground. The little African American girls at Louise Day Care Center, who were three and four years old, sang this for me:

> If you happy and you know it clap your hands (*Clap clap.*)
> If you happy and you know it clap your hands (*Clap clap.*)
> If you happy and you know it, then you really ought to show it,
> If you happy and you know it clap your hands (*Clap clap.*)
> If you happy and you know it stomp your feet. (*Stomp stomp.*) (*Repeat as in the first verse.*)
> If you happy and you know it shout hooray! (*Shake head, or raise arms.*) (*Some said, "Shake your head."*)
> —*Louise Day Care Center, African American girls, New Orleans*

The tiny preschool girls who sang this, Angelique, Quintella, Patricia, and DeShawn, were four of the sharpest and most verbally adept children I ever recorded.

At Happy Face Nursery School in Chalmette, Louisiana, I recorded three little white girls who insisted they were in second grade but looked like toddlers. After singing several nursery rhyme songs, one child shouted, "People on the Bus!"

(JS) Y'all play that here at Happy Face?

(Girls) Yeah! We all sing it!

(JS) Do they do it at school?

(Girls) They bring it here from school. We learn it at dancing school. Go get Jasmine outside. (A playmate leaves and then comes back trailing Jasmine.)

The people on the bus go up and down (*Standing behind one another, hands on hips of girl in front, they go up on their toes and crouch down.*)
Up and down, up and down
The people on the bus go up and down
All over (One child says "around") the town
The money on the bus goes clink clink clink (*Drop "money" into cash box.*)
Clink clink clink, clink clink clink
The money on the bus goes clink clink clink
All over (around) the town
The driver on the bus goes, move on back, move on back, move on back (*Push sideways with hands.*)
The driver on the bus goes move on back
All over the town
The horn on the bus goes beep beep beep (*Push on "horn."*)
Beep beep beep, beep beep beep
The horn on the bus goes beep beep beep
All over the town
The baby on the bus goes waa waa waa (*Put fist to eyes.*)
Waa waa waa, waa waa waa
The baby on the bus goes waa waa waa
All over the town
The lady on the bus goes woo woo woo (*Shake mightily.*)
Woo woo woo, woo woo woo
The lady on the bus goes woo woo woo
All over the town
The ladies on the bus go yack yack yack (*Open mouth from side to side.*)
Yack yack yack, yack yack yack
The ladies on the bus go yack yack yack
All over the town
The fat man on the bus goes ho ho ho (*Hands on sides.*)
Ho ho ho, ho ho ho
The fat man on the bus goes ho ho ho
All over the town
The door on the bus goes open and shut (*Open arms wide, then close.*)
Open and shut, open and shut
The door on the bus goes open and shut
All over the town.

(JS) When y'all do this, do you make 'em up as you go along sometime? Do you change 'em? Or do you sing the same ones every time?

(Worker at Happy Face) Same ones! (*And she rolls her eyes.*)
(Girls) Patty cake!
(JS) OK.
(Girls)

> Patty cake patty cake baker's man
> Make me a cake as fast as you can
> Roll 'em up and pat 'em up
> Put 'em in a pot for baby and me.

(Happy Face worker) That's interesting. I've heard kids say "Pat a cake pat a cake
　　make a man." I've never heard that said here.
(Girls) Can we do cheers?
(JS) Yes.
(Girls)

> Firecracker firecracker
> Boom boom boom
> Firecracker firecracker
> Boom boom boom
> The boys have the muscles
> The girls have the brains
> The team has the (Mumble.)
> To win this game
> Yeah!

(JS) I like that.
(Girls)

> Push 'em back push 'em back waaay back!
> Push 'em back push 'em back waaay back!
>
> (Repeat many times.)

Then:

> California sunshine Alabama traction
> We think your team needs a bit of action
> Put them in the bathtub

Pull out the plug
There goes your team glug glug glug
Hit 'em once (*Clap clap.*)
Hit 'em twice (*Clap clap.*)
Make 'em quick (*Clap clap.*)
Make 'em nice. (*Clap clap.*)
—*Happy Face Day Nursery, Chalmette, La. white girls*

The following camp song was one I had never heard. The girls who sang it for me were a group of middle-school African American and white Girl Scouts at St. Catherine of Siena Catholic School in Metairie, Louisiana, 1977. The girls sang the song in unison, but it is clear that it could be an "echo" song:

My Aunt came back
My Aunt came back
From old Japan
From old Japan
She brought me back
She brought me back
An old man's hand
An old man's hand
My Aunt came back
My Aunt came back
From old Algiers
From old Algiers
She brought me back
She brought me back
Some sewing shears
Some sewing shears
My Aunt came back
My Aunt came back
From Holland too
From Holland too
She brought me back
She brought me back
A wooden shoe
A wooden shoe
My Aunt came back
My Aunt came back

From the county fair
From the county fair
She brought me back
She brought me back
A rocking chair
A rocking chair
My Aunt came back
My Aunt came back
From Italy
From Italy
She brought me back
She brought me back
An itchy flea
An itchy flea
My Aunt came back
My Aunt came back
From the Brooklyn zoo
From the Brooklyn zoo
She brought me back
She brought me back
A nut like you! (*All shout.*)

—*St. Catherine of Siena Girl Scouts, 7 white, 1 African American, Old Metairie, La.*

The St. Catherine of Siena Girl Scouts had a copy of their songbook with them. They consulted the book and then sang a few bars of the popular camp song "Barges."

Out of my window
Looking through the night
I can see the barges
Oh, what a sight.

Then they launched into a parody of "Barges":

Out of my window looking through the night
I can see the counselors, oh, what a sight
Counselors, I would like to go with you,
I would like to see the Boy Scouts too
Counselors, would you throw me in the lake,
I would like to be bitten by a polka-dotted snake.

This was only one of the many camp song parodies current in the 1970s. When I heard the girls singing their parody, I recalled one we had sung at Girl Scout camp when I was a preteen in the early 1950s—I began, "Do your boobs hang low / Do they wobble to and fro . . . ?" and I glanced at the troop leader and saw the expression on her face, and I stopped. The Metairie Girl Scouts were not finished, though. They had barely heard me as they were all talking at once. They consulted their camp song pages, and then asked, "May we sing a song?"

Then, all together, they chanted:

> Peanut butter, peanut butter and jelllly
> Peanut butter, peanut butter and jelllly
> First you take a peanut and you break 'em, you break 'em
> You break 'em, break 'em, break 'em (*"Break" peanut open.*)
> Then you smoosh 'em, you smoosh 'em (*"Smoosh" between palms.*)
> And you smooosh 'em, smooosh 'em, smooosh 'em
> And you roooll it out and you roooll it out, and you have peanut peanut butter and jelly (*Roll motion.*)
> Peanut peanut butter and jelly
> First you take the berries and you pick 'em, you pick 'em (*Pick motion.*)
> First you take the berries and you pick 'em, you pick 'em
> You pick 'em, pick 'em, pick 'em
> Then you smoosh 'em, you smoosh 'em (*"Smoosh" between palms.*)
> You smoosh 'em, smoosh 'em, smoosh 'em
> And you spreaaaaad it out (*Spread motion.*)
> And you spreaaaaad it out
> Then you have peanut peanut butter and jelly
> Peanut peanut butter and jelly.

(Girls stop singing and giggle.) One girl touches my hand and says, "Can we sing "Flamin' Mamie'?"

(JS) What is that? How does "Flamin' Mamie" go?

(The girls scream) Flamin' Mamie!

(JS) Is that one you sing on the playground?

(The girls shout) No! At Girl Scout Camp. At the bonfire! That's when the big girls get to do it. (Lots of noise, while the girls select who will sing.) Then they begin:

> They call me (umf) Flamin' Mamie (*Sexy hip thrust.*)
> I'm a sugar baby
> I'm the hottest baby in town.

(An argument breaks out, and the next few moments are full of cries of, "You messed up. It doesn't start like that!" and "Amy doesn't do it right." "Amy don't know nothin."") Then one girl struts forward and begins, "It goes like this":

I style my hair (*Brushes back forehead hair.*)

The clothes I wear (*Runs hands down her sides.*)

I walk down the street (*Does "sexy" walk.*)

Boys at my feet (*Indicates feet.*)

They call me (umf) Flamin' Mamie (*Sexy hip thrust.*)

I'm a (umf) Sugar Muffin

I'm the hottest baby in town

And when it (umf) comes to lovin'

I'm a (umf) cookin' oven

I'm the hottest baby in town

And when the honey gets the letter that it's time to retire retire

I said Grandma you're the hottest since Chicago fire

They call me (umf) Flamin' Mamie

I'm a (umf) Sugar Muffin

I'm the hottest baby in town

Hottest baby in town

Flamin' Mamie!

(*Girls all giggle.*)[8]

—*St. Catherine of Siena Girl Scouts, Old Metairie, La.*

Every collecting session had an atmosphere all its own. When I collected from children in an outdoor setting, the sessions usually had a relaxed, informal feeling. When I held recording assemblies in classrooms or cafeterias and a teacher was present, there was usually a strained sense of "Oops, can I really say that?" At Ursaline Academy, in New Orleans, in 1977, the air was heavy with watchfulness. There were two nuns in the classroom, and they hovered, alert to every word the students and I exchanged. The girls, twelve white and two African American, were slow to feel comfortable. But when they relaxed, they volunteered these:

(JS) Oh, you have a prayer? Could you come say your prayer for me? (Two girls step forward.)

(Girls)

Now I lay me down to study

I pray the Lord I won't go nutty

And if I fail to learn this junk
I pray the Lord that I don't flunk
But if I do, don't pity me at all
Just lay my bones in the study hall
Tell my teacher I've done my best
And pile my books upon my chest
Now I lay me down to rest
To pray I'll pass tomorrow's test
If I should die before I wake
That's one less test I'll have to take.[9]

(JS) Where did you learn it?
(Girl) Uh, it was on a piece of paper that was going around in government class.
(Girls break into embarrassed laughter.)
(JS) Do you know any other prayers? (Girls think a while.) Are there any more
things that you did?
(Girls) We have a folklore prayer that's a Sioux prayer.
(JS) OK. Oh, well . . .
(Girl) It's, uh, it's a serious prayer. It's an Indian prayer.
(JS) Where did you learn it?
(Girl) From Pam. It's old.
(JS) I would like to hear it.
(Girl)

We are the mighty Sioux
We're strong and true
We always try our best
In everything we do
Our hearts are filled with memories
Of every church thought and deed
And may St. Joseph stay with us
In every time of need
A Sioux prays in every class
Where we get to stay
And may our class of '78 forever lead the way.

(JS) Where did you learn it? Is this traditional? Did your mother know it?
(Girls) No! It's by class. Each class has a class name, and when you graduate, you
get to keep your class song
(JS) I collect jokes. You know a good joke?

(Girl) Why are fire engines red?

(JS) I don't know. Why are fire engines red?

(Girl) Fire engines are red because they have three speeds and four wheels, and three times four is twelve and twelve inches are a foot, and a foot is a ruler, and a ruler is Queen Elizabeth, and Queen Elizabeth has ships, and the ships sail the seas, and the seas have fishes, and the fishes have fins, and the Finns fought the Russians, and the Russians are red, and that is why fire engines are red.

The girls immediately chant in unison:

> The more you study
> The more you learn
> The more you learn
> The more you study
> The more you study
> The more you learn
> You have to study.

(Girl) Erin, Erin knows one. Come on, Erin, sing it!

(Erin) Awwww. This is a song my little nieces always used to sing. It is . . .

(The girls get rowdy.)

(JS) Sing it!

(Erin)

> What's today?
> Today is Happy Birthday
> What's today?
> It's time to celebrate.
> Come enjoy
> The Happy Birthday party
> Come enjoy
> Before it gets too late
> All day long the doorbell rings
> Rings and rings and rings and rings
> After all the ding-a-lings duly stand in line
> All the friends and all they greet
> Bring us something new to eat
> "How are you?" And "How dee do?"
> And "Thanks, I'm feeling fine."

Oh, everybody's fine, hurray
They're really not in touch, OK.
Talk talk talk so much to tell each other
Then the games with blindfolded eyes
Donkey's tails are crowding one another
Are you last to win the booby prize?
Now the Birthday cake is here
Everybody claps and cheers
Have the candles for the years
Blowing as they go
Boo hoo hoo
Now we have the counted years
Now we can go home
It's really time to go
Now we leave the Happy Birthday party
Say goodbye and wave her at the door
Thank you for this Happy Birthday party
And we wish you many happy more.

(JS) Where did your little cousins learn that?

(Girl) I have no idea. I think . . . I think they may have learned it . . . they have lived
everywhere. My sister's husband is in the air force, and I think they might
have picked it up either in Germany or somewhere else. They have lived all
over.

(JS) Yeah, I think it reminds me very much of a speech that is made, "Ladies and
gentlemen, dogs and cats . . ."

(Girl) Yes! It goes

One bright day in the middle of the night
Two dead boys got up to fight
Back to back facing each other
They drew their swords and shot each other.
A deaf policeman heard the noise
And came and shot the two dead boys.
If you do not believe this rhyme is true
Ask the blind man, he saw it too.[10]

(Girls in the class make appreciative noises at end of this speech.)

(JS) That's a delivery that children do on the playground. We used to say, "Starkle
   starkle little twink . . ."Do you say that too?
(Girls laugh and look around to see how the nuns will react.)
(Girl) I'm not as drunk as thinkle peep I am?
(Another girl volunteers.)

> Starkle starkle little twink
> I think I had too much to drink
> The drunker I think here the longer I stand . . . (Girl pauses.)

(JS) "I'm not as drunk as thinkle peep I am" is in there somewhere. I love that line.
(Girls) Yeah.
(The two nuns are frowning by now.)
(JS) Does anybody else know any others?
(Girl) I do.
(JS) Yes?
(Girl) Here's one my sister taught me.

> We are brave we are bold
> Lots of liquor we can hold
> In the cellars of old Ursaline
> Guzzle guzzle guzzle
> We've no muzzle muzzle muzzle
> Mother had a heart attack in fear
> More Beer!
> In the cellars of old Ursaline.
> Never fear, we say, Sister have a beer
> In the cellars of old Ursaline![11]

(JS) Who has another song for me?
(Girl) How about school?
(JS) OK. School.
(Girl)

> Mine eyes have seen the glory of the burning of the school
> We have tortured all the teachers
> We have broken all the rules
> We plan to hang the principal
> Tomorrow afternoon

The year is blasting on (*Clap clap clap.*)
Glory glory hallelujah
Teacher hit me with a ruler
Met her at the door with a loaded .44
And she ain't my teacher no more.
—*Ursaline Academy, teenage girls, New Orleans*

So, even in the most constricted of classroom circumstances students can volunteer lore that is wonderfully new, gleefully satirical. The girls at Ursaline Academy were ninth graders and gladly shared what they knew of teen lore on tape, in spite of the frowning of the nuns and the stricture of the stuffy classroom.

In 1980, I recorded several freshman students at Tulane University, New Orleans. One white girl, Ruthanna, who was reared in Cooperstown, New York, told me, "We used to sing songs a lot on the busses. We almost got thrown off the bus once for our dirty songs."

(JS) Do you remember any of those?
(She laughs) The one they really didn't want us to do was "Throw Me Over in the Clover, Lay Me Down and Do It Again." (Sings):

This is number one and I think we're going to have some fun
Roll me over lay me down, do it again.
Roll me over in the clover, roll me over, lay me down, do it again.
This is number two and I think we're gonna screw
Roll me over lay me down, do it again.
Roll me over in the clover, roll me over, lay me down, do it again.
This is number three and his hand is on my knee
Roll me over lay me down, do it again.
Roll me over in the clover, roll me over, lay me down, do it again.
This is number four and I think he's locked the door
Roll me over lay me down, do it again
Roll me over in the clover, roll me over, lay me down, do it again.
This is number five and his hand is on my thigh
Roll me over lay me down, do it again
Roll me over in the clover, roll me over, lay me down, do it again.
This is number six and I think I'm in a fix . . .
This is number seven and I feel like I'm in heaven . . .
This is number eight and, boy, I'm feeling great . . .

> This is number nine and I'm feeling mighty fine . . .
> This is number ten, I think we're gonna do it again
> This is number eleven and I think we should have stopped at seven
> This is number twelve and my stomach is beginning to swell
> This is number thirty and this song is getting dirty . . .[12]

(JS) I've never heard that.

(Ruthanna) I can't believe it. (Laughs.) There's a clean version of it too, but we used to change the words to it, and we used to make it as filthy as we could. We did a lot of things like that.

(JS) Um, what were some of the other ones?

(Ruthanna)

> I'm a juvenile delinquent
> Can't go home any more . . .

(Ruthanna) OK, I don't know how it works out. It goes on about "my father slept in and my mother stayed out all night / My brother is a Kamikaze pilot and my grandmother gets caught swinging on the outhouse door waiting for the milkman to come."

Ruthanna then recalled several songs she learned at various summer camps she attended as a child.

(Ruthanna) Let's see . . . my favorite was about underwear—

(Sung to the tune of "Bye Bye Blackbird.")

> I just lost my underwear (*Hands up in surprise.*)
> I don't care (*Shakes head.*)
> They go there (*Makes throwing motion.*)
> Bye bye long johns (*Waves good-bye.*)
> They were always good to me
> Tickled me (*Tickles ribs.*)
> Hee hee hee (*Holds sides.*)
> Bye bye long johns (*Waves good-bye.*)
> I remember the little trap door behind me (*Motions behind.*)
> Look inside and there you'll always find me (*Hand to forehead.*)
> I just lost my underwear
> I don't care
> I'll go there
> Long johns good bye.

(JS) Wow! That was a parody of "Bye Bye Blackbird."

(Ruthanna) Yeah?

(JS) Any more?

(Ruthanna) Uhhhhmmmm . . . goodness gracious . . . there was one . . . however, it was short. (Sings):

> Hallelujah I'm a bum
> Hallelujah bum again
> Hallelujah give us a handout
> To revive us again.

And there were other verses, but I can't remember all of them. Um, it's an old . . . it's from the Appalachian Mountains.[13]

(JS) Um hum.

(Ruthanna) I learned it from traveling minstrels that traveled through town kind of thing a long time ago. And then I heard it again at a camp a couple of years ago. There's another one:

> I'm a little acorn brown
> Lying on the cold cold ground
> Everybody steps on me
> That is why I'm cracked you see
> I'm a nut (*Cluck cluck.*)
> I'm a nut (*Cluck cluck.*)
> A nut nut nut nut nut nut nut
> Took myself out on a date
> Careful now don't stay out late.

I can't remember just how it all goes. Do you remember?

(JS) I don't know it.

(Ruthanna)

> Every time I squeeze, I slap my face
> I'm a nut (*Cluck cluck.*)
> I'm a nut (*Cluck cluck.*)
> I'm a nut, I'm a nut
> A nut nut nut nut nut nut nut.

There were other songs we played. That was a cute one. There was another . . .
um . . . How does it go? It was about an English sparrow . . . oh . . . it goes:

Oh I wish I were a little English sparrow sparrow
Oh, I wish I were a little English sparrow
I would sit up in the treesies and sprinkle all with feces
Oh, I wish I were a little English sparrow sparrow
Oh, I wish I were a little striped skunk striped skunk
Oh, I wish I were a little striped skunk striped skunk
I would sit up in the treesies and sprinkle all the breezies
Oh, I wish I were a little striped skunk . . .

I can't remember any more, but there were all kinds of verses, and we used to
make up all kinds of animals and have them do all kinds of things, and we
used to sing it all the way to the store.
(JS) Did you sing one that went da da da da da duh da duhhhhhh?
(Ruthanna) Yes, I think I remember—

The ants go marching one by one hoorah hoorah
The ants go marching one by one hoorah hoorah
The ants go marching one by one
The little one stops to shoot his gun
And they all go marching down in the ground to get out of the rain
Dum dum dum
The ants go marching two by two hoorah hoorah
The ants go marching two by two hoorah hoorah
The ants go marching two by two
The littlest one stops to tie his shoe
And they all go marching down in the ground to get out of the rain
Dum dum dum
The ants go marching three by three hoorah hoorah
The ants go marching three by three hoorah hoorah
The ants go marching three by three
The little one stops to cry at a tree
And they all go marching down in the ground to get out of the rain
Dum dum dum.

Then number four "shut the door" and number five "played with a beehive"; six
"picked up sticks," seven "looked at heaven," eight "shut the gate," nine . . . uh

. . . what did nine do? "Marched in time," I think. And ten, "begin again" I think . . . something like that. We used to do "This Old Man."

(JS) How does it go?

> This old man, he played one
> He played knick-knack on my drum.
> Knick-knack paddy whack give your dog a bone
> This old man came rolling home
> This old man he played two
> He played knick-knack on my shoe
> With a knick-knack paddy whack give your dog a bone
> This old man came rolling home
> This old man he played three
> He played knick-knack on my knee
> With a knick-knack paddy whack give your dog a bone
> This old man came rolling home.[14]

We did that for a long time. We used to change it though. We used to always use the same tune, but we tried to change it every time we did it. Like for number one, instead of shooting his gun . . . shooting his gun—we had him do something else.

(JS) Uh huhhh, you remember any of those?

(Ruthanna) Not really. It depended on who was there. We changed things around so we could include people, and get them to do changes of the songs, just to see if we could do it.

(JS) Um hummm.

(Ruthanna) I'm trying to think if there's another song we used to do. There's one we used to do . . . we used to do it basically for our counselors.

> We will roll the old chariot along
> We will roll the old chariot along
> We will roll the old chariot along
> And we will get on behind . . .

And this . . . we would stop and pick them up or we would roll right over them.

> Whoever's in the way we will stop and pick them up
> Whoever's in the way we will stop and pick them up
> Whoever's in the way we will stop and pick them up
> And they'll get on behind.

And we would go through all the counselors that way. If we didn't like them, we
would always say we would "roll right over them." (Laughs.) Nice kids, I know.
Let's see . . . oh, goodness . . . um . . .

(JS) How about anything to the tune of "Glory glory hallelujah / Teacher hit me
with a ruler?

(Ruthanna) Yeah, we used to sing that. Let's see, we used to sing:

> From the shores of Lake Otsego
> To the walls of Cooperstown High
> We will fight for right and reason
> And to keep our desks a mess . . .

No . . . It went . . .

> First to fight for rights and reason
> And to keep our desk a mess
> We are proud to claim the title of
> The teacher's number one pests.

There's a verse in there . . . a line there that I have forgotten. We used to sing that
all the time, and we used to make the teachers so mad. And when we used to
do it the most was when we were in elementary school, like, when we were
in fourth grade, and we were supposed to be learning how to take proper
care of our desks and stuff. Nobody wanted to clean their desks. We used to
have desk inspections. We used to sing it all the time. I remember my third-
grade teacher used to put us in the corner if we got caught singing it. We got
the whole class to sing it, and she got so flustered, she made us write five
hundred times, "I will not sing that song again." (Laughs.)

(JS) Wow—she sounds like a real . . .

(Ruthanna) She was. Actually, she was a real nice person, but she didn't like the
song we did. Rotten kids, what can I say?

(JS) Cheers?

(Ruthanna) We used to make up our cheers ourselves. I was on a championship
field hockey team for four years, and we used to make up all our cheers
ourselves, like, when we got there. We would have a certain contest. What
we did was we'd start with the captain of the team, and we would say her
name, and "She is our captain," and we would say, you know, "of outstanding
fame," and then we would say something she had done, like, in the last game.
Uh, we used to do that all the time, 'cuz it would psych the other teams out

because we could do that. We would just make it up as we went along. But, they could never . . . they couldn't understand how to do it. Funny. We had a real sense on that team. Um, one of the cheers that we used to do in high school was, like, the basketball, and the football team, was

> Choo choo bang bang
> Got to get my boomerang
> Ungawa great power
> Redskins are the best
> Better than the rest
> All you gotta do
> Is dance the boogaloo.

And then at the end they had a whole dance that went with it. And everybody used to get up and do it. It was crazy. Everybody was getting up in the stands and doing this dance because everybody wanted to do this dance.

(JS) Any more songs?

(Ruthanna) Oh, yeah . . .

> I know a weenie man
> He owns a weenie stand
> He sells them anything from hot dogs on down
> Someday I'll be his wife
> I'll be his sweetie wife
> Hot dog I love that weenie man
> We'll build a bungalow big enough for two
> Big enough for me and my honey
> Big enough for two
> And when we marry, happy we'll be
> Under the bamboo
> Under the bamboo tree
> Boom boom, boom boom, boom boom boom boom boom boom
> Boom boom, boom boom, boom boom boom boom boom boom
> He'll be m-i-n-e mine
> We'll be f-i-n-e fine
> And I will always love you all the t-i-m-e time
> We'll have the b-e-s-t best of all the r-e-s-t rest
> We'll l-o-v-e love you all the t-i-m-e time
> We're the b-e-s-t best of all the r-e-s-t rest

Any ole time
Match in a gas tank
Boom boom![15]

(JS) Was that a handclap? Or did you sing it?

(Ruthanna) We sang it. Yeah, we used to sing it on the busses. Yeah, that was a
favorite because everybody knew it. We used to do . . . what was that? "Noah's Ark"?

(JS) How did that go? (Then Ruthanna sings her version of "Rise and Shine" Carol
sang at St. Joan of Arc bingo.)

(Ruthanna)

So rise and shine and give God your glory glory
Rise and shine and give God your glory glory
Rise and shine and give God your glory glory
Children of the Lord
The Lord told Noah there's gonna be a floodie floodie
The Lord told Noah there's gonna be a floodie floodie
Get those animals out of the muddy muddy muddy
Children of the Lord
So, rise and shine and give God your glory glory
So, rise and shine and give God your glory glory
Rise and shine and give God your glory glory
Children of the Lord
The Lord told Noah to build them an arkie arkie
The Lord told Noah to build them an arkie arkie
Build it out of hickory barkie barkie
Children of the Lord
So, rise and shine and give God your glory glory
So, rise and shine and give God your glory glory
Rise and shine and give God your glory glory
Children of the Lord
The animals they came on, they came on by twosies twosies
The animals they came on, they came on by twosies twosies
Elephants, cats, and kangaroosies roosies
Children of the Lord
So, rise and shine and give God your glory glory
So, rise and shine and give God your glory glory
Rise and shine and give God your glory glory

Children of the Lord
It rained and rained for forty daysies daysies
It rained and rained for forty daysies daysies
Drove those animals nearly crazy aysie
Drove those animals nearly crazy aysie
Children of the Lord
So, rise . . .
The sun came out and dried up all the landy landy
The sun came out and dried up all the landy landy
Everything was fine and dandy dandy dandy
Children of the Lord
So, rise.[16]

With that one we used to stand up and raise our hands like a sun was shining.
(JS) Was that a camp song or did people do it on the bus?
(Ruthanna) Everybody sang that. We did it everywhere because everybody knew
it just because it was real cute, and it was real easy to learn because it all
rhymed. What else did we do? We used to try to do popular songs. There was
one that was real cute and we used to do it on the busses, because everyone
was developing their first crushes on everyone else. It would be like . . .

Oh, Ann has a little box
She keeps her Gregie in
She takes him and NASTY
And puts him back again
Harumph harrumph oh la daa daa de ay ay ay
Harumph harrumph oh la daa daa de ay ay ay
Oh, someone has a little black box
They keep their baby in
They take him out and NASTY
And put him back again
Harumph harrumph oh la daa daa de ay ay ay
Harumph harrumph oh la daa daa de ay ay ay.

We used to go on, and do that for hours, and hours, and hours . . . It was terrible.
It was fun, though, because it made everyone that had a crush on someone
able to sing the song with their name.
(JS) Um hummm.

(Ruthanna) That was exciting. What else did we used to do on the bus? Most of
them were general songs; like we used to try and copy songs from the radio.
And most of us were usually in, like, the chorus, so we would do songs that
we were doing in choir. We did this a lot. I'm trying to think. (Pause.)

(JS) Did you play jump rope when you were in grade school?

(Ruthanna) A little bit.

(JS) It wasn't a big thing where you were?

(Ruthanna) No . . . we used to . . . when I was in school . . . we didn't . . . our school
didn't have any toys or anything really to play with, and we weren't big jump-
rope people. I think mostly because we had to play on black top, and whenever we did anything like that somebody always ended up having to go see
the nurse, so they didn't let us do it that often. Um, what we used to do . . .
what we used to do is, um, we'd play, like, dodge ball. Things like that. If we
didn't do that, we would always play tag or something. And there was always
the little girl who would take all the boys off into a corner and play dress-up
with them. (Laughs.) Well, they did it. There was a little boy at our school
who always wanted to play daddies and mommies, and he was always the
mommy.

(JS) Hummm, that's interesting.

(Ruthanna) When I was real small . . . before we moved to New York, and we
still lived in Massachusetts, they had a big hill by the side of our house that
ended in a barbed wire fence. And we had a porch . . . a side porch, we used
to play on. I used to sit up on the end of it and sing "Jesus Loves Me" and take
my clothes off. (Laughs.) I was a strip teaser from way back when, see. And
then we had apple trees, too. And we had a stream that ran through the back
of our house. We used to get on, like, a couple of kids on each side of the
stream, and have apple fights until we got caught.

(JS) What did you do? Pick apples, and throw them?

(Ruthanna) Yeah, they hurt, too. We used to see if we could smash them against
the other person's face.

(JS) Yeah, apples hurt.

(Ruthanna) We used to have a board across the stream, a small board across, and
we used to have to try to walk across the board without falling in. We invari-
ably fell in, and somebody got in trouble.

(JS) There's something else I didn't ask. With jump rope . . . did you ever play any
kind of games where you did this? (I demonstrate a handclap.)

(Ruthanna) Yeah, we did . . . (Sighs.) Not real well . . . we had one about Lizzie
Borden, and we had one about a little Dutch girl.

> Lizzie Borden took an axe
> Gave her mother forty whacks
> When she saw what she had done
> She gave her father forty-one.

(The tape ends.)

—*Tulane University Freshman, white girl, New Orleans*

Ruthanna, who was nineteen at the time, was a wellspring of lore. I could have continued the taping session and enticed even more items from her, but classes had begun, and she had to run. Like the Girl Scouts and the campers from Camp Ruth Lee, Ruthanna recalled singing in group situations, more than playing on the school ground.

JUST FOR FUN

Camp songs are fun! I Googled "Camp songs," and literally hundreds of possibilities appeared, from "A-Camping We Will Go," to "We're going on a (lion, bear) hunt." Try going to YouTube, typing in the first line of a camp song you remember, and seeing if it is featured well. Maybe you can create a video for YouTube that is even better.

CHAPTER 6

Running and Imaginative Games

In January of 1979, I found myself at Gates of Prayer Hebrew Synagogue on West Esplanade Avenue, in Metairie, Louisiana, a suburb of New Orleans. Armed with my tape recorder, I was collecting verbal lore from children who attended Hebrew School. Just as the nuns stood sentinel in the classroom at Ursaline Academy, the teacher remained at the front of the class at Hebrew School. The teacher, whose name was Rochell, later joined the session and became a participant in some of the folk games. The session began with the children, who were all white, demonstrating play with a dreidel.

(Boy) It's a Hannukah game. Uh, you put some things in the pot, and uh, you spin the dreidel. Then, then, you get some of the stuff in the middle . . . Like you spin "gimel," you get all the stuff . . .

(JS) All right, tell me again.

The children played with the dreidel. I watched for a while, but they were speaking so fast in Hebrew, I realized I would need to videotape the game to begin to understand it.[1]

(JS) How do you choose who's first?

(Boy) The number comes up on the top.

(JS) But how do you choose who's first? When you are outside, and you are going to play a game, how do you choose who's first?

(Boy) You put out your hands, and you do potatoes.

(JS) OK. How do you do it?

(Boy) You say: "one potato two potato, three potato" until you get to seven, and the first one out is "it."[2]

(JS) First one out is "it." OK. What do you do?

(Boy) We divide into boys and girls.

(JS) When . . . when you play tag?

(Boy) Yes.

(JS) What kind of tag are you going to play when you divide into boys and girls?

(Boy) "Freeze Tag."

(JS) How do you play "Freeze Tag?"

(Everybody begins to talk at once. The teacher calls for order. I cannot tell her that everybody talking at once is exactly what I want to record.)

(Boy) You gotta freeze when someone touches you. You run, and when someone touches you, you gotta freeze, and then you're "it."

(JS) You ever play "Stuck in the Mud"?

(Boy) When you chase and you touch somebody, they have to stretch their legs out like they are stuck in the mud. And the only way they can get away is if they crawl under somebody's legs.[3]

(JS) Oh—to get free.

(Boy) And if you are tagged three times, you're "it."

(JS) If you're tagged three times, you're "it." Who is keeping track of who is getting tagged?

(Boy) Everybody.

(JS) Any other games that you play? What's "Chinese Freeze Tag"? (In the first few moments of the interview, before I had set up the microphone, the children had named many running games they played.)

(Boys all shout at once.) It's like someone's "it," and it's like "Freeze Tag", but when you get frozen, but it's like wherever someone touches you, you have to put your hand. Like, if they touch you on your head, you put your hand there. Then someone touches you, and you are unfrozen.[4]

(JS) Any more games? (A boy touches my arm.) Yeah?

(Boy) King of the Mountain with pillows in my house on my bed. Right in the middle of my two beds they got a water, and the one who gets over, and gets on the bed first, wins.[5]

(JS) Uh huh. How many pillows does this take?

(Boy) Two.

(JS) Does your mother like this game?

(The children laugh and begin to shout, "I know one!" "I know one!" The class is beginning to relax. The teacher becomes wary.)

(Boy) My mother tells us when we have nothing to do to go get our pillows and think us a game.

(JS) Uh huh.

(Boy) She tells us to use our own pillows and to play long until we're too tired. We get the pillowcases off the pillows, and slide down the steps and destroy them.

(The other children hoot and laugh at this boy, and eagerly jump out of their seats to get to the microphone.)

(JS) (I turn to another boy.) What about you? You have a game you play?

(New boy) Uh uh.

(JS) You don't play?

(Boy) Not at home. No.

(JS) OK. What *do* you play?

(Same boy) We play, like, something neat, like, Cylons, like, Battlestar Gallactica, you keep the Cylons from getting the good guys. We try to shoot each other, and, you know, fight.

(JS) Yeah.

(Boy) Rough game . . . fighting.

(JS) OK. I'm sure it is . . . OK.

(Another boy) My brother, he plays superheroes.

(Laughter)

(JS) OK. What does he do?

(Boy) He plays with the twins next door and (laughs) He always makes me (laughs) . . . He always makes me be the bad guy, and they always chase me . . . Play for about two hours!! He shoots me . . .

(JS) And you always wanna get shot? What do you do when . . . ?

(Same boy) Oh—hooh—the bad guy gets to sneak inside . . . and then you have trouble finding him . . .

(JS) (A different boy is patting my arm.) (I turn to him.) What do YOU play?

(Boy) We have a two-story house, and we always play like the stairs are at bottom and is the hell, and the top is where the witch is.

(JS) Uh huh. Does anybody play "Witch in the Well"? Speaking of witches . . .

(Boy) No.

(Another child comes forward and stands in front of me.)

(JS) Do you play it?

(Boy) No, but I know one similar to it. One person is the witch, and if she says, "Seven o'clock," you don't get to run. But if she says, "Twelve o'clock midnight," you do get to cross the mountains.[6]

(JS) Does she chase you when you cross the mountains?

(Boy) Yes.

(JS) Uh huh. Where do you go to school?

(Boy) Newman.

(JS) And do you play that at Newman?

(Boy) Uh huh.

(JS) I'd like to get to Newman, and I want you all to play it for me. (I turn to a new boy.) What do you play?

(Boy) I play at my house, and I really don't do it no more, but I play this game, and it is a spy—you know, like, going out, and spying on people. It's sort of like a game. You go out and spy on people, and the one who doesn't get caught, you run away. It's sort of like a game, you know. We used to grab someone by the neck and just start shaking them.

(JS) Who do you spy on?

(Boy) Uh . . .

(Another boy) Your sister!! (Everybody laughs.)

(Boy) Me and my friends, Steven, and, like, Jeffrey over here, we spy on his sister. Like, you know, Steven takes stuff, removes it out of their room, and put it in his room. And when he goes in, and his sister . . . she goes in mine, and we get caught.

(JS) Um huuum.

(The boy who has said "Your sister!" points to his friend, and says,) My games are better than yours, but I can't tell you about them!

(Students laugh.)

(JS) What games do YOU play?

(Boy who said "Your sister!" rushes to speak.) One time when we were at Steven's place, we played "Freeze Tag", and we had, um, we had that hiding place. We hide over there. Every minute we hide, every place we hide on . . . we hide over there. First, everybody comes. We run up, and we hide all over there, and Steven comes, and he catch people before they go to base. They got, um, secret passageways over there . . .

(JS) Oh, you have secret passageways?

(Boy) You have to sneak up and run because the phantom can swing close to them.

(JS) Um hum. (Turning to a new informant.) And what do YOU play?

(Boy) There's this game called Mr. Fox, and there's four people and one fox. Mr. Fox stands against the wall, and the four people have to ask him, "Mr. Fox, Mr. Fox, what is the time?" And if it is lunch time or breakfast time or suppertime, you gotta run. And if he says it is any other time, you just stay there and keep on asking what time it is. And then you gotta run until he catches you.

(JS) What does he do if he catches you?

(Boy) He eats you.

(JS) All right. So, do YOU know a game? (Children are crowding closer.)

(Boy) Electronic football.

(Group laughs.)

(JS) That's an electronic game. I'm trying to think of games that people play on the school ground without electricity.

(Boy) We play football. We play football on the schoolground at school. We play spank tag. We have to spank them on the behind for the other person to be it.

(Group yells and laughs.)

(JS) Ahhh, there's also "Kiss and Chase," where you have to kiss somebody before they can chase you.[7]

(Group shouts, "Eeeuuuuw!")

(Boy) We do Red Rover.

(JS) How does Red Rover go?

(Too many people are shouting by now for the boy to describe Red Rover.)[8]

(One student shouts.) Ghost in the graveyard!

(JS) I don't know ghost in the graveyard. Tell me, how does it go?

(Boy) You need a flashlight, and somebody's got to be the ghost. Ghost in the graveyard—you play it at night—and the ghost, he has to run around in the back yard somewhere . . . And the other people have to run around and try to find him, and if the ghost flashes the flashlight in your eyes, you are dead.[9]

(JS) Oooo, that's spooky. It's like playing hide and seek at night?

(Boy) Um, at home we have a (Mumble.) in my back yard, and when we play . . .

(JS) You have a what?

(Boy) I have a (Mumble.) (Swimming pool?) in my back yard, and when we ride my bike, we go around and around and around it, and there's a shipwreck in the middle, and if we go around too close there's a witch in the middle of the shipwreck, and she can pull you in.

(JS) Is there a witch really there?

(Children) NOOOOO! (Explosion of laughs.)

(JS) All right. Just thought I'd ask. Yes? (I turn to a different boy.)

(Boy) We have one like, um, Blind Man's Buff, and we tie a cloth around his head, and we turn him round, and turn him round, and he tries to find us, and we try to get him to bump into a door or something.

(JS) You know how old that game is? That's a very old game. They used to play that in the fifteenth century, and in the nineteenth century grown-ups used to play it.[10]

(The children are more interested in clamoring about games they know. They shout and gabble.)

(Boy) Spear the Ring . . .

(JS) How does it go? Spear the Ring?

(Boy) All you need is a stick, and a ring, and a string. And you tie the string on the stick, and you tie the ring on the string.

(JS) Yes?

(Boy) And you have to try to get the ring on the stick.

(JS) Are you walking, or riding a bike, or what are you doing?

(Boy) You can run, or you can walk, or you can stand still.

(JS) Hummm, people used to do that on horses. They would ride a horse and try to spear the ring. (I had not envisioned exactly what the child was describing, until I read it over again later. It seems that the child was describing flipping the ring tied on the string *onto* the end of the stick, not having the ring hung somewhere, and trying to run at it to spear it.)

(Same boy) Sometimes me and my friend have potato-sack races.

(JS) So you do that at home? What do you use?

(Boy) Pillow cases.

(JS) Pillow cases??

(Boy) And sometimes we have a bowl game. We put peanuts in one bowl on one end of the table, and peanuts in another bowl on the other end of the table, and then we pick it up with a spoon, and run to the other and then . . .

(Teacher) They do that at a Halloween party!

(Boy) Um hum . . . they brought it home.

(JS) OK. Anybody else? Yes?

(Boy) At school at gym we play "Thumbs Thumbs Here We Come," and . . .

(JS) What's "Thumbs Thumbs Here We Come?"

(Boy) It's chase, and everyone's "it," and you take the tip of your thumb, and you touch someone on the back, and when you touch them, then they're frozen. Then, like, if you're standing near someone, and you take his thumb, and you touch him somewhere else on the other person . . . and then they're . . . and then you're unfrozen.

(JS) (Mystified by this description.) Um hum—That's a lot like "Freeze Tag"?

(Boy) And my cousin and I, in his room—we play kickball.

(Children shout with laughter and make noise throughout this child's delivery.)

(Boy) My cousin's closet is home, the drawer is first, his record cabinet is second, and the top of his bunk bed is third.

(JS) And how far can you kick the ball?

(Boy) As far as the wall.

(Lots of noise follows.)

(JS) What to *you* play? (I turn to another boy.)

(Boy) Well, like, I take a ball, it's like a basketball, but I take the ball, and I start to dribble it and, when I come to . . . uh . . . we have this television, and there is a channel with this circle in the . . . it . . . and usually I throw it, uh, the basketball right through without the TV being on . . .

(JS) Uh huh. I can't imagine anybody doing that without their mother getting very upset. I have some questions. I have some specific questions about Hebrew

games. Is this Rochell's class? (In the few minutes before the taping session began, the teacher, Rochell, had suggested that I ask about Israeli games.)

(Children) Yes.

(JS) Have you ever played the "Name Game"? It's an Israeli game.

(Children) The what? I think we played it last year.

(JS) Does anybody remember how it went? How did it go?

(Children) I don't really know, but we have it on a record.

(JS) Well, then you don't know about a dreidel either?

(Girl) YESSS!

(JS) All right—tell me how it works.

(Girl) The way we do it was we get potato chips and we get . . .

(Children yelling.) Pretzels! Pretzels!

(JS) OK. You use potato chips, and everybody else uses pretzels. And then what
would you do?

(Girl) OK. We get pretzels, and we make groups, and some used pretzels, and
some used potato chips and . . . (Noise breaks out.) What we do is we'd get
about ten each or something, and then we'd each put one in, and then we
would spin the dreidel, and if it lands on something like "gimel," you'd get it
all. I don't know all the other names.

(Children shouting.) I know! I know!

(Child) And you spin again, and you keep those, and the one who has the most
chips at the end wins.

(JS) What does a dreidel look like? Who wants to tell me what it looks like?

(Child) It's, like, it comes like that (Makes a square shape with her hands.) And
has a point at the end.

(JS) Is it like a top?

(Child) A top with four sides.

(JS) A top with four sides. And you spin it with your hand?

(Child) Yes.

(JS) On the four sides, are there pictures?

(Child) No—letters.

(JS) What do the four letters mean? Let your teacher tell me. Maybe . . .

(Teacher) Well, it depends. If you're in Israel the letters stand for shin, hey, gimel,
and nun. That's what they stand for. It means, "A great miracle happened
there." And if you're in Israel, and you have relatives, and you play, you go,
"Haya po," "A great miracle happens here." So, if it lands on a "nun," it's none.
"Nun" means "none," so if it lands on that, you don't get anything. If you land
on "gimel," you get everything in the pot. After every . . . and after everybody
spins, you have to have everybody anteing up, or otherwise you won't have

anything in the pot. If you land on "hey," you get half of whatever's in the pot. And you land on "shin," it means you have to put in more.

(JS) OK. Could the children play that game for a videotape crew?

(Teacher) Sure. I need to know that before you come, because I need to make a date for the group to come in.

(Teacher) OK. There's a game that is an Israeli Simon Says.

(JS) Could you play that for me?

(Children) Oh yeah! We love that!

(Teacher) You want me to play it?

(Confusion as the players sort themselves out.)

(Teacher) OK. Does anyone want to be Shimon? Shay, do you want to play Shimon?

(Shay) No.

(Children) I do! Me! I do!

(Teacher) OK. Anybody that wants to play, stand up. Whatever the leader says is in Hebrew. So basically, the command is just in Hebrew. It's the same exact words. It's just that the person in command doesn't have to do the correct motions. It's just to get everybody listening.

(JS) Uh huh. For learning.

(Teacher) Yes, learning—You should say (in Hebrew), "Hand on your head." And she might put her hand on her legs, and you will see a lot of the kids put their hands on their legs, but the fact that more than thinking, you're just watching them for their reaction.

(JS) Uh huh . . . Yes?

(Teacher) (In Hebrew) "Put you hand on your nose." (She directs the students to put their hands somewhere on their body, instead of their nose, so it will misdirect the listeners, and make them practice listening skills more carefully.)

(The teacher then guides the children through several more "Shimon says," routines. After a short time, the children begin to grumble and complain that they are tired.)

(One student says) Tic tac toe?

(A handclap begins to be played in the back of the room.)

(Teacher) OK. So, let's see (She gives the students another direction in Hebrew. They try to follow, arguing among themselves as to what precisely to do.)

(Teacher) So, that's it!

(JS) What about the other game you mentioned. (We had talked about another particular game before the taping session.) A shoe game? What?

(Teacher) Um hum.

(Children) It's called an Israeli shoe game! And we have some shoes . . . We have two shoes . . . And . . .

(Children begin to shout.) I'm not gonna take off my shoes!

(Teacher) Quiet!

(Child) You have some shoes . . . You take, like, four . . . and you put . . . and you put them certain distances, like, first you put them all together, and then they try to . . . and you put them scattered . . . Then you try to put a space where you jumped wider . . . and then you jump over each shoe . . . and then they get wider, and you try to jump over the wider . . .

(JS) Can they play that?

(Teacher) I think it's too wild.

(JS) How did you . . . Where did you learn that game?

(A child from the back.) We play it at school.

(Boy) Well, one year I went to camp, and an Israeli came, and showed us . . .

(JS) Show us how to do it. Everybody, contribute a shoe!

(Shouting) OK. No!! I can't, I have boots on!

(JS) OK. We got one . . . two . . . OK. We got two . . . three . . . shoes. We got four shoes. All right, I think we have enough shoes now.

(Teacher) OK. We have enough shoes. We don't need Shoshanna to give a shoe. (Shoshanna is struggling to get her boots off.)

(Boy) I have foot odor! I have foot odor!

(Teacher) Then push yourself back. I don't want odor under the chair. That's easy.

(A child asks me, bewildered.) What is she doing?

(JS) She is going to demonstrate an Israeli shoe game where you line the shoes up on the floor, and then you jump.

(Child, still confused.) Oh.

(Boy) That's easy! (Boy jumps the line of shoes.)

(Teacher) It gets harder.

(JS) OK. Everybody gets up in a line, runs up, and jumps through the first part of the shoes.

(Boy) That's easy!

(JS) Then you spread the shoes out wider.

(Child) Then, when everyone goes, you spread them out wider.

(JS) Like hop scotch? But gets bigger every time?

(Child) But you keep the middle ones together.

(JS) But you keep the shoes in the middle together, so you have to take a little step in the middle?

(Teacher) You can take only one step.

(JS) You keep making them wider and wider!

(Teacher) Um hum.

(JS) So you keep making them wider after each person jumps through, to make it harder and harder. And the first person to touch a shoe is out?

(Teacher) Um hummmm.

(Girl) Then you go like this. (The child demonstrates wildly jumping around sideways.)

(JS) Then you're silly. (The teacher quits directing the shoe game.)

(Girl) Yeah!

(JS) OK. So, what's your name? Melissa? . . . And where do you go to school?

(Girl) Newman

(JS) Newman, OK.

(JS) And what is your last name? (I cannot make out her response.) OK. Any more games that are specifically Hebrew games?

(Girl) It's not a Hebrew game, but it's sort of a shoe game where there's, like, three over there, and one over here, and one person jumps over a shoe, and then where his foot lands, you put the next shoe, and so the next person jumps, and he moves the next shoe, and so on.

(JS) Um hum. And what do you have? (I turn to a new student.)

(Girl) Um, there's this Hebrew tic tac toe.

(JS) How does it go?

(Girl) OK. It is like ordinary tic tac toe, but you fill in the spaces with Hebrew words. Then, like, when you get a word, when you get an x, you put an x. Then when you get an o, you put an o. It's easy.

(JS) Wow! I'm getting chains! (A girl has walked up to me with a long paper chain. Each link in the chain has a Hebrew letter, or a Hebrew word on it. The child presents me with the paper chain, and I put the chain in my bag.) I'm stuffing that in. OK—you.

(Girl) There's another Hebrew game.

(JS) All right.

(Girl) It's another shoe game. Everybody gets a shoe, and they put it in a large bucket.

(Child next to her.) I hate that game!

(Girl) Then you all run, and the first person who puts on his shoe to match the other, and runs back to his place where the other person is, wins.

(JS) Oh!

(Girl) We played that at camp!

(JS) Uh huh.

(Girl) Do you know Hebrew Hangman?

(JS) How does Hebrew Hangman go?

(Girl) It's when you play Hangman, but you use Hebrew words.

(JS) Hebrew words!

(Girl) That's right. We had another game. It was like labeling. Each girl had to bring her father's shirt, and her father's shoes, and each boy had to bring his mother's dress, and his mother's shoes, and the students had to stand over here, and the teacher threw them all in the middle, and the boys and girls had to run in, and put on our father's clothes, and our mother's clothes, and see who wins.

(JS) Um hum.

(Girl) And when we played Hebrew Tic Tac Toe, our teacher used to give us a letter, and then when we wrote the letter, he would come and see, and we got a check on it 'cause we got it right.

(Boy) Hebrew baseball is just like regular baseball, and you play it on . . . you play it . . . and you write again just like—one—two—three, and home base.

(Boy) And one team is up to base, and the teacher asks questions, and if you get it right, you get to move up a base.

(JS) Um hum. So, the first person to get all the right answers makes a home run?

(Boy) You divide into teams, and you take turns. Like one has a question, and another has a question—you take turns.

(JS) It's a good way of teaching—a good teaching technique. (I turn to another child.) Yes?

(Boy) At school we play "Devil in the Ditch."

(JS) Ahhh, "Devil in the Ditch," how does it go?

(Boy) Well, uh, one person is "it," and a lot of people are in two groups on the sides, and when the devil says, "Go," they each have to run. The people on this side have to run to that side, and the people on that side have to run to this side. And if somebody touches . . . the devil touches them, they are "it," and the first devil is still in.

(JS) So you end up with a bunch of devils after while? Is that it?

(Boy) Uh huh

(Child sneezes.)

(JS) God bless you.

(Boy) Well, at school, it's like, um, "Uncle Sam, Uncle Sam, May I Cross the River Dam?" And we have three people on each side, and Uncle Sam in the middle, and then . . . and then you say, "Uncle Sam, Uncle Sam, may we cross your river dam? "And then Uncle Sam will say, "Yes you may. Yes, you may, like, if you're wearing red today." And if you have red on, then you try to cross the space where Uncle Sam is standing, and rush to the other side, and if he catches you, you're "it."

(JS) Um hummm—I haven't heard that one around here . . .

(Teacher) It's like Red Rover. Instead of saying "Red Rover," you say "Uncle Sam."

(JS) Yeah. Anybody have another one? I saw a hand up.

((Boy) I forgot it.

(Boy) You forgot it!

(JS) Yes—which?

(Boy) At camp we play this game. Um, it's named "Shark Bite." And we dive into the deep part of the pool, and then there'll be a shark in the middle, um, a person in the middle, and the others are minnows, and if he catches you, then you are helping the shark catch the other minnows.

(JS) Uh huh?

(Boy) We play football at school, and Andrew is the quarterback.

(JS) Um hummm?

(Boy) That's right. We have two fifteen-minute recesses, and one twenty minutes.

(JS) And you play football the whole time? What happens to your clothes?

(Boy) Sometimes we play soccer.

(JS) Oh.

(Boy) A lot of times we're covered with mud.

(Teacher) My son does too. He comes home covered with mud. Yes?

(The teacher has turned to a boy.)

(Boy) Well, we do . . . We . . .

(Another boy) He just remembered.

(Boy who remembered.) We did it in P.E. We had two lines, and we had to stay that way in the line, and the teacher called out "blue," and if you were wearing blue, like, a blue shirt, you have to run, and if the guy runs after you, he touches you, like, you're, like, with him. And when the line is all full, and there is only people wearing, like, red, then they win. Then, when the whole line is with him, he has to win, because there's no other person who could get through.

(JS) Uh huh?

(A boy shouts.) You could . . . It's called "King," and you stand, and face the wall, and you call out "k-i-n-g," says "king," and then you turn around, and all the people behind you take steps, and when you turn around, they have to stop. And if he sees you, he can say, "Take ten steps back." And the first person to reach the wall gets to . . .

(JS) Win?

(Boy) No, he has to touch him, and then the king gets to chase him, and if he touches him, he's the next king, unless the first king touches him back.[11]

(JS) Ahhhh.

(Boy) And there's another game where you play with letters. There's the king, and he says, "I can see the letter "M" and if your name begins with "M" you get to take one step.

(JS) Um hummm. Yes?

(Boy) Queenie.

(JS) I don't know "Queenie."

(Boy) Some people are standing in a line, and one person is the king or queen. So, they take—the king or the queen—they take the ball and throw it in back, and the people that are standing behind them, they catch the ball. In back—the king or queen has to guess who has it.

(JS) Um hum. And everybody stands there with their hands behind their backs like they have it?

(Boy) Yes.

(JS) What happens if he makes a guess, and the person doesn't have it?

(Boy) If he gets it wrong, then the person who has the ball gets to be king. If he gets it right, he gets it again.

(JS) Oh.

(Boy) Last year, at the end of the day, we would play "7Up." And it has seven people off in a locker room, and you have to turn off the lights, and everyone would put their head down with their thumb up, and if someone touches you on the back, then you raise your hand so no one will touch you again, and when seven people are picked, and everyone is back to the blackboard . . . After they turn on the lights, and they stand up, every person who is touched has to guess who touched you.

(JS) And if you are right?

(Boy) And if you are right, you get to go up and take the place of the person who has touched you. And the game begins again. And if you are wrong, you have to sit down and wait for the person who picks you again.[12]

(JS) Yeah?

(Girl) There's a Hebrew guessing game, and there's someone who has a nickel, and she goes around, and everyone's in a circle, and she comes around, and sticks the nickel in someone's hand, and the other person that doesn't even get the chance to get the nickel, he has to guess . . . she or he has to guess who has the nickel, and then she goes (Hebrew phrase I cannot understand.), and you have to put your hands down, and then you . . . if it is a girl, she says, "Ot," and if it is a boy, she says, "Ta" . . .

(JS) Did you learn that here? Where did you learn that?

(Girl) At Al Judea.

(JS) Where?

(Girl) At Al Judea.

(Teacher) It's a youth group.

(JS) Oh! It is a youth group. You learned it there?

(Girl) Yeah.

(JS) It is related to "Button, Button, Who's Got the Button." We play . . . English people play that one.

(Girl) And she goes, like, and if she comes around you, and you have the nickel, and she says, "Ot," you have to pick your hands up, and if you have the nickel, then she wins.

(Teacher) You can play that with a button or a ring.[13]

(JS) Or with anything else, for sure.

(Boy) We play TV tag.

(JS) OK. How does TV tag go?

(Boy) A person is "it," and when the person comes around, you have to think of a TV channel, and if you can't think of one in about five seconds, you're out.

(JS) Oh, I get it.

(Boy) Yeah, like, you have to say "Starsky and Hutch," and I'm safe.

(Boy) Around the world.

(JS) OK. How does around the world go?

(Boy) There's a basketball and a goal . . .

(Children shout.) Oh yeah, now I remember!

(Boy) You have five kids, and you take a shot, and if you make it, you run around, and try to make it again. If you miss the first time . . . you have to take a risk . . . and if you risk, like, right here, and if you risk, and you don't make it, you can try to make it again.

(JS) OK. And how do you play this game again? Do you have a real basketball, and a real goal? Do you play it in the gym?

(Children) Yeah! Yeah! We play it at my house!

(JS) I don't understand the game. Do you have your own goal?

(Boy) Yeah!

(JS) Uh huh. Let's start again.

(A child tries to tell me the game again, but speaks so softly that it does not come out clearly. Children are talking at the same time, and a game called "Wink" is mentioned.)

(JS) Uh huh. How do you play "Wink"?

(Boy) Everybody sits in a circle, and there is one player who stays in the middle, and then if you wink, and he sees you, you have to sit back. You have to wink at somebody, and if you do, they have to lay back, and they are dead.

(JS) Uh huh. They wink, and if you see them, they have to lay back.

(Boy) Um hum. If they wink, and you see 'em, and you get it wrong, you're dead.

(JS) If you see 'em, and you get it wrong, then *you're* dead? Oh boy. Do you all play this?

(Children) Yeah!

(Boy) There's this game called "Colored Eggs."

(JS) How does "Colored Eggs" go?

(Yelling and laughter.)

(One child shouts) Peter, Peter, Pumpkin Eater!

(Boy) There's this wolf, and all the children get to choose their colors . . . And the wolf comes and he says, "I want colored eggs." And then he calls out the colored eggs he wants, like, he wants "red," and the . . . the one with red runs, and the wolf tries to catch him . . .[14]

(JS) What school is that?

(Boy) Newman. Really around . . . everywhere . . .

(JS) Really, everywhere, that's right. I've gotten that game from everywhere. It's a good one.

(Boy) We have a game called "Ching Chong Chock," and lots of people can play it. It's a good one . . .

(JS) OK. How does "Ching Chong Chock" go?

(Boy) You put your hands behind your back, and one person says, "Scissors, paper, rock," and you put your hands out, and scissors cuts paper, paper covers rock, and rock breaks scissors, so you get points for when one person has something stronger than the other. And ten points wins.[15]

(Girl) And then there's this game we play at school called "Teddy Bear Teddy Bear."

(JS) How does "Teddy Bear Teddy Bear" go?

(Boys screaming) TEDDY BEAR! TEDDY BEAR!

(Boys) We say, "Teddy Bear Teddy Bear brush your teeth," and you have to play like you are brushing your teeth. And we say, "Teddy Bear Teddy Bear go to sleep," and you have to play like you are going to sleep . . .

(JS) Yeah, that's right out of the "Teddy Bear Teddy Bear" jump rope game . . . anybody plays Teddy Bear Teddy Bear jump-rope game?

(Girl) No . . . I never heard of it.

(JS) OK?

(Boy) I forgot mine.

(JS) You forgot yours? It's been so long since you had your hand up.

(Boy) Yeah.

(Boy says loudly.) In Sunday school we play "Around the World," and then the teacher, she would put up some Hebrew words, and she would write, like, um, something under it, and if you get that word right, then you keep going until you miss, and if you miss, you start all over. And if you make it, you get to go to Israel, or New Orleans, or something, and if you make it there, then you win. And, um, um . . .

(JS) We'll get back to you, OK?

(Boy hurries on.) There's another game called "GaGa," and you need a ball, and there's a lot of people. And you don't really have a team, and one person has the ball, and every time they throw it down, they say, "GA," and every time it bounces, they say "Ga," and they say "Ga ga ga," and everybody tries to get the ball, but they can't touch it, you just kick it, and you try to hit someone's ankles, and if they get hit, they out.

(JS) Hummmm!

(Girl) We got a game we call "Beaver," and we have to play it in a car. It's with "Bugs," and it's called "Bugs," that's a kind of car. And we watch for Volkswagens, and if we see a color, we have to say, "Beaver," like, we see a red one, we say "Beaver."

(JS) Volkswagens? OK so what do you do with "Beaver"?

(Girl) Like, they have different kinds. If there's a green, then, like, you get a one . . . and if you get a white . . .

(JS) So you're watching cars go by? If you get a green Volkswagen you get a certain . . .

(Teacher) I've never heard of this.

(Boy) You can play license plates . . .

(JS) Wait, she's telling me about the other game . . . it's called "Beaver." Is that the name of the game? Why is it called "Beaver"?

(Girl) I don't know. My friend taught it to me.

(JS) So, different Volkswagens of different colors gets different points, and at the end of the trip you add 'em up, and the person with the most points wins?[16]

(Girl) Yeah.

(I heard a boy discussing playing "Poker With License Plates.")

(JS) How did you play "Poker With License Plates" when you were a little boy?

(Boy) You get the numbers, and the letters off the license plates, and you try to get a flush.

(JS) You do this to try to keep busy?

(Boy) Yes.

(JS) We used to stamp white horses when we were on a trip. We went (Lick thumb, and stamp it on palm, and slap it.) Like that.

(Teacher) OK. It's break time.

(Tape off)

—*Gates of Prayer Hebrew School white boys and girls, Metairie, La.*

This recording of the children from Gates of Prayer Hebrew School in Metairie, Louisiana, revealed a number of things. The children were there for
religious education, and they certainly knew a host of Hebrew games that
the teacher guided them to learn. They also knew many schoolyard games
prevalent among children throughout New Orleans and Metairie, Louisiana,
where they mixed with all sorts on the playgrounds. Most of the children I
interviewed at Hebrew School attended Isadore Newman College Prepara-
tory School in uptown New Orleans.

RUNNING GAMES FROM THE NEW ORLEANS AREA

The transcript from Gates of Prayer Hebrew Synagogue was recorded in 1979.
In their rambling fashion, the children contributed approximately forty-eight
running and chasing games. Before I had ever thought of visiting Gates of
Prayer Hebrew Synagogue, however, I had been skipping around the city
of New Orleans and its suburbs, Chalmette and Arabi, and making recordings as I went. What follows is another transcription of around forty-eight
running and chasing games collected at different New Orleans area schools,
from 1974 to 1978. Many of the games are variations of those played by the
children at Hebrew school.

Tag is by far the most varied and popular running game around. For the
outsider, tag games might look like total confusion, especially when there
is one entire group running after another, as in "Kiss and Chase." "Kiss and
Chase" looks like total chaos. The whole schoolyard might already be crowded
with other children playing their own games, and here is this mass of children
running helter skelter, screaming and grabbing, hastily kissing, then breaking
away, and settling at the "safe" spot, only to suddenly run again.

Teachers use running games for physical education classes, and as the
students tell it, these games initiated by the teacher are sometimes adapted
into the everyday play of schoolchildren. Kindergarten teachers are especially
fond of "A-Tisket-a-Tasket, a Green and Yellow Basket," and this was adapted
into play citywide in New Orleans by schoolchildren on playgrounds and
after school. The game is quite old, and was included in Lady Alice B. Gomme's *The Traditional Games of England, Scotland, and Ireland* Vol. 1, 109–12,
as "Drop Handkerchief" (1894).

Running games fall easily into four types: those played in a ring, like
"A-Tisket-a-Tasket"; those played in which one player is "it," and all the others
have to keep away from him; those games in which there are strict rules, like

baseball, football, dodge ball; and finally, dramatic play with a story line. This chapter will follow those four divisions.

The descriptions of these running games appear in the words of the child informants. The descriptions are sometimes hazy, muddled, or scrambled. I allow the children to speak because their words convey both the outline of each game, and the energy of the teller.[17]

Circle running games

A-tisket a-tasket a green and yellow basket
I wrote a letter to my mother
And on the way I dropped it
A little girl picked it up and she put it in her pocket, her pocket.

(The players sit in a circle and one player skips around it. She drops the letter, usually a handkerchief, behind one player, who then chases her around the outside of the circle. The object is to catch her before she gets back to her place.)[18]
—*Andrew Jackson, 3rd-grade African American girls, New Orleans*

"Duck Duck Goose" or "Goose Goose Duck"—In the words of a fifth-grade white boy at Lacoste Elementary, "They gotta get a circle, everyone sits in a circle. Then one person goes around taps everyone on the head, and he says, "Duck, duck, duck, duck, then goose." When he says "goose," the person jumps up and starts to run, and the person who tapped him has to chase him around the circle until he can get back to his place." (I observed the game played at Lusher Elementary in New Orleans.)
—*Lusher Elementary, white 3rd-grade boy; Lacoste Elementary, white 5th-grade boys and girls; Adolph Meyer, African American boy 5th-grade, New Orleans*

"Yella Duck"—Another fifth-grade white boy in the Lacoste Elementary group explains, "The people make a circle. Then one child goes around tapping people on the head saying, 'Blue duck, green duck,' like that, until he says 'Yella duck.' On 'Yella duck' the tapped player jumps up, and runs around the circle. If he is caught, he's put in the center of the circle in the pot. If he gets back to his place, he's safe."
—*Lacoste Elementary, 5th-grade white boy, Chalmette, La.*

"David Come Home, or Mary Come Home"—"David come home or Mary come home, if it is a girl. Well, there's got to be a circle of people, and then, uh, this one person, he goes around and taps two people on the head, and they have to be sittin' down, and then, and then, uh, the person who is to the right of the circle, they run after him, and then, when the person goes back to their, um, um, the person that takes his spot, that means he wouldn't win, so he gets to pick the next person."

—*Adolph Meyer Elementary, 5th-grade African American boy, Algiers, La.*

The speaker above, from Adolph Meyer Elementary, had some problems making the object of the game clear, but in the following description of "Duck Duck Goose on Roller Skates," the speaker showed a *complete* inability to express himself. He punctuates his logical lapses with the catchword "awright," while he tries to think the game out.

"Duck Duck Goose on Roller Skates"—"Awright, and you have one . . . awright, this guy goes around . . . awright, and then the person next to you on the right side, you have to play this in a ring . . . awright . . . the guy on your right side . . . awright . . . when you get tagged, he will guard you while the guy is chasing you on the roller skates. So, you know, and you go around twice, and then you sit down in your place.

—*Lusher Elementary, 5th-grade white boy, New Orleans*

If you did not know what the game "Duck Duck Goose" was all about, you might never figure it out from the above description. Unfortunately, there were a number of games, which had to be left out of this collection because the children described them in an even more scattered manner.

"Steal the Bacon"—"You make a circle, and you put something in the middle. Everybody gets a number. Then somebody calls out a number, and that person has to go to the middle, and steal the 'bacon,' and the others have to catch him before he goes back to his place."[19]

—*John Dibert Elementary, 6th-grade African American boy, New Orleans*

"1–2–3 Sugar Baby Stop"—"You pick numbers like, 1–2–3–4–5 and 6, you know, and somebody gets in the middle, and they throw up the ball, and then they call out the number, and the one that catches the ball, he yells 'Stop.' And then he comes in to catch it, and the first person to catch it, and turn around, and hits somebody, they got an 'S.' Then, when they hit somebody again, he got a 't'; and then the one who gets to s-t-o-p, is out." (I was not exactly sure how this is played, but the next informant made it a bit clearer.)

—*John Dibert Elementary, 6th-grade African American boy, New Orleans*

"Sugar Baby"—An Xavier University freshman girl wrote down this version of "Sugar Baby," in 1980, and it was more detailed and made more sense:

> Three or more players—each player is assigned a number. The player who will start the game is number one, and the other players are numbered two, three, four, and so on. Each player is a Sugar Baby. Sugar Baby number one takes the ball, and throws it up in the air, while at the same time hollers, "Sugar Baby _____," and whatever player number he wished to call. The called player must obtain the ball and holler, "Sugar Baby stop!" If the called player catches the ball *before* it hits the ground, he throws it up again, and calls out another number. Those players whose number has not yet been called, should scatter as far away as possible from the ball. The player who obtains the ball and has not caught it before it hit the ground, must take three giant steps to the Sugar Baby closest to him, or any other Sugar Baby. If he hits the Sugar Baby with the ball, the Sugar Baby must go through the "Patty Wack." If he misses, *he* must go through the "Patty Wack." Patty Wack—All Sugar Babies line up in two straight rows facing each other. The player who is to receive the "Patty Wack" must run straight through the two lines. When he does, each player is allowed to pat him on his behind with their hand. Once he has run through, he starts the next game over. All players keeping their same numbers."[20]
>
> —*Twenty-year-old African American Xavier University freshman student, New Orleans*

"One and Twenty"—"One person has to stand in the middle with a lot of people around. And you have to count to a hundred—like, 'One and twenty, two and twenty, three and twenty,' you know. The circle people get partners, then the person in the middle has to take their partner away, and the one that's left has to go and get another partner. And whoever gets to a hundred is the one that's 'it.'"

> —*Lusher Elementary, African American 5th-grade boy, New Orleans*

The crew from Channel 26, WGNO television and I videotaped a wild game of "Kiss and Chase" at Lacoste Elementary in Chalmette, Louisiana one cold winter day in 1977. The players were fifth and sixth graders, mostly white. However, the game "Kissing Chase," or "Kiss and Chase," was played all over New Orleans, by both African American and white elementary school children:

"Kiss and Chase"—Groups of boys chase groups of girls between the goal posts on the basketball court. The two posts are safe places. If a player touches the posts, and remains near them, he is safe. But if he runs, and gets caught and kissed, he is then escorted back to the safe place. After a while the players switch roles, and the girls get to chase and kiss the boys. I saw this played at Lacoste Elementary, at Eisenhower Elementary, and at Andrew Jackson Elementary. The junior high students at Beauregard Junior High told of playing it when they were "kids."[21]

—Observation, Jeanne Soileau, New Orleans

"Red Rover"—"A bunch of people line up on one side of a yard, and a bunch of people line up on the other side. It has to be even. Then you call out, 'Red Rover, Red Rover, let Mary come over.' And the person who's named has to run across, and try to break through the people's hands. If she does, one of their people has to come over to Mary's side. If she can't break through, she has to stay on that side."[22]

—Lacoste Elementary, 6th-grade white boy, New Orleans

"Freeze Tag"—was played all over New Orleans. Several students described the game to me, but most descriptions were too illogical to use. In essence, the game goes like this: One person is chosen "it." The other players scatter, and the one who is "it" has to chase them. If he tags someone, the tagged person has to freeze in the same position he was in when tagged. Another player on his side may come up, and touch him, thus unfreezing him to run again. In most schools, a person has to be tagged, "frozen," and "unfrozen," three times before he is the next "it."[23]

"Freeze Tag with Flashlights"—"We play "Freeze Tag" in the house at night with flashlights. Everybody has a flashlight except 'it,' and they flash on and off, and he has to tag them three times."

—Adolph Meyer Elementary, 5th-grade white boy, Algiers, La.

"Chinese Freeze Tag"—The same boy told me that in "Chinese Freeze Tag," the "it" chases the group, and if he touches somebody, that person is "frozen" in the position he was in at the time he was touched. But he is released if one of his teammates comes along, and "lets him run between his legs."

—Adolph Meyer Elementary, 5th-grade white boy, Algiers, La.

"Chinese Freeze Tag 2"—In this game "the person tagged has to hold on to whatever part of his body is tagged when he is touched, and he has to continue to run holding on to himself."

—Adolph Meyer Elementary, 5th-grade white boy; John Dibert Elementary 5th and 6th graders,
African American and white, New Orleans

"Jailbreak"—"All the girls chase all the boys, and when a girl catches a boy, she takes her captive over to the "boys monkey bars" (or any other specified "jail"), and the captives have to stay there until another boy runs by, and taps them, and frees them. Then the chase continues."

—Lusher Elementary, 6th-grade white boys, New Orleans

"Jailbreak 2"—"You get some people, and then you get another group of people, and then you get a base, like a jail, and then your whole group runs out while the other group's countin,' and you go hide, and then you try to catch the people. If you catch a person, he goes to jail, and then you gotta try to get the person out of jail. If they catch you three times, then you're it."

—John Dibert Elementary, 5th-grade white boy, New Orleans

"Jailbreak 3"—This variant of Jailbreak involved three separate bases where people could be safe, as well as in jail.

—John Dibert, 5th and 6th-grade boys, New Orleans

"Dungeon"—"You have two teams. You choose who's 'it.' There's a jail. Somebody runs, and if he's caught, the catcher has to say, '1–2–3 dungeon!' And he has to freeze. Then they take him to the dungeon, the base. She can be rescued by someone on her team." (The change from "he" to "she" in the account is not unusual for small children.)

—Second-grade white girl, Lacoste Elementary, Chalmette, La.

"No Man's Land," or "King of the Mountain"—"You go stand up on a hill, and, like, uh, somebody's gotta come up there and push you off, and then they're the King, and you gotta push them off." A Lacoste Elementary white boy described "King of the Mountain" verbally, but I witnessed it played at Andrew Jackson Elementary (1976), where it was a wild and dangerous pushing and pulling contest high up on the monkey bars. Boys got injured so many times, the principal finally forbade playing the game.

—Lacoste Elementary, 5th-grade white boy, Chalmette, La.; Andrew Jackson,
3rd-grade African American boys, New Orleans

"Devil in a Teapot"—"You have a devil, and you have fruits, ice cream, any food, like, all that . . . Then you name 'ice cream,' and you have all kinds of ice cream. Then the devil comes up, and he says, 'Do you have vanilla?' And the person gotta get up all the way to the front, and the devil, he gotta count out how old the person is to the front. Then, when he gets out how old the person to the front is, he gotta take out after him and run."

—Eisenhower Elementary, 5th-grade African American boy, New Orleans

"Bloody Mary"—The same Eisenhower student told me, "You gotta put something over one person's eyes, and everybody goes and hides, and the house be dark, and the one with eyes covered gotta try and catch you. Then you gotta be it." This is a version of the ancient game "Blind Man's Buff."

—Eisenhower Elementary, 5th-grade African American boy, New Orleans

"Lion's Den"—A white boy stepped forward, "In my other school in Illinois, I played "Lion's Den." This one person had to have, like, a little rock, or sumpin,' and we get a whole bunch of persons, like, ten or sumpin,' and then all the persons gotta put in their han' and they choose the lion, and the hens, and the lion gets in the middle, and the lion and all the hens hold up their hands, and the captain of the hens gets the rock, and put it in one of their hands, and the lion has to hold his eyes so they don't see, and, and, then they all run, and the lion has to take somebody, and then open their hands to see if they have the rock. If they don't, they let them go. If they have the rock, the guy with the rock has to be the next lion."

—Eisenhower Elementary, 5th-grade white boy, New Orleans

"Bear in a Cage"—"When I was a Cub Scout we used to play 'Bear in a Cage.' There's about five people around, and one in the middle, and this one in the middle tries to break through. The cage is all holding each other's hands, and make a strong cage."

—Eisenhower Elementary, 5th-grade white boy, New Orleans

"Big Bear"—A fifth-grade girl from Lusher Elementary in New Orleans described "Big Bear." She said, "There would be a lot of kids, and there would be a biiiig bear, and they would all run up, and they would all start picking on him, and he would have to go in his cage. Then, they would go close to him, and he would pop out, and go, 'AAAAAAGH!' and he would chase everybody." I asked, "Does the guy who is the bear . . . does he like being the bear?" Her answer was, "With tag games, if the person is like a witch or a bear, then he likes it. If you choose the person to be 'it,' and make the person chase you, they don't like it so much. If you say, 'Hey, you're "it,"' and make the person chase you, they don't like it so much."

—Lusher Elementary, 5th-grade white girl, New Orleans

"Hot Tail"—At Adolph Meyer an African American fifth-grade boy told me the following three games, "Somebody has to find a belt, and when they find it, they get to whack you. (Much laughter from the group.) They all get on base, and they choose somebody to get the belt, and they go hides it. Everybody go, and they—when they see somebody getting' closer, they say, "Warmer," and "Warmer," then they say, "Ya hot!" Then they find it (the belt), and everybody runs back to the base, and whoever that don't get there in time, they get whacked." The class loved this game and shouted and laughed over it.

—Adolph Meyer Elementary, 5th-grade African American boy, Algiers, La.

"Catch One-Catch All"—The boy continued, "It's 'Catch one, catch all'—One person is it, and then he catches another, then they help him catch other people."

—Adolph Meyer Elementary, African American 5th-grade boy, Algiers, La.

"The Blob"—And he concluded with, "The Blob"—"You see, they touch somebody, and they gotta hold they hands, and then they go all run after somebody, and they holding hands, and they keep touching until they touch everybody. So, at the end there is a long line of people chasing others."

—Adolph Meyer Elementary African American 5th-grade boy, Algiers, La.

"The Blob 2"—This inspired another child to add, "You have people, and they all gotta run around, and the first person tries to knock everybody down, and they wiggle a lot." I asked, "Do they hold hands?" "Yeah, they hold hands, and the leader tries to knock all the rest down, and if he does, they out." To me, this sounds suspiciously like the game "Pop the Whip."

—Adolph Meyer Elementary, African American 5th-grade boy, Algiers, La.

Pop the Whip"—We used to play "Pop the Whip" when I was a child in the fifties. A strong child headed the "whip," and a series of smaller children ran in a line behind the leader, holding hands. The leader stopped, and swung the line in an arc, and the child running at the end of the line often was jerked off his feet and into the air.[24]

—Observation, Jeanne Soileau, Lafayette, La.

"Octopus"—A girl from John Dibert described several running games that they played in her physical education class. Some were too garbled to include here. One, which was pretty clear, was "Octopus."—"Half of the group stands on each side, and there is a person in the middle, and what happens is, the

teacher blows a whistle, or something, and then they try running to the other side, and a person touches them, doesn't say anything—just touches them, and they need to sit down, and when the other people cross, they try to touch them, and they'll have to sit down with the people that are sitting down, and there's still . . . there's only one person running around."
—John Dibert Elementary, 5th-grade white girl, New Orleans

"Hide and Seek"—"One hides his face and counts to a number—25 or 100—while everybody hides. Then he goes seek."
—John Dibert Elementary, white boys and girls, New Orleans

"Hide and Go Seek Ghosts"—Well, there's bushes, and there has to be five people. One person's the ghost, and they have a white sheet over them. And you have a plastic baseball bat, and you go—everyone's hiding in one place—and um, if the ghost walks by, and they hit him on the head, um, they touch base before the ghost does, or if the ghost touches base before they do, they all out."
—John Dibert Elementary, African American 6th-grade boy, New Orleans

Ruthanna, the Tulane Freshman student from Cooperstown, New York, remembered several running games.

"Ghosts in the Graveyard"—"We used to play 'Ghosts in the Graveyard' in the graveyard at our church at night on Thursday . . . it was basically like hide and go seek, only you would try to scare the person who was trying to find you. We would hide behind gravestones and whoever was 'it' would come out to find you, and when they were right near you, you would, like, jump up, and then you would run, and it was very scary."[25]
—Ruthanna B. Tulane University freshman student, Cooperstown, N.Y.

"Sardines"—Ruthanna continued—"We played all kinds of hide and go seek—like 'Sardines.'"

(JS) What was "Sardines"?

(Ruthanna) It was a lot like hide and go seek, but instead of one person . . . everybody hiding, and one was "it,"—ONE person would hide, and everybody had to . . . they sent *everybody* out to find them, and when that person found the person who was "it," he had to hide with him. And you ended up everyone was all in one place, and one person finding everybody in the basement. We had basements, and people in New York had a lot of antiques and stuff in their basements and attics, and they were always good hiding places.

(JS) We don't have basements here in New Orleans; they flood.

(Ruthanna) Yeah, and you don't have snow. We used to play snow games.

—Ruthanna B., Tulane University freshman student, Cooperstown, N.Y.

"The Fox"—"One of the snow games we used to play," Ruthanna continued, "was 'The Fox.' What you did was, one person went out, and he made trails in the snow . . . and, you know, he made it within a reasonable space. And he tried . . . you know, like, he made all these snow patterns with his feet, and then somebody else would try to follow, and he would try to get to him. And if they made a mistake, then they were chickens, and they got thrown out. And then, somebody else would try."

—Ruthanna B., Tulane University freshman student, Cooperstown, N.Y.

"TV Tag"—"When you touch someone, they gotta holler out something that is on TV when they fall down on the ground—like 'Dukes of Hazard!'—and when someone touches them, they free again."

—Ruthanna B., Tulane University freshman student, Cooperstown, N.Y.;
Eisenhower Elementary 5th-grade white girl, New Orleans

"TV Tag 2"—"You got a group of people, and you have to get one person that's it, and you, um, the person that's 'it' has to go, and touch a person three times, and if you chase him after, you have to kneel on one knee, and say a name of a TV show, and if you get picked three times, or if he touches you before you kneel down and say a TV show, you're 'it.'"

—John Dibert Elementary, 5th-grade white boy, New Orleans

"Cigarette Tag"—"In Cigarette Tag, you have . . . everybody takes the name of a cigarette, and the person who is 'it' has to run up, and if they are about to get tagged, they can squat down and yell the name of a cigarette. And then they are not "it," and the person who is "it" has to go, and try to tag someone else."

—Ruthanna B., Tulane University freshman student, Cooperstown, N.Y

"Trees"—And then we used to play "Trees." Um—One person—you start off one person would be "it." And you would have to play it in an established area, like, between two trees. The person who was "it" would stand in the middle, and he would yell, "Tree!" and they'd run from one side to the other, and whoever "it" touched had to stand still, and they couldn't move except that they could move their arms, and everybody had to keep running, and that's how "it" could catch another person. We'd just do that until everybody was caught, and the first person, who was caught, would have to be the next "it."

—Ruthanna B., Tulane University freshman student, Cooperstown, N.Y

"Cramps"—When a white boy began to talk about "Cramps" in his classroom at John Dibert Elementary, everybody in the class brightened up. It was obviously a well-liked game, but frowned upon by adults.

(Boy) You get a lot of people, but not people who's gonna cry right easily, 'cause you gotta go 'round punchin' people.
(JS) OK, what do you do?
(Boy) And you gotta hit people.
(JS) Different people?
(Boy) Yeah, kids just go 'round hit people. (The class grunted approval, grinning and laughing.)
(Boy) Well, sometimes you "teams," and sometimes you don't, and when you got your teams, you gotta catch all of 'em, and you clips 'em. Like, when we play around my house, we play like they gotta jack, and we give 'em cramp, and they gotta run, and we hit 'em on the legs, and all that, and soon, we hit 'em all over."

—John Dibert Elementary, 5th-grade white boy, New Orleans

"Bread and Butter"—One boy said, "One person goes hide something. When he hide it, he say, 'Bread and butter,' and the other people gotta go find it. Then, if they find it, they gotta . . . they gotta go hide it."

—Eisenhower Elementary, 5th-grade white boy, New Orleans

SCHOOLYARD VARIANTS OF RUNNING GAMES WITH STRICT RULES

"Dodge Ball"—"We play 'Dodge Ball' in the space between the basketball goals. A whole bunch of people get in the middle, and two people get on each side. Everybody runs back and forth, and they try to hit them with the ball. When somebody is hit, he has to be with the guys throwing the ball. The last one in is the winner."

—Lusher Elementary, 6th-grade white boys, New Orleans

"Touch Football"—This is a favorite game on and off the school ground. In my neighborhood, the grown men and the older boys played in the empty lot in the middle of the block almost every afternoon. African American and white boys from Lacoste, Lusher, Andrew Jackson, John Dibert, and Adolph Meyer all told of playing "Touch Football." The rules were simple: The teams choose sides, designate goals, choose a passer, offensive, and defensive players.

The passer falls back, his receivers follow whatever plan has been decided on, and the opposing team tries to prevent a touchdown.

—Observation, Jeanne Soileau, New Orleans

"Basketball"—"Basketball" is popular among both African American and white students and young men, but much more noticeably played by African American young people on public playgrounds, and in neighborhood yards. It is sometimes played one on one, sometimes in sets of twos, or even odd numbers, the weaker players being assigned to the weaker side. When enough players are available, it is played full court, but the majority of after-school games involve from two to six players using half a court. Makeshift goals made from metal hoops, plastic baskets, or nailed-up buckets decorate some city yards.

—Observation, Jeanne Soileau, New Orleans

"Volleyball"—"Volleyball" is played by groups in playgrounds and yards after school. I have observed volleyball players using a fence as a net, using a parked car as a net, and sometimes, using no net at all, just an imaginary line between two stationary objects. "Volleyballs" are anything from soccer balls to beach balls.

—Observation, Jeanne Soileau, New Orleans

"Tetherball"—The following is my condensed version of several minutes of rambling, much interrupted, explanation of "Tetherball" from John Dibert fifth- and sixth-grade children, both African American and white: "There's a pole, and they have a ball attached to a string on it, and you have to hit the ball a lot, and run around, and try to get the ball around the pole. Somebody else runs to the other side, and tries to block the ball and hit it back to you."

—John Dibert Elementary, 5th- and 6th-grade boys and girls, New Orleans

"Kick Ball"—One white boy stepped forward out of the crowd of informants at John Dibert Elementary and spoke, "You need two teams, but you don't *have* to have two teams, and, uh, if you have two teams, one team is 'it.' You kick the ball, and if they don't catch it, you have to run to a base, and you have to go to first, second, third, and back home. And then, if you make it all the way around, if you kick it hard enough, you come back home, and you get a point. If you can't make it all the way around, you just run to first base. If they catch it without a bounce, it's a 'fly,' so that's one away, and they out. Kinda like 'Baseball,' but you kickin' it." Notice he said in the very beginning that "you don't have to have two teams." Like any other schoolyard version of an organized game, as few as two or three can play; one kicks and runs, the other(s) try to catch flies, or put the kicker out.

—John Dibert Elementary, 5th-grade white boy, New Orleans

"Baseball"—Several children interviewed spoke of playing "Baseball" with friends after school. At Eisenhower Elementary, one boy said, "We play 'Baseball' at my house on Sunday. My cousins come over, and we play girls against the boys, and we all get to play and hit the ball. Sometimes we play a real game, and if the other team loses, we have to serve them drinks, and after, if we win, they have to serve us drinks. Sometimes we just hit the ball and practice."

—Eisenhower Elementary, 5th-grade white boy, New Orleans

DRAMATIC PLAY WITH A STORY LINE

This section involves more than choosing an "it" and running from him/her. Of course, most tag games seem to have a theme of some kind, TV program titles or prisoners breaking out, but the following games have a rather elaborate structure, a structure that is, in some cases, very old.

"Jailhouse"—At Eisenhower, a fifth-grade white boy told me, "OK, then there's one certain place where there's about seven people can play, and about two people are the guards, and the rest are prisoners. First thing you have to do is you have to walk around, and play like you are doin' something bad, like shoplifting, or something, and then they'll catch you, and bring you to jail, and then they'll lock you up. Then you gotta play like you have a machine, and you gotta pretend like you excape. And then, you run around, and then the guards have to try to catch 'em, and if you do that three times, and they catch you, then you have to be one of the guards. Then they do that again, and see how the other persons run."

—Eisenhower Elementary, 5th-grade white boy, New Orleans

"Monsters"—The group I observed at Lacoste Elementary in Chalmette, Louisiana, was large, and racially mixed. A fifth-grade white boy described playing the game: "A boy has to be a monster, and he lies down, and the girls walk around them and pick flowers, and if they pick the monster, the monster gets up, and chases them." I watched the children play this game, and I found it was based on two contrasting modes. While a boy lay on the ground on his side, and hid his face, and pretended to sleep, the girls circled around him, singing softly and pretending to pick the flowers. Then, when one girl circled in close, she touched him, and he rose up roaring. All the girls screamed in real, not mock, terror, and ran away. I felt a tingle of shock myself when he jumped up. It was an enactment of a primal fear we all carry deep within us.[26]

—*Lacoste Elementary School, 5th-grade white boy, Chalmette, La.*

"Murder"—"The object of the game is they have one detective, one murderer, and all the other people have to hide, and the murderer goes around, and if you come out, the murderer touches you, and you fall dead on the floor. Then there comes the detective, and the group has to tell him what happened."

—*Eisenhower Elementary, 5th-grade white boy, New Orleans*

"Batman"—I observed children playing "Batman" at Lacoste Elementary in Chalmette, Louisiana. In Batman, there are two heroes, Batman and Robin. The players tie their coats over their shoulders by looping the sleeves in a knot around their necks. Then the two run around shouting, "Batman da da da da da da da da Batmaaaaaan!" The rest of the group gets together, and plots some kind of evil, and Batman and Robin have to figure out the story. Some of the other kids take the part of Penguin, Joker, or other characters, who are evildoers on the original Batman series on television.

—*Lacoste Elementary, 5th and 6th graders, Chalmette, La.*

"Charlie's Angels"—"Charlie's Angels" was extremely popular at Lacoste Elementary in 1977. Three girls were the Charlie's Angels, and part of the fun was getting the group together and discussing whatever storyline was to be enacted. Sometimes the story line followed the television episode that week. The girls who got to be Charlie's Angels pranced around and acted sexy and seductive in their roles.

—*Lacoste Elementary, 5th-grade white girls, Chalmette, La.*

The following three games involve a "wolf" as chaser. The "big, bad" wolf is found as a folklore fright figure in many cultures. In Europe, the wolf has been almost eradicated, possibly due to its reputation as evil. In the United States, wolves have been poisoned, trapped, and snuffed out in many areas where cattle ranchers fear them.[27]

"Colored Eggs"—"The 'it' is the wolf, and all the other players are chickens. The chickens tell each other what their colors is of their eggs; then the wolf comes up, and he call out colors, and when he calls out a chicken's color, he has to run, and the wolf chases him." The children argued over what happened next. Some children said the caught chicken became the next wolf; while others said the caught chickens were taken over and put in a "pot" with all the other caught chickens. Then, at the end of the game, when all the chickens were caught, the first caught became the next wolf.

—*John Dibert Elementary, 5th-grade white girl, New Orleans*

"Colors"—"You get some people, and um, you give each a color. You gotta have a mama and a wolf. And the wolf comes over and he says, 'Knock knock.' And you say, 'Who is it?' and he says, 'The dirty-faced Devil, yaaahh!' And you say, 'Go home, read the Bible, eat a banana, kiss your wife!' and all that. And then he comes back, and he knocks on the door again, and you say, 'Who there?' And he say, 'The clean-faced Devil.' And you say, 'What color you want?' And he have to guess some colors, and then, if he gets the color that one of the persons is, um, he gotta run. And you gotta give the wolf how old the person is."[28]

—*Adolph Meyer Elementary, 5th-grade African American girl, Algiers, La.*

"Bread and Butter"—The following explanation is very confused and may seem to be a bit strange, but as you will see, the African American fifth-grade girl who recounted it to me at John Dibert Elementary was recalling the basic elements of a traditional English game, which the English folklorist Lady Alice B. Gomme had collected and published in 1894.

(Child) I know one called "I Went Downtown to See Mr. Brown."
(JS) Oh?
(Another child) No, it called "Bread and Butter."
(JS) How does it go?
(First child) I went downtown to see Mr. Brown . . . wait . . . yeah . . . I went downtown for a cockfight at daylight . . . (Then the child goes off into a confused explanation. I make her start again.)
(JS) There's a particular way that game starts. It is a tag game, right?
(First child) Yeah.
(JS) How does that game start?
(First child) You go like . . . alright . . . you have Monday, Tuesday, Wednesday, Thursday, Friday, and Saturday. And then, um, you say, like, you have to hold on tight, tight, tight, and say, "I went downtown to see Mr. Brown, I won't be back 'til tomorrow night." And then, like, the mama go, like, downtown, or sumpin'. Then,

the wolf come, and the wolf, say, he try to grab you away, and he eat you, and then you say, "Mama, the bread and butter is burnin." And the mama comes back and try to whup the wolf, and whoever he get, they gotta be on his side."[29]

—*John Dibert Elementary, 5th-grade African American girl, New Orleans*

"Witch in the Well"—At Lacoste Elementary a sixth-grade white girl began,

OK, you need a witch, and you need a mother and some children, and the Mama goes out and says, "Going out to smoke my pipe, and I won't be back until Saturday night, and don't get dirty."

Then they play in the dirt. Then she turns and she says, "I saw you! I saw you playing in the dirt!"

Then the children say, "No Mother, we wasn't."

Then, um, then the mother says, "Lemme see your hands." "Dirty, dirty, dirty" to all of them, and then, um, she says, "Go wash your hands in the well!"

The witch scares 'em, and they go back and they say, "The witch in the well! The witch in the well!"

And then she (the mother) says, "I don't have no time for no jokes. Go back and wash your hands."

Children: "The witch in the well!! The witch in the well!!"

And then she comes back, and they come back, and she (the mother) says, "If you insist!"

And, um, she goes, and the witch tries to scare her, and the mama goes, "What you doin' in my well?"

And the witch goes, "Sweepin' out."

And she goes, "What you doin' in my well?"

And the witch goes, "Smokin' my pipe."

And she goes, "What you doin' in my well?"

"Sharpenin' a knife so I can kill ya!"

Then they all gotta run, and the one the witch catches is the next witch.[30]

—*Lacoste Elementary School, 6th-grade white girl, Chalmette, La.*

"Ghost in the Bathroom"—A Lacoste white boy volunteered "The Ghost in the Bathroom" after listening to the girl recount "Witch in the Well." His game closely resembles "Witch in the Well":

Well, they have a ghost in the bathroom; then they have a mother and a few kids. The mother sends the kids to play outside; then she calls 'em in to eat, and she says, "Go wash your hands in the bathroom."

And the ghost scares 'em, and they go back and say, "Mommee, Mommee, there's a ghost in the bathroom."

And she says, "There's no such thing as a ghost. Go back and wash your hands."

And then they go back, and then they go over there, and they say, "Mommee, Mommee, there's a ghost in the bathroom."

And then their mother says, "If you come and say this one more time, I'm gonna whip you."

And then, they go back, and they wash their hands, and then the ghost scares them, and they say, "Mommee, Mommee, the ghost in the bathroom!"

Mommee (says), "Now I'm gonna come with you!"

And so the Mama goes with 'em to wash their hands, and then the ghost scares 'em, and whoever she touches is the one who's gonna be the ghost.[31]

—*Lacoste Elementary 6th-grade white boy, Chalmette, La.*

"Can I Buy Some Eggs?"—At an earlier session taped in the Tulane University neighborhood, a fifth-grade girl from Lusher Elementary in New Orleans volunteered, "And there's this thing where you need five people. There's four corners, and it's called 'Can I Buy Some Eggs.'" (She points to the four corners of the room. Then she points to the middle of the room for number "five.")

(JS) Hummm—I never heard this one.

(Girl) Yeah, four corners—you need four people, and you go this way, "Can I buy some eggs?" And someone goes, "No, I don't have any. Sorry, I don't have any; you'll have to go to the next corner." And then this person ("it" who is stationed in the middle of the room) has to go to the next corner. Then he asks someone else in the next corner. Then, when he goes to the next corner, then the other players have to run to each other's corner. Like that.

(JS) OK. So, this one asks for eggs . . .

(Girl) Um hum.

(JS) Then, when the first one has none, he has to go to the next corner, and these two switch?

(Girl) No . . . no. When this one changes, the other ones change too, and they *all* run at the same time . . .

(JS) And does the fifth player have to try to catch them?

(Girl) Um hum. So, one person is switching to another corner at the same time the fifth person is running after the first corner. So, he trades with this one (She indicates the right corner of the room.), and *this* person is going to *this* corner. (She indicates two other corners of the room.) They trade. And, it's

like, he's in the middle of here, and he's over here—then he runs back, and
gets over here, and it goes on and on like that.

(JS) So the person that is "it" has to ask for eggs—

(Girl) Um hum

(JS) Are there bases marked? Does it have, like, a can or something marking the
bases?

(Girl) It all depends.

(JS) It doesn't have to? It can have just a spot?

(Girl) Yes. You can say, well, (points) that, that, and that. And you can say, "That's
the corners."

(JS) I never heard that one. It's a good one.

—Lusher Elementary, 5th-grade white girl, New Orleans

"Blowing Bubbles"—The same girl from Lusher Elementary said: "And there's
another one where one person's 'it,' and he blows bubbles, and all the others
try to pop 'em. And they have to count them when they pop 'em. They have
to keep the number in their head, and the person, after all the bubbles are
gone, and it's the first round, he asks them, 'Who has the number in their
head?' And whoever hasn't the number in their head, they out."

—Lusher Elementary, 5th-grade white girl, New Orleans

CHAPTER 7

Teases

I wondered how to introduce this section. Then I read the following statement by C. W. Sullivan III, in "Children's Oral Poetry: Identity and Obscenity." Sullivan explained teases better than I could:

> In addition to regulating their own games, children have a series of rhymes that attempt to enforce conformity. Children have their own ideas, independent of (but to some extent derived from) the adult culture that surrounds them, and they have rhymes that make fun of or insult transgressors within the group. Overweight children hear "Fatty, fatty, two by-four," a child hastily dressed might hear, "I see London / I see France / I see [name]'s underpants," informers to authorities hear, "Tattletale, tattletale / Hanging on the bull's tale (sic)," liars hear "liar, liar, pants on fire," and, of course, immature or sensitive children hear, "Cry, baby cry, stick your finger in your eye." There are many more such rhymes, and the point is that they are circulated by children, not taught by adults, and address what the child's folk group considers proper or, more to the point, improper behavior.[1]

An Andrew Jackson Elementary sixth-grade African American boy said:

> Fat and skinny was jumpin' in the bed
> Fat turned over and skinny was dead
> Fat called the doctor and the doctor said
> That's what you get for peein' in the bed.[2]

His friend then shouted, "Do your funky titty thing!" and the boy added:

> Cry baby cry
> Suck your mama's titty.

Then he finished with:

> He wears such funny clothes
> And everybody knows
> A scarecrow has to look that way
> To scare off all the crows.
> —*Andrew Jackson Elementary, African American boy, New Orleans,*

There were several teases I remember from my childhood (1940s). One was a variation of "Cry baby cry":

> Cry baby cry
> Stick your finger in your eye
> And say it wasn't I.

Another is when the teacher made the mistake of putting a large box in front of the class for us to slip Valentines into. I have never forgotten that I received:

> Roses are red
> Violets are blue
> Skunks stink
> And so do you!

> Roses are red
> Violets are blue
> You look like a monkey
> And belong in the zoo.[3]

When asked my name I answered:

> Puddin' in tame
> Ask me again
> And I'll tell you the same.

For us, in the nineteen forties, finding an object elicited:

> Finders keepers
> Losers weepers.
> Dropping food on the ground:

(Make the sign of the cross)
God's dirt don't hurt

(Then eat it.)

Name-calling was answered with:

Sticks and stones may break my bones
But names can never hurt me.

The answer to a nosy person was:

Ask me no questions
And I'll tell you no lies.
Shut your mouth
And you'll catch no flies.

And we would sing this little song to people who complained:

Nobody loves me
Everybody hates me
I'm going to the garden to eat worms.
Big fat juicy ones
Itty bitty skinny ones
I'm going to the garden to eat worms.[4]
—*Jeanne Soileau, Lafayette, La.*

A senior student at Chalmette High School (1978) recalled these quips from his elementary days:

Act like a tree and leave.
Take a long walk off a short pier.
Act like an orange and peel.
Act like a dancer and go go.
Act like a tumor and cut out.

CHAPTER 8

Jokes

Telling jokes and stories is an art form for both children and adults. The teller has to have good logical order, precise timing, and entertaining delivery to keep everyone's interest. This section is an examination of children's jokes— some that succeeded and some that failed—complete with listener's comments, the "hums," and the "ums," and the logical lapses that happen when a neophyte tells jokes. Children I recorded helped their friends along on the path to joke telling—in one way or another. Sometimes listeners encouraged tellers. Sometimes listeners broke in and took over. Children can be brutal audiences and don't allow too much leeway when the speaker is stumbling.[1]

In my recordings of children learning to tell jokes, I encountered struggles for clarity, audience dominance, and verbal control repeated again and again. My grandson was four years old when he came home one day from preschool and asked me, "Why does the chicken cross the road?" Being a dutiful grandmother, I replied, "I don't know. Why *does* the chicken cross the road?" His reply was, "Uh—maybe because he was going to the store?" I laughed heartily both from recognition of the logical struggle he was going through and his answer. At age seven, the same grandson told me another "joke." As I was parking the car to go to the supermarket, I heard him say from the back seat, "Did you hear about the kidnapping in the park?" "No," I said in a voice of concern, "What happened?" "Then you ought to wake him up," said my grandson, and it took a half a second for me to realize that he had uttered a joke. I glanced around, and his eyes were twinkling. He had bridged the logical leap from his question to the correct answer.

The chapter that follows is transcriptions of "joke" patter told in racially mixed sessions. The race of each teller is indicated. The format is organic, rather than numbered and ordered. It seemed better to include everything surrounding the jokes as they were told, so that an overall view of how they were told, and how the group reacted to them, might be shown. Warning— these jokes are uncensored.

The first is an example of failure. Children are involved listeners. They grunt and "um hum" when the speaker is successful, and they break in and take over the narrative if the speaker is doing poorly. This beginning joking attempt is by David, a white boy from Adolph Meyer Elementary School, Algiers, Louisiana:

(JS) Who knows a joke?
(Children) David! (The group points to a white boy with his hand up.)
(JS) What's the joke?
(David) There was this man, and there was this other man, and see, they was
    walkin' up, and then, they was in the woods. They was walkin' around, and
    this man sees a bear, and he looks around, and he says, "Gimme the gun!
    Gimme the gun!"
(One listener shouts.) Too many people around!
(David) Up your nose with a rubber hose!
(Group) We wanna do another song.
(Pause. Grumbling. "We know "Fire!")
(JS) All right, "Fire"—Let's go.

And the children go on to sing the song "Fire," beating out the rhythm on the tops of their desks, while the girls sing the words. David was ignored. David's rambling narrative was not able to hold the group's attention. He was interrupted, and he got irritated about it. He sulked.

The next jokes succeeded. At the International Year of the Child Festival, Lafayette Square, New Orleans, in October 1979, I stood in line with a group of children who were waiting to get their faces painted.

(JS) Where are you from?
(Group) New Orleans Free School.
(JS) Do you know any jokes?
(White boy) I think I know one. Why do birds fly south?
(JS) I don't know.
(Boy) Because it's too far to walk.
Everybody responded well to this. It is an old, corny joke. Maybe that is part of
    its charm, but the child's timing was good, which is essential, even in a short
    joke. The same white boy told me this one:
(Boy) What has two ears and a point on top?
(JS) I don't know, what?
(Boy) A mountain.

(JS) A mountain does not have ears.
(Boy) Haven't you ever heard of mountaineers?
The same boy told a third joke.
(Boy) What did the big chimney say to the little chimney?
(JS) I don't know.
(Boy) You're too young to smoke.[2]

These simple, well-worn jokes elicited grins, giggles, and chuckles. The teller was liked, the jokes were comfortable, and the group of listeners welcoming.

The next transcription of a recording comes from Myrtle Place Elementary School in Lafayette, Louisiana (1998). It took place in a loud, echoing cafeteria where an after-school group made up of kindergarten white girls, a few older African American and white girls, and African American and white third-grade boys waited for their parents to pick them up. One large African American boy named Michael often dominated the taping by yelling, pushing people, and grabbing the microphone off the table where I had placed it. The transcription begins with the kindergartners singing a song about "Fried bugs."

(Kindergarten girls)

Put your feelers on your head (*Put fingers up like antennae.*)
Then your mama and your papa
Will feed you fried bugs

(Kindergarten girl) Want me to show—um—that goes?
(JS) Do y'all sing that on the playground?
(Kindergartner) Uh huh.
(Children arrange themselves—they are making a line, putting each other's
    hands on the shoulders of the person in front.)

Come out come out
Put your feelers on your head (*Put their fingers up.*)
Then your mama and your papa
Will feed you fried bugs.

While a few of the kindergarten group continue to sing about "fried bugs" and supply a continuing musical background, a small girl standing close to the microphone looks up and says, "I know a joke." I say, "OK. Tell me your joke." What followed was the sound of very young children struggling to make their way through the mental gymnastics of telling jokes:

(Girl) Um—why did the chicken cross the road?

(JS) Why?

(Girl) I mean—why did the K cross the road?

(JS) Why?

(Girl) To go to K-Mart.

(JS) Haw haw haw.

(Second girl) I know one. Why did the penny cross the road?

(JS) Wait—what?

(Girl) Why did the penny cross the road?

(JS) Why DID the penny cross the road?

(Another girl breaks in and shouts.) To go to J. C. Penny's!

(JS) Yes! (Laughter)

(Kindergartner) I know one. Why did the chicken cross the road?

(JS) I don't know.

(Kindergartner) 'Cause he wanted to go get some beer. (Pause and a sprinkling of laughter.)

(Second child) That's NOT a joke!

(Third grader) Why did the turkey cross the road?

(JS) Why DID the turkey cross the road?

(Third grader) It was the chicken's day off.

(Laughter)

(JS) That was a good one.

(Kindergartner) Why did the chicken cross the road?

(JS) I don't know.

(Kindergartner) To get some—um—chicken legs. (She giggles and puts her hand over her mouth.)

(Third-grade boy steps forward.) Why did the chicken cross the road?

(He supplies his own answer.) To get to the other side!

(JS) Awwww, that's the usual . . . OK. Yes?

(Michael, the large, dominating boy.) Why did the chicken cross the road?

(JS) I don't know.

(Michael) To go to the K-Mart, and go get—uh—no—to go to Walmart and go get him some chicken.

(Kindergarten girl) I know one.

(JS) All right.

(Kindergarten girl) Why did the—why did the turtle cross the road?

(JS) Why did the turtle cross the road?

(Girl, shyly) 'Cause they wanted to try to see how to get runned over.

(Loud raucous laughter from the group, followed by an even louder burst of laughter from Michael.)

(Older boy) Knock knock.

(JS) Who's there?

(Boy) Tuna fish.

(JS) Tuna fish who?

(Boy) You can tune a piano, but you can't tune a fish. (Giggle.)

(JS) That's a good one.[3]

(Another older boy.) I know one.

(JS) Yes.

(Boy) Why does the chicken cross the road?

(JS) I don't know.

(Boy) To see what the cars look like.

(Michael shouts.) He can see from the sidewalk! What a . . .

(Kindergarten girl) Why does a skeleton cross the road?

(JS) I don't know.

(Girl corrects herself.) Why DIDN'T the skeleton cross the road?

(JS) I don't know.

(Girl) He didn't have enough guts.

(Michael and the kindergartners guffaw very loudly.)

—Myrtle Place Elementary School, kindergartners and 3rd-grade African American and white boys and girls, Lafayette, La.

I learned much transcribing taped sessions such as this one. Telling a joke well is a gradual learning experience. Good joke tellers might start out tentatively sending out a line. The audience reacts in positive or negative ways. A tenacious child works his / her way through the rough commentary, the corrections of others, and the mocking of hecklers, to achieve poise and timing, along with a stockpile of ready jokes. As is demonstrated above, kindergartners and other very young children do not always "get" the connection between the beginning of a joke, and its necessary punch line. At this point, the other children in the group often supply the right comment, the correct boost, the slight push, which encourages their fellow classmate to plunge on and gain confidence.

Just when I thought the collecting session at Myrtle Place Elementary was winding down, a little white girl said, "I know a story. It's a scary one."

(JS) Tell me a story. Tell me a scary one.

(The second-grade girl stepped forward.) It's called the Mo . . . It's called the
Monkey's Paw. Once upon a time a boy, he . . . um, moved into a new house.
(Group shouts, "Yeah!") It was late at night, so he went to bed, and he heard
some noise. He went to see. They were coming from the closet. He found out
that they were—they were—just his dad getting some boxes inside of the
closet. So, he went back to bed. Next morning . . . uh . . . he went inside, to
look inside the closet and—um—there was a box, and (Giggles.) he opened
it up, and there was a monkey's paw in it. ("OOOOOOO," sounds of disgust
from the listeners.) There was a note said, "Wish three wishes with this—uh—
monkey's paw, and you will die."

(JS) And what happened?

(Second-grade girl) And he went to bed with it, and he did three wishes, and the
morning came . . . The first wish he said for his grandmother come back from
the dead—from the dead—and he went to sleep. (There is absolute silence
during this part of the story.) Then he heard a knock at the door, and he
opened it, and there was his grandma from the dead, and his grandma tried
to kill him, but then he wished that she would go away, so she went away.
(Some child screams shrilly in the stillness, maybe Michael?)

(JS) But the other wish was still there, huh?

(Second-grade girl continues.) But then he wished for a million dollars, and then
the next morning it got—it didn't turn light from night—so—

(JS) The next morning it didn't turn light? Oh, it stayed nighttime?

(Second-grade girl) Uh huh—so he went back inside, and when he opened the
door, he died.

(JS) Whoa!

—Myrtle Place Elementary School, white girl, Lafayette, La.

The second grader who told this story handled it beautifully. She kept her
voice soft and thrilling. She made eye contact with her listeners. Most of
all, her story flowed logically. By the second grade she was already a gifted
storyteller.[4]

Sometimes the success of a joke-telling session relies more on the rela-
tionship between the spoken words and the group bandying them about. At
J. W. Faulk, in Lafayette, Louisiana, the African American girls sharing jokes
and stories played on words they shared as a clique:

(JS) OK—What's yours?

(Girl) Knock knock.

(JS) Who's there?

(Girl) Boo.

(JS) Boo who?

(Girl) Don't cry—it's just a joke. (OOOOOO! From girls.)

(JS) Oh, that's a good one. Who's next—who knows a joke or anything like that?

(Girls) Me! Me! Me!

(JS) OK.

(Girl) Knock knock.

(JS) Who's there?

(Girl) Ashley.

(JS) Ashley who?

(Girl) Ashley, who likes to pick on everyone.

(Girls) Ooooo! Aw (Laughter.) Oh! Oh! (Pointing at Ashley, who puts her hands over her face.)

(JS) OK?

(Girl) Knock knock.

(JS) Who's there?

(Girl) (Long pause.) Uh . . . duh.

(Girls) (Laughter.)

(Girl) Knock knock.

(JS) Who's there?

(Girl) Bald.

(JS) Bald who?

(Girl) Bald Campo.

(Screams of laughter—it had to be an "in" joke.)

(JS) I missed that one.

(Girls scream even louder, laugh, and pummel each other.)

I later learned that "Bald Campo" was their teacher. "Knock Knock" jokes were popular when I was in elementary school in the 1940s. They were, apparently, still very much in vogue in the last third of the twentieth century.

—*J. W. Faulk Elementary, African American 3rd-grade girls, Lafayette, La.*

In 1997 I had the opportunity to record second graders at St. Genevieve School in Lafayette, Louisiana. We held our session in the cafeteria, and it looked and smelled exactly the same as it had when I was a student there in the late 1940s.

This time the assembled children were all white, except for one African American boy named Harold. This transcript begins with second-grade repartee between the boys and the girls and then gradually proceeds to jokes.

(JS) What grade y'all in?

(Group) Second!

(JS) Y'all all in second?

(Lead boy) All three . . . all of us right here—we're all in the same class except him. And we're all in . . . we're all friends.

(JS) And you are all friends.

(Boy) Me . . . except for them (Indicating the girls standing on the other side of the table.). We're not friends with THEM!

(JS) Oh no—y'all are boys!

(Boy) Us three are real friends (Indicates the two boys nearest him.).

(Girl) You talked me into playing soccer, and I got hit in the nose! (Giggles.)

(JS) Do you play jump rope? Tell me a jump-rope game.

(Girls)

> I like coffee
> I like tea
> I like the boys
> And the boys like me.
> (Boys in chorus)
> The boys make girls
> The girls is like them
> The girls is stinky little poo faced wimps.[5]

(Girls fall all over each other and giggle helplessly.)

(JS) Ah hah!

(Girls) We know another one—

> Registration registration
> Sign your name
> T-a-y-l-o-r
> Pre-K, kindergarten first grade
> Second grade third grade fourth grade
> Fifth grade sixth grade seventh grade
> Eighth grade ninth grade tenth grade
> Eleventh grade twelfth grade
> College, marriage, old Grandpa.

(Boys) Wait—I got one.

(Boys as a group) We got one! We got one!

(JS) You jump on each one? Wait—wait—wait, wait.

(Girls all talking at once.) We jump on each one . . . We jump like until it stops . . . until we . . . until we get out. And we . . . and then, like whatever, we go one—two—three—four—five—six—and if we land on A—we go like "Hi A."

(JS) OK. When you do the game—the game—I've always heard people do games differently. Do you go first grade, second grade . . . do you jump each time?

(Girl) We go

Registration registration (*Jump twice.*)
Pre-K Kindergarten, first grade (*Jump one time for each grade.*)
Second grade, third grade, fourth grade, (*Jump twice, then thrice, then four times.*)
(*As each grade is called, jump that number of times.*)

At the end, the girl says, "High School, college, marriage, old Grandma" and jumps twice for each word.

Note the change in the last line from one telling to another. The small change from "Old Grandpa" to "Old Grandma" demonstrates the manner in which chant lines subtly shift from one performance to another.

(JS) OK.

(Everybody shouts) We have one! I know one! (Boys are shouting twice as loudly as girls.)

(JS) OK. You tell me one now. OK. Young man—give it to me.

(Boy) I ate a booger
Tastes like sugar

That's it—I forgot the rest—They know the rest. We learned it from them.
(Points to the girls.)

(JS) Do you know one like that?

(Girls) Yeah.

(JS) How does it go?

(Girls) Booger booger on the wall
Do you think it's gonna fall?

(JS) What? What?

(Boy) Then you go y-e-s spells yes, and you are not it.

(JS) Wait—is booger booger on the wall a count out?

(Boy) Yeah.

(JS) Show me exactly how you are counting?

(Boy) Booger booger on the wall—and then you take your feet—and you put
   them in . . .

(JS) You put your feet in?

(Boy) Yeah—watch—

Girls line up and put their feet into a circle. They chant, "Booger booger on the
   wall / Do you think it's gonna fall / y-e-s spells yes / and you are not it." (*Point
   to each girl's foot on each word and letter.*)

(JS) OK. That's how it looks.

(Boy) Wait! I got a joke.

(JS) OK. Gimme your joke.

(Boy) There's this little boy, and he was sleepin', and then a ghost said, "I'm a
   (Mumble.) green ghost and I'm gonna eat ya'." And so, he called his mama,
   and she went in his room, and then she heard it too. And she . . . and then he
   said, "I'm a ghost and I'm about . . . I'm gonna eat you." . . . He didn't say, "I'm a
   ghost." I just remembered, he said, "I'm gonna eat ya." And then his dad came
   in, and he heard it too. And then he said, "I'm gonna eat ya'" And then they
   opened the closet, and it was his little brother eating his boogers.[6]

(JS) Aww!

(Group shouting.) I got one! I'll tell you one! I'm going next! (Indecipherable
   comments.)

(JS) What?

(Boy)

Girls eat their poo
What does it taste like?

(A chorus of screams from the girls.)

(JS) OK.

(Boy) I got something.

(JS) Go.

(White boy) It's a ghost story. Uh, there were two brothers and . . . and their
   . . . uh . . . wives kicked them out of the house. And they went to a hotel,
   and they said . . . and one of them said, "Can I have a room?" Then he goes,
   "There's a ghost in the bathroom." They go, "Oh, I'm not afraid of no ghost."
   And they go in, and they sleep and they go . . . and they hear, "I've got ya and
   I'm gonna eat ya." (The girls chime in on this line.) And then . . . and then they
   jump up . . . they jump out of the window, and then his brother comes and
   says—um, "Can I have a room? 'Cause, uh, 'cause his (MY—someone corrects
   him.) wife kicked me (HIM—someone shouts.) out. And—um—yeah—but

one man already—uh—killed hisself out—jumpin' out the window because
a ghost, there is a ghost in there. He says, "Oh, I'm not afraid of no ghost."
And when he goes to bed it goes (Chorus of all the group.) "I've got you and
I'm gonna eat ya," and he jumps out the window. Then . . . and then . . . and
a smart one comes and says, "Can I have a room?" And she says, "No, I'm not
afraid of no ghost." And then he goes in, and he says, "I've gotcha and I'm
gonna eat ya.'" So, he goes hides in the closet, and it's a little boy sayin' it.[7]

By this time my head is spinning trying to follow that last joke. The boys are
shouting, "I know a ghost story!" "I have a story!" "I got the best story!"

(JS) OK. Just a minute—I'll get your one.

(The same boy who stumbled through the last joke.) I have a . . . I have a . . . um
. . . these two jokes.

(JS) OK when you think about it, you get to tell it. *He's* gonna tell one in the
meantime.

(New white boy) OK. There's two brothers, two sisters, a mom, a dad, and a baby
and they forgot the baby's (Mumble.).

(JS) The WHAT?

(Boy) They forgot the baby's Pampers, and then they were drivin' to go to their
new house, and then the first brother went in, and the other brother was already—and he said, "I'm the ghost of the (Mumble.)."

(JS) He said what?

(Boy) I'm the ghost of the big black guy. So, the other brother ran out, and then
the sister came in, and she said, "I'm the ghost of the big black guy." And the
brother that had scared the other brother ran out. And then the other sister
came in, and she said, "I'm the ghost of the big black guy." So . . . um . . . the
other sister . . . so then the mom came in, and she said, "I'm the ghost of the
big black guy." And the mom ran out, and the dad walked out of the house,
and then the baby went out. And then the real ghost of the big black guy
said, "I'm the ghost of the big black guy." And she said . . . and the baby said,
"I'll give you another black eye if you don't give me my Pampers." (Giggles.)

I was surprised that the children let this story go by without any interruption or
heckling. I think it was because several of their mouths were repeating the
line "I'm the ghost of the big black guy," every time it was said.[8]

(JS) OK. What?

(Boy) If you don't give me my Pampers.

(JS) (I turn to a large boy waving his hand, and jumping up and down.) All right,
tell me a joke.

(Boy) Once there was this boy named Texas, and then this little boy . . . he was
runnin' to the store, and this little boy said, "Tell me who you are, and I will

send you to the teacher." And he said, "Texas." So, he told him . . . he told his
teacher, and the teacher said, "If you don't tell me your real name, I'll send
you to the principal." So, he said, "Texas." And she sent him home. And then
when he was walkin' home, this guy said, "If you don't tell me your name, I'll
kill you." And then he said, "Texas." And then the whole group came by, and
then one of the guys stuck a knife in him. And then the leader said, "Where's
my knife?" And they said, "Deep down in the heart of Texas."

(JS) Aw aw aw aw OK.

The boys are climbing all over one another trying to get a chance to speak, so I
pick the nearest one.

(JS) All right—very good. (I point at the boy.)

(Boy) I have something—it's a joke. There was three boys, and they were Crazy,
Shut Up, and Stupid and . . .

(JS) They were Crazy, Shut Up, and Stupid?

(Boy) Yeah—Crazy got lost, so—um—then there's—no, wait . . . Crazy got lost
in the forest, so then they were walkin' through the forest . . . um . . . Shut Up
and Stupid . . . um . . . Stupid. So *Stupid* got lost, and then Shut Up went to the
police, and then he said . . . he said, "My two friends Crazy and—um—Stupid
got lost." And then he said, "Well, what's your name?" and then he said, "Shut
Up." And he said, "What's your name?" And he said, "Shut Up." And they kept
on, and he kept on asking the name, and he kept on saying, "Shut Up," 'til he
never shut up, and the policeman didn't understand.[9]

(JS) OK. I gotcha.

(The lead boy edges closer.) I got one.

(JS) You got one too?

(Boy) (He is another white second grader, and he tells the joke in a manic rush.)
It's a Boudreaux and Thibodeaux joke. Boudreaux bought a helicopter, and
Thibodeaux said, "I could drive. I could fly it." He goes, "No, you gonna crash
it, 'cause you crash everything else I got. You even crash my other helicopter."
And he goes, "I promise, I'm not gonna crash it." And he goes, and he's flying
it, and he goes, "I'm not gonna get caught—I'm wearing one hundred pairs
. . . I'm wearing one hundred pairs of pants." And, he gets hot up there, and he
goes . . . and it was cloudy, and the airplane was carrying him so he wouldn't
fall, and he was getting hot up here, and, and, he turns that big propeller at
the top off . . . on . . . and it chopped the ropes, and it fly, and it go run into
. . . and he turnin' it off, and he comes down, and he turnin' it back on, and
he landin' on top of that airplane, and he's goin' in the airplane say we lost,
and the airplane lifts up in the air, and then he sees that helicopter, and goes

AAGGGGH! He jump out there, and the helicopter drops the airplane, and the airplane makes a safe landing, and Boudreaux says, "I'm getting so cold I'm gonna turn this thing off immediately." And he turns it off, and right whenever he said that, and he came all the way down, and he crashed, and he goes, "Boudreaux, I crashed it. What should I do?" "You crashed it? You said you wouldn't crash it, Boy! I'll kill you!"
(Giggles from the group.)[10]

To my surprise, no one kibitzed on this rambling joke. Perhaps that was because it was told at such a speed that no one could have interspersed even one comment. But maybe it was because the boy who told it was a leader in the group and no one dared to interrupt him. Whatever the reason, the other second graders listened attentively and laughed at the correct moment.

The time was over for the second graders, and a couple of white fourth graders came in to be recorded.

(JS) Fourth graders? OK. Fourth graders—What's your name?
(Boys) Luke, Michael.
(JS) Can you sing any songs? Songs that you sing on the playground?
(Boys whisper between themselves.) We know lots of jokes.
(Boy) Boudreaux and Thibodeaux worked at the airport and they—uh—went to a plane, and they found this thing that said, "Plane fuel." So, then they said, "What is plane fuel?" Then they smelt it. They said, "This smells just like that red wine we drink." So, they go home to drink it. They put it in a bottle. And then ... um ... uh ... at the end they, they go say—Boudreaux calls Thibodeaux said, "You drank that wine yet?" He said, "No, just about to drink it." He said, "Well, don't—it gives you gas." He said, "How much gas?" Said, "A whole bunch. I'm calling you from San Antonio."

This is the difference between logical order at the fourth-grade level, and logical order for a second grader. By the fourth grade, the boy's story is organized and well ordered. The telling is a bit too staccato, but the idea is fully developed.
—*St. Genevieve School, 2nd-, 3rd-, and 4th-grade white boys and girls, Lafayette, La.*

Following are more jokes told by another fourth-grade boy. These all were learned from schoolmates in middle school at Holy Cross High School in Arabi, Louisiana (1981). The speaker was white and nine years old.

(JS) Jokes?

(Boy) Once there were these three English people. They were captured in Africa. And of course, they were kept by an Indian tribe there. And the tribe says, "OK. You can get two choices, death, or boola boola. The first says, "I don't like death. I'll take boola boola." OK, so they tie him down on the ground. They start putting their weenie in his behind. He is screaming, "Agh! Agh!!" And he is bleeding, and getting hemorrhoids, everything. So, the second says, "I don't like death. I'll take boola boola." And they stick him with a spear. And the third guy says, "I don't like boola boola. I'll take death." So, the tribe says, "OK men. Death by boola boola!" Hee hee—get it?

(JS) Yes.

(Boy) There's this little boy named Johnny. And the teacher says, "OK. We gonna go through the alphabet, and for each letter I'm gonna call on somebody to say a word. She says, "A." Johnny raises his hand. "OK Johnny." And he says, "ASS—Big fat ass as big as four feet wide." So, she does not call on Johnny for a while. She says, "B." And another boy says, "Boy." And she says, "C." And another boy says "Cat—as in kitty cat." So, she gets to "R," and she figures Johnny can't say anything bad about "R," so she calls on Johnny. He says, "RAT—big fucking rat with a dick two feet wide!"

(JS) Aha. Next joke?

(Boy) Yeah. So, there's this guy, and he goes into a bar, and the waitress is fine, really beautiful. And he says to the bartender, "Bartender, give me a beer." He gives him a beer, and a frog comes out of his pocket and, SWOOP! That's the end of the beer. Then he says, "Give me another one." And SWOOP! The same thing happens. The frog jumps out of his pocket, drinks the beer. This happens again, and the waitress says, "Man, that's neat. How'd you teach him to do that?" The guy says, "Oh, you think that's cool? There's something else he can do. He can lick pussy like something you never seen." And he says, "OK you meet me at ten o'clock tonight, and I'll show you how it's done." So, he goes where the girl lives, and he takes off all her clothes, and he lays her down, and he puts the frog in between her legs. He goes "Ribbit ribbit ribbit ribbit . . . OK Give him time. He has to get used to it." So, he goes "Ribbit ribbit ribbit ribbit ribbit." Then he sighs, and says, "OK but this is the last time I'm gonna show you how to do it."

This boy has reached the ability to tell a perfectly organized, logically sequential joke. The content is of a type that some readers might find reprehensible, but the delivery works well. I interviewed the same boy a few years later. By the eighth grade, this same student had moved on to:

(Boy) What is a ****** on a bicycle?

(JS) I don't know.

(Boy) A thief.

(Boy) How do you kill a black person?

(JS) I don't know—how?

(Boy) Shoot him in his radio. OK, here's a Polish joke. Why do you feed a Polock beans on Friday?

(JS) I don't know—why?

(Boy) So he can have a bubble bath on Saturday.[11]

(JS) OOoooh.

(Boy) OK. The foot and the penis were talking, and the foot goes, "You know my master's real mean. He puts me in socks and, you know, all this." And the, um, the penis goes, "Oh, that's nothing." And the foot goes, "And he puts me in a sneaker, you know, a real smelly one." The penis says, "Oh, that's nothing." And then foot says, "Then he ties me up real tight so it hurts." And the penis goes, "That's nothing. My master puts me into a rubber jacket and hides me in a black cave and makes me do push-ups 'til I throw up."

(JS) Awwww. That's awful.

(Boy) Wait, I got another one. Well, there's this baby-sitter, you know, who's a girl, and the parents are coming home?

(JS) Um hummm.

(Boy) And, you know, and the boy who is being baby-sit says, "Hey, do you want to play with my puppy?" And the girl goes, "Yeah, OK." And the boy does this. (Imitates undoing his fly.) And when the parents come home, they see cop cars and paramedics all around the house. And, you know, they ask the girl, "Hey, what happened?" And she goes, "I was playing with his puppy, and it spit in my face, so I bit its head off."

Then the boy sings a few songs he has learned from his eighth-grade friends:

Mr. Leaner had a ten-foot wiener
And he showed it to the lady next door.
She thought it was a snake
Hit it with a rake
Now it's five foot four.[12]

Jack and Jill ran up the hill
Each of 'em had a quarter
Jill came back with fifty cents
They went up for water?[13]

There was once a man from Crockett
He stuck his dick in a socket
His wife was a bitch
She turned on the switch
His dick came out like a rocket.

(I reach to turn off the tape recorder.)

(Boy) Oh wait—wait—I got more jokes—

(JS) Um—OK.

(Boy) These three guys walk in a whorehouse. Their names were Ben, James, and Scotty. Ben walks in, and he comes back out with a big smile on his face, and he says, "I went in, and they put a donut on my dick, and she ate it off." So, then, James walks in, and he comes back out, and he says, "The lady put a do- nut on my dick, and she ate it off." Then Scotty walks in, and from inside they heard the cry, "Break out the Cheerios!"

(The boy continues with) Ben, James, and Scotty are walking into this bar, and then there is a device for measuring the size of your dick. So, Ben goes in, and sticks it in, and it says six inches. James walks in, and sticks it in, and it says six inches. Scotty goes and sticks his in it, and it says three inches. And then he comes out, and they ask him what it said. He says, "Oh, mine said three inch- es. Boy, was I glad it was on a hard."

(I reach to turn off the tape recorder again.)

(The boy rushes on with.) All right—These three guys, Ben, James, and Scotty walk into a whorehouse. And Ben walks in, and walks out with a huge smile on his face. He says, "For five dollars, Boy, they put whipped cream on my dick, then she licked it off." Then James walks in, and ten minutes later he comes out, and he says, "For ten dollars, they put whipped cream, and nuts, and a cherry on top, and licked it all off." Then Scotty walks in with twenty dollars. He says, "They put whipped cream, nuts, a cherry, and some other stuff, and it looked so good I licked it off."

(The boy's final joke was political.)

Edwin Edwards, Buddy Roemer, and Jimmy Swaggart are in a boat. And Buddy Roemer jumps out the boat, and Edwin Edwards says, "Where you going?" And Buddy Roemer says, "I'm going to save Louisiana." And Edwin Edwards says, "Fuck Louisiana." And Jimmy Swaggart says, "Can I watch?"

—*Holy Cross Elementary white boy, Arabi, La.*

I never knew what a kid would say when he or she volunteered a joke, and I did not act as a censor. The next story came from an eighth-grade African American boy from Beauregard Junior High School in New Orleans. His teacher, also African American, was monitoring the session when the boy launched into this tale. I watched her become increasingly fidgety as the joke went on:

(Boy) There was this white boy walking through the project, and he had to use the bathroom. So, he goes up to this house and asks this boy, "Can I use your bathroom?" The boy goes, "Wait." And he goes upstairs and asks his mother, "There's this boy outside wants to use the bathroom, can he?" And since the boy was white, and the people was black, the mother goes, "No." So he goes, finds some black paint, and paints himself. He goes back. "Can I use the bathroom?" Kid goes, "Yeah, come on in." So, he goes up, and the maid sees him and says, "Bless my heart, bless my soul / Never see a ****** with a white ass hole."[14]

—*Beauregard Junior High School, 8th-grade African American boy, New Orleans*

In 1987 I spent two hours interviewing a Redeemer High School (New Orleans) ninth-grade class. The students knew me well because I was teaching most of them at the time. In the classroom were thirteen African American boys and girls and two white students, one boy and one girl. Most of the class arranged themselves into an audience. Four chose to speak.

(JS) Who wants to do a "Knock Knock"?
(Boy) I don't know any.
(JS) No "Knock Knock"? Oh, come on.
(Boy) What's a dog official at a wrestling match?
(JS) I don't know.
(Boy) A ruffaree.
(JS) A ruffaree! Oh no! Anybody got another one?
(Boy) Yes. Knock knock.
(JS) Awwww. Who's there?
(Boy) Orange
(JS) Orange who?
(Boy) Orange you glad I'm not saying orange again?
(Girl) You didn't?
(Boy) Not yet.
(Laughter and teasing.)

(Boy) Wait, wait . . . knock knock . . .

(Girl interrupts) I got one Miss Soileau . . . What did the Indian say when the dog fell off the hill?

(JS) I don't know. What did the Indian say?

(Girl) Dog gone.

(Lots of laughing and people saying "Knock knock" in the background.)

(Boy) Knock knock.

(JS) Who's there?

(Boy) Gray—knock knock.

(JS) Who's there?

(Boy) Blue (Somebody yells, "Blue who?" and others laugh.)

(Boy) Knock knock.

(JS) Who's there?

(Boy) Yellow.

(JS) Yellow who?

(Boy) Knock knock.

(JS) Who's there? (I'm laughing by now.)

(Boy) Orange.

(JS) Orange who?

(Boy) Orange you glad you're not another color?

(Students laugh, and point at him.)

(Boy) I got another one, nah. Knock knock.

(Somebody shouts, "Your Maw!")

(Girl shouts) "Can I say it?" "Can I say it?" "It's not a knock knock joke."

(JS) OK. Go 'head.

(Girl shouts) "There's this man . . . !" (And everybody immediately laughs. She says again) "There's this man, all right?" (And everybody says, "OK." So she continues . . .) There's this man, OK? And he walks into a bar, and there's this guy, and he was gay . . . OK? He was gay . . . (The group laughs, and says, "Uh huh" in encouragement.) And he says, "Can I have a beer?" And the bartender says, "Sorry, we don't serve your kind in here." So, he says, "Well, I'll go sit here all by myself." And the bar is real, real busy. And then a big truck driver comes in, and he is all sweaty, and he says, "Man, I'm so hot I can lick the sweat off a . . . a cow's nuts." And the gay guy goes, "Moo moo." (Group bursts into laughter, one student claps.)

(Boy) Ohhh, all right. Yup! We can say nasty jokes?

(JS) I'd rather not.

(Girl) We can't say nasty? All right.

(Boy) It's not nasty; it's just y'all heard it before.

(JS) All right.

(Boy) It's about the lady, um, that wanted her baby to be kind. And the doctor said, "Rub your stomach every day and say, "Kind." All right, so she went home, and she was pregnant, and so she rubbed her stomach every day and said, "Baby, be kind. Baby, be kind. Come on Baby, be kind." And after a year she went back to the same old doctor and said, "I been pregnant for a year, and I ain't had the baby yet." And the doctor listened to her stomach, and the baby said, "I'm so kind, you go first."

(Students laugh appreciatively.)

(Boy) I got one. I got one.

(JS) OK.

(Boy) There's this lady, and everywhere she go, people are, you know, movin' away from her. So, she go to the doctor, and the doctor told her, "Well," he couldn't find nothin' wrong with her. "Come back next Wednesday when the x-ray man here." So she came back, and he said, "Well, I found a cure" . . . No, that's right . . . he said, "I found out what was the matter with you."

(People laugh encouragingly.)

(Boy) And she said, "Well, what is it?" And he said, "You got bat." And she said, "What in the hell is that?" And he said, "Your breath smells exactly like gas from a bat."

(Class laughs uproariously.)

(JS) OK. I never heard *that* one before! Anybody got any more?

(Boy) Yeeeup. I got another one.

(The class laughs and points to the joke teller.)

(JS) I don't know. Another joke teller is on his way. (Another boy is elbowing his way to the front.) OK. You tell yours, and he will tell his.

(Boy) Oh, all right. They had this, uh, cucumber. They had this pickle, cucumber, and they had a pig . . .

(Another boy interrupts.) They had a WHAT?

(Boy) They had a cucumber . . .

(The class bursts into laughter.) A cucumber and a pig!!

(JS) (Laughing.) Come on. Come on, finish it up.

(Boy) Nah. They had a cucumber, a pickle, and a DICK. And the cucumber said, "When I grow up, I'm gonna be in a salad." And the pickle said, "When . . . (The class bursts out laughing, and interrupts.)

(Another boy) Come on, let him finish.

(By now, the whole assembly is laughing and coming up with alternate lines. The noise continues while the joke teller continues.)

(Boy) And the dick says, "When I grow up, they gonna put a bag on my head and put me in a dark cave, and make me do push-ups until I throw up."

(By now the class is completely out of control. They are laughing, repeating the last line, and falling all over each other giggling.)

(JS) OK. Who's got one?

(Same boy) I do. Now they had this dude, right? He was in school, right? And he was runnin' late for school, and he came in and, um, and the woman say, "Where were you?" And he says, "I was on top of Blueberry Hill." This other dude came in. The lady say, "Where were you?" He say . . . he say, "I was on top of Blueberry Hill." This girl came in. Say, "Now don't tell me you was on top of Blueberry Hill again." "No, I'm Blueberry Hill."

(Class laughs, but not as uproariously as they did for the "cucumber" joke, but boy chuckles at his own joke.)

(Cucumber joke teller.) I got another one.

(JS) Is it the same kind again?

(Boy) No, it is about a Coke bottle.

(JS) Oh, all right.

(Another boy) Oh, yeah. I know that one.

(Boy) There's a Coke bottle. And there's a Dr. Pepper. And the Dr. Pepper said, "What are you doing, Coke?" And the Dr. Pepper said, "I'm feeling me a Seven-Up."

(I must have looked baffled, because one girl speaks out.)

(Girl) Miss Soileau, you ain't get that? You ain't get that? Just you think about it. (The girl bursts out laughing.)

(The boy who told the joke sings.) I'm feeling Seven-Up, I'm feeling Seven-Up. You ain't get it? Think about it.

(JS) Oh, all right. (I am flustered because I really didn't get it!!)

(Girl) OK. All right, now think about it, Coke and Seven-Up was together, and they was holding something in they hand, and they ask Dr. Pepper what he doin,' and he say, "I'm feeling Seven-Up."

(JS) All right. All right. I got it. It takes me a looong time.

(Another child) Me too!

(Everybody laughs.)

(Boy) OK, all right, they had . . . they had this lady and, uh, they had this farm, and they had this man, that was a hiker, and he needed a place to stay overnight, so the man say, "Well, I'll, um, I'll let you stay in my barnyard as long as you don't have sex with my wife, 'cause I have to go to work on the farm in the morning."

(Second boy) Oh, yeah, I heard this one.

(Boy continues.) So he said, "All right." And the next morning the black man, he pulled down his pants, and nuttin' was wrong wit him. Oh yeah—and he was

all cut up. And then the white man did it, he pulled his pants down, and he
was all right, and he asked the black man, "Did you do it to my wife?" And he
said, "No, I didn't." And his tongue was all cut up.
(Everybody chuckles in an embarrassed way, not because of the joke, but because of the mangled telling.)
(JS) I think you missed half that joke, but OK, and that was just the last part.
(Tape off.)

The next day, April twenty-eighth (1987), I interviewed another group of
ninth-grade students at Redeemer High School. There were eleven students
in this class, and four African American boys and one African American girl
stepped forward to speak. The taping began with the girl telling a variant of
the "polite baby" joke.

(Girl) OK this lady went to the doctor, and she was pregnant, right?
(Boy) I don't know if it is recording.
(JS) Oh. No, I can hear it.
(Girl) OK. And she was pregnant, and the doctor, the lady, she wanted her baby
    to come out polite, and she wanted her baby to come out fast. So, doctor
    said for her to rub her stomach every hour and say, "Politeness." So, she was
    rubbing all these years, and the baby hasn't come out. So, she is eighty years
    now. And she went to the doctor's, and the doctor looked in there, and she
    got twins, right? So, the doctor said, "Now they still ain't comin' out." And he
    listened to them and he hear, "No, you go first. No, you go first." They was so
    polite. You get it?[15]
(The class giggles, and chuckles, and repeats the last line for a while.)
(JS) OK. I think we got an Ethiopian joke. Come on?
(Boy) What you got with a Ethiopian with a bush—a great big old bush?
(JS) I don't know.
(Boy) Mister Microphone.
(Class laughs.)
(JS) You got more Ethiopian jokes?
(Boy) What's the fastest thing in the world?
(JS) I don't know.
(Boy) An Ethiopian with a lunch check.
(JS) What's the fastest animal in the world?
(Boy) A cheetah!
(JS) It's an Ethiopian chicken.

(Class hardly responds. It seems it was unwise for me to volunteer a joke. One
    girl says, "What!" and there is a murmur of other comments, like, "He was
    afraid to get paint on his hands." "I got one." "I got one about the jumper.")

(JS) Oh, they got an Evel Knievel joke?

(Boy) Yeah!

(JS) What's the greatest trick Evel Knievel ever did?

((Boy) Yeah?

(JS) He rode through Ethiopia with a ham sandwich on his back.

(Boy) Yeah!

(Class laughs at this one. Class continues to talk among themselves. They wait
    for someone to step forward. Someone says something about "What kind of
    wood don't float?" "Natalie Wood." And the class laughs.)

(JS) OK class, there used to be some Michael Jackson jokes?

(Boy) Michael Jackson?

(JS) Yeah, do you know one?

(Boy) Awwwww girl. I can't remember them. I gotta think.

(JS) There was one about NASA. What does NASA mean?

(Boy) Need another seven astronauts.

(JS) What does FILA mean?

(Boy) FILA means "found in left Adidas." And Adidas means "All day I dream about
    sex."

(Class laughs among themselves, and throws lines around.)

(JS) What does Ford stand for?

(Boy) Oh, I know. I know that one.

(Girl) What *does* Ford stand for?

(JS) I don't know. You have to tell me.

(Boy) Oh, no, I can't say that one.

(JS) Oh?

(Boy) "Fucked over rebuilt Dodge."

(Girl) Fucked over rebuilt Dodge?

(Class "haw haws" like they do when there has been something forbidden said.)

(Girl) Can I tell you something about tennis?

(JS) Come over here.

(Girl) You not gonna fuss at me?

(JS) You come over here.

(Girl) OK they got . . . BK.

(Me mystified.) OK. I don't know what you're talking about. These are tennis shoes?

(Boy) Yeah.

(JS) Oh, my God.

(Class laughs and cackles.)
(Girl) And MBA means "many bodies against." Yep. And FILA means "Fags in LA."

The taping session ends with the class throwing out a jumble of lines that mock brand names.
— *Redeemer High School, African American 9th-grade boys and girls, New Orleans*

A few years earlier, in 1977, I interviewed a white student who was a boarder at Sacred Heart Academy, Grand Coteau, Louisiana.

(JS) What's your joke?
(Girl) How did the cupcake get pregnant?
(JS) How?
(Girl) It fell into a box of Dingdongs.
(JS) And how did the Dairy Queen get pregnant?
(Girl) How? She went to bed with the Burger King, and forgot to cover his Whopper.
(JS) OK. Tell me some more.
(Girl) Oh, yes, . . . um . . . this is a joke. Once there was two nuns, and they had to go out all day, and they really had to go to the bathroom. So, they go to the hotel room, and they never went to the bathroom, and they had to go real bad, 'cause they happened to have diarrhea. So, one of the nuns says, "All right, I know what I'll do. I'll go to the bathroom, and you take the sheet off the bed, and I'll go to the bathroom in the sheet." And the other one says, "All right." And she goes to the bathroom in the sheet, and rolls the sheet all up and throws it out the window. Well, there happens to be a man passing by who is blind, and so the sheet falls on him, and he starts fighting with the sheet, and he don't know what's going on—he's blind. So finally, he feels this yicky stuff, and he says, you know, he starts screaming and hollering, and later on when he tells this story, he told his friends, "You know, I scared the shit out of that ghost."
(JS) All right. You said something about an ant and a log?
(Girl) Oh, this is another bathroom joke. Um, there were these three ants, and they went to the bathroom to rest for the night, and one ant took the sink, and the other ant took the tub, and the other ant took the toilet. And the next morning the first ant said, "Oh, man, I really was comfortable. Nothing wrong with it at all." And the second ant, who was in the bathtub, said the same thing. Well, the third ant, who was in the toilet said, "Aw, just had the roughest night! All of a sudden these things fall down look like logs, and

then they have this gigantic rainstorm. If it wasn't for those logs I would have drowned."

(JS) That's the joke?

The student then begins a narrative of boarding school "pranking" behavior that is at least as old as the 1920s. The stories the girl relates were first told to me, almost verbatim, by my mother and her sisters, who all were boarding school students at Sacred Heart Academy in the early part of the twentieth century.

(Girl) (Giggles) That's it. All right—oh yeah, now this is a complicated joke, but first you have to go, and you set it up. Somebody goes into one of the rooms at school, and, you know, she's talking to somebody, and then another person walks in and says, "Listen, do you have something?" You know, like a pair of scissors or a pencil or a pen, or something like that, of mine? Like say, "Do you have a pencil of mine?" And the other person will say, "No I don't." And she'll whisper to somebody, and they'll say, "Oh, what's this I hear about your mother being a famous roller skater?" And then you put on a real serious face, and say very hurt, "That's not funny. My mother doesn't have any legs." And everybody feels embarrassed, and gets all squinched up. It usually works, but every now and then somebody catches on.

(JS) OK.

(Girl) Uh, this is a long one. It's a "little old lady" joke. Well, this is a long, complicated joke, and it's all . . . it goes like this:

Do you know the other day we went down to Ivy's. That's a little store near our school. We went to Ivy's about last year, I'd say, and while we were down there we met this little old lady. This is the weirdest thing that's ever happened to me. We met this old lady in the store. She just kept following us around, following us around. We just couldn't understand it. So, you know, one of us said, "Go ask this lady." "I'm not going to ask her—you go ask her." So finally, I went and asked her, you know, what—what—what it was that she liked so much about us. And she looked at us and she gave us this weird look, and says, "You look . . . y'all both look just like my long-lost daughters who died in a car accident two years ago." And, uh, we all said, "What a weird person." So we tried to avoid her the whole time we were in the store, and we don't buy too much, you know, just some nail polish, and some emery boards, and some remover, and a pair of stockings. And, you know, the lady, she just buys all this stuff. And we get, we get in front of her, and I forgot something. I don't know what it was—I think it was something to eat—and I had to go back and get it, so we let the lady through. And she turns around while the man is ringing up the groceries and asks my friend if she would please say goodbye to her, and kiss her, like—just like she was her mother, and it would be just like her daughters saying goodbye to her. So, my friend says, "Sure."—So she doesn't want to get in a fight with this weird person or anything—so I'm in the back getting my stuff, and I come back. The little old lady is going towards—out the door. We're by ourselves, and the man at the store says, "That's forty-two dollars." And we stare at him, and say, "That's not possible for just the few items we bought." He said, "Well—your mother told us—your mother told me to charge it to you." We said, "Well, wait a minute—we don't have a mother." And he just looked at us, and said, "Well, you just told your mother good-bye. You just waved good-bye to that lady, and kissed her, and said "Good-bye Mama," and all that." When he said that we didn't know what to do. And so my friend, she just runs out the door, and the only thing she could grab onto was her leg, and she pulls, and she pulls on it, just like I'm pulling yours.

(JS) Aha! (I chuckle.)

(Girl) We had two or three others just like that that ended the same way, but they are pretty much the same thing.

(JS) Do you remember the skating rink joke?

(Girl) It's pretty much the same thing, you know. Um . . . They're both about these two girls who go into a roller-skating rink—and somehow, they get into this fight with these two other girls—and they run into the bathroom, and they lock the doors, and just when they—and they climb out the window, and these two other girls start pulling on their legs, just like I'm pulling on your leg. They had two or three of them that ended like that.

(JS) Do you know any others?

(Girl) Uh huh—boob fights. I—they don't want us to do that too much this year at school, but, uh, last year we had boob fights. You'd run up and pinch somebody on the boob and say, "Boo beep!" or something like that. You know, something weird. You'd run by and go PINCH! And they used to have mass boob fights, and everybody would be running all over the place pinching everybody on the boob. Oh, it was hilarious. And they had one or two this year, but they weren't nothing like the ones from last year.

(JS) Did you say something about "lick 'em if you like 'em"?

(Girl) Oh, that's pretty much a last year thing, too. You'd walk up to somebody and go (licking sound) and lick 'em on the face or sumpin' and if you liked 'em a lot. And lots of people would walk around really wet. (Giggles) You know, with licks all over their face. It was real cruddy.

(JS) OK. Now tell me about some of the practical jokes you play on each other. You were telling me about short sheeting beds, and . . .

(Girl) Oh, yeah. We short sheet beds and ransack beds . . .

(JS) How do you do that?

(Girl) We just take a sheet and fold it over and make it look just like a normal bed, but when they get in, they can't.

(JS) Why? What do they do?

(Girl) Because we take a top sheet, and fold it over like was the top sheet and the bottom sheet . . . do you know what I mean? So, when they get in, there's no room for their legs.

(JS) Oh, in other words, you've got the bottom sheet, and you put it up so that it looks like two sheets, but it's really one turned up?

(Girl) No, you take your *top* sheet, then, you pull the top sheet up, and tuck it all around just like it was the bottom sheet over the bottom sheet . . .

(JS) Yeah?

(Girl) 'Cept you can't tell, and then you take the other sheet part of it . . . and you fix it like it's a top sheet, and you just make the whole bed up again so that that night when they get in, they can't.

(JS) Uh huh. (I am puzzled, because I have heard this explanation before from my mother, who used to gleefully recall "short sheeting" girls when she was at Sacred Heart Academy in the 1920s. I could never picture the exact ritual, and I have difficulty now.)

(Girl) (My informant sees my questioning face and continues.) "Cuz their legs don't go anywhere except right in the middle of the crease. There's no place to go. We did that for one girl, but she never did . . . she didn't find out for three or four days . . . she doesn't sleep in the sheets. She sleeps on top of her bed. (Giggles) We kept waiting for her to say something, and it was three days passed, and finally she says something. We said, "Why didn't you say something earlier?" "Oh, last night I decided to sleep in my sheets."

(JS) Why does she sleep on top of her bed?

(Girl) So she can sleep late, and she doesn't have to worry about making up her bed. A lot of people do that. You have to be at school for eight . . . All right now . . . ya see, we have to be at school for eight fifteen . . . and if you wake up at eight o'clock, you only have fifteen minutes to get dressed, eat, and everything. So, most of the time, you don't have enough time to make up your bed and clean up your room, so you clean up your room the night before. You can't sleep on the sheets, so you don't worry about it. You just get on top of your bed and cover up with your blankets and Sister will never know, if she, ya know, she can't tell if you're all covered up with a blanket.

Now this habit of sleeping on top of the already made bed makes sense to me. My roommate and I did that very thing in 1957 when we had to get up at eight, eat, and run to class for eight fifteen. However, during the one year I boarded at Academy of the Sacred Heart, no one pranked anyone by "short sheeting," or "boob fighting," so I was unfamiliar with those.

The Sacred Heart girl ended her recording with this rhyme:

> Excuse me please
> That was so rude
> That was not me
> That was my food
> It got so lonely down below
> It had to pop up and say hello. (Burp!)

And later, she added this Christmas Carol, which she wrote down for me at Christmas of 1978. I reproduce it as written:

> Hark the Herald Angels Shout,
> Three more days 'till we get out!
> Three more days 'till we are free,
> From this penitentiary.
> Grab your ball and grab your chain,
> Run like hell to the nearest (plane or train),
> Hark! The Herald Angels Shout!
> Three more days 'till we get out!
>
> Back to smoking; back to drinking,
> Back to sex and evil thinking
> No more pencils. No more books;
> No more teacher's dirty looks,
> Grab your ball and grab your chain;
> Run like hell to the nearest (plane or train)
> Hark! The Herald Angels Shout!
> Three more days 'till we get out!
> —*Academy of the Sacred Heart, 9th-grade white girl, Grand Coteau, La.*

This final section on jokes and pranks involves Ruthanna, the white Tulane freshman student from Cooperstown, New York, who, like the teenagers at St. Joan of Arc bingo babysitting session, was able to remember hours of "stuff." The taping gets started jerkily with:

(Ruthanna) OK. This is a good one. Why is a man . . . no, what is the difference . . .
  no, why does a man NOT want to be like an egg?

(JS) I don't know.

(Ruthanna) He only gets laid once. He only gets eaten once. And it takes fifteen
  minutes for him to get hard. And there was this one about Disneyland . . .

(JS) Oh, yeah?

(Ruthanna) Why did Disneyland close for a week? Because Cinderella was sitting
  on Pinocchio's face saying, "Lie to me. Lie to me!"

(JS) What is another one?

(Ruthanna) Why did Ronald McDonald get sent out of McDonaldland? Um, he
  got caught eating Wendy's hot and juicy. I got another one . . .

There were these two little ovaries. They're having a conversation. One little ova-
  ry says to the other, "Is it getting crowded in here?" The other says, No, why?"
  The first one says, "Well, there's two nuts pushing an organ in here."

(JS) OK. What's the next one? I gotta get 'em all.

(Ruthanna) OK. Now, it's Christmas Eve. Santa Claus comes down the chimney,
  and there's this lady waiting for him in her nightgown. She says, "Santa, I'd
  like you to stay a while." And Santa says, "Ho ho ho gotta go. Gotta make a delivery now." So, she tries again, "Santa, I'd really like you to stay a while." Santa
  says, "Ho ho ho gotta go. Gotta make a delivery now." So, she takes off her
  nightgown and lies down in the opening of the chimney and says, "No, Santa, I don't think you really understand. I want you to stay a while." And Santa
  says, "Hey hey hey gotta stay. Can't get up the chimney now."

  —*Ruthanna B., Freshman, Tulane University student, New Orleans*

Looking through my scraps filed in a manila envelope titled "Folklore notes,"
I came across these scribbled-on faded note cards:

From June 1978, told to me by my Italian American babysitter's 17-year-old son:

What did one wall say to the other wall? Meet you in the corner.

How many ***** does it take to rape a lady? Ten to hold her down, and one to
read the instructions.

If Mississippi let Missouri wear her New Jersey to the fair, what would Delaware?
I don't know, but Alaska.

How many ***** does it take to paint a house? 101—One to hold the paintbrush, and 100 to turn the house.

Why were the two strawberries crying? 'Cause their mama was in a jam.

What did one strawberry say to the other? If you wouldn't be so fresh, we wouldn't be in this jam.

What animal needs oil? A mouse—it is always squeaking.

How do you keep a herd of elephants from charging? You take away their credit cards.

What's black and white and red all over? Answer 1—a newspaper. Answer 2—A zebra with a rash. Answer 3—A nun that just got hit by a car. Answer 4—A skunk with a diaper rash.

When does a teacher wear sunglasses? When she has bright pupils.

Two ***** came off a banana boat. They wanted a car. They went to a Volkswagen dealer. They went for a ride. When they got back to the dealer, they looked in the front. "Hey, this car don't have no motor!" The other one looked in the back of it and said, "That's all right, It has a spare."

Three Americans in a pickup truck picked up a ****. Somebody sideswiped them and they went into a river. The three Americans survived, but the **** didn't. Why? He couldn't get the tailgate open.
—*Seventeen-year-old Italian American boy, Chalmette, La.*

Children's jokes, more than any other aspect of child lore, often make adults uncomfortable. It seems it is acceptable for a child to ask, "Why did the chicken cross the road?" But when a child jokes about sex, drugs, rock n' roll, or racism, frowns form on adult faces. I noticed that certain adults express shock that children find the same things amusing that lots of adults around them also find amusing.

Attaining the ability to tell a joke and have listeners hang on every word comes only to some, and only after much trial and error and persistence. A combination of word choices, logical delivery, and physical presentation are features of good joke tellers, and only a few achieve master–joke-teller status.

Conclusion

Stepping out of my role as teacher and assuming the role of interviewer taught me many things. For one, being an interviewer was not easy, and I saw, as indicated in the text, that I made many mistakes. Gradually, I learned that an interview succeeded best when I had a well-planned, but flexible, questionnaire at hand. Interviews went best when I spoke the least; when I simply urged those questioned along with minimal suggestions like, "That's good. And you, do *you* know one?" And, most important, I learned that interjecting my own stories or jokes into the narrative was unwise and tended to make the children uneasy.

I learned to allow the self-appointed leaders among the group of children to take over and manage the flow of talk. My recording sessions held in schools and on playgrounds became for many children the only instance they had ever encountered where an adult had shown the least interest in what they shared with their friends in their free time. Most volunteers proved eager to have their verbal art recorded.

And what did this "verbal art" consist of? Many collectors of child lore, from William Wells Newell to Peter and Iona Opie and from Roger Abrahams to Brian Sutton-Smith, have noted how conservative rhymes, songs, tag games, and counting-out rhymes, remain over the centuries. A look through the notes following the chapters on counting out and rhymes and songs shows how enduring certain elements of verbal formulas are. "Eenie Meenie Miney Moe" alone has been catalogued for at least two centuries. Girls have been recorded singing variations of "When I Was a Baby" from as early as 1894, and variations of it still remain a standard ring play song at recess.

I learned that popular songs, political rhymes, and parodies of commercials come and go. For a while, I found children singing adaptations of the hit song "Rockin' Robin," by Michael Jackson and the Jackson Five, in almost every collecting venue from 1972 to 1990. Now, one has to search the Internet and YouTube to encounter performances of children singing "Tweedle

tweedle dee / He rocks in the treetops . . ." Its popularity has dwindled. Yet, certain older songs persist on the playground. Girls clap hands to "Playmate, Come Out and Play With Me," and Girl Scouts strut their stuff to "Flamin' Mamie." There is no way to predict whether or not a popular song might become a much-performed speech play.

As I accumulated more and more lore, I asked myself a question other folklorists have posed to themselves. What should we call children as a group? Are they a "tribe"? Are they "little adults"? I turned for an answer to the writings of a folklorist I respect immensely, Iona Opie. I wondered how the Opies referred to children, and I found the answer in Iona Opie's final book-length publication, *The People in the Playground*. In the first three lines of her preface to *The People in the Playground*, Iona Opie states, "I tried to explain to the people in the playground why I turned up every week and wrote down whatever was happening. (They always call themselves 'people,' never 'children')."[1]

I wondered if the use of "people" was an English thing, since Iona and Peter Opie collected for the most part in England. I searched through my own transcripts, and there it was! I had recorded children saying, "You get some *people* together . . ." and "OK *people*, let's do this." Somehow it makes sense that when children get together in groups, they form their own rules of conduct. They police themselves and function as self-regulated units. They are a people.

I found that children tended to gather in gangs and cliques and to defend those units both verbally and physically. Lead boys might say something like, "C'mon, you guys!" or "We friends. Just us three." Lead girls often used hand signals to order their friends to make a circle for a ring game or put their hands up, palm to palm, to indicate the beginning of a handclap. A lead girl could rush forward at recess time, appropriate the jump rope, and then limit the number of participants in her jump rope line by waving her hand to govern the lineup of players.

I discovered that boys bunched together when delivering jokes or counting-out rhymes. They tended to touch and poke each other, laughing loudly to urge one another to speak. I found that when faced with a rival set of girls in a taping session, young boys often resorted to screeching, howling, huffing, and snorting to try to drown out the girls who were chanting their jump-rope rhymes or performing their handclaps. In more than one taping session, boys had to be sent out of the room because they were so disruptive.

For a little over fifty years, I have recorded children as they struggled to speak clearly, as they willingly attempted to convey to me what they played.

Some children spoke eloquently and in excellent, logical patterns even from the age of two or three. Others stuttered and wrestled with words, changing tenses, speaking in half-sentences, even when they were in the fifth or sixth grade. I watched their classmates correct their friend's mistakes, smoothly ironing out logical twists or supplying forgotten punch lines. Children, I learned, are quite good at teaching one another.

Child lore has passed into a new dimension with the introduction of the Internet, and other technological advances. By 2019, nearly all the verbal lore found in my collection appeared in some form or other on YouTube or other sources on the Internet. The childhood network, which used to involve passing on lore verbally, or by demonstration, is now much wider. Now anyone can look up a handclap game, watch it performed by two or more players on YouTube, and then, of course, read all the comments that follow the production.

One final note: I have heard people say again and again over the last few years that children do not play any more. I have heard people say that all children do is watch TV and doodle on their phones and computers. I have heard it said that children's folklore is dying out. Well, maybe not yet. I submit two items for the reader's perusal. My nine-year-old grandson, Max, came home from school a few days ago (2020) and said to me, "Grandma, I have something for you. WE made it up at school. We choose who is 'it' like this!"—He wrote it down:

> Enie—mienie—minie—moe
> Catch a tiger by the toe
> My mom said to pick the very best one
> And you are shurly not it.

Then he giggled and said, "And we made this up too."
He chanted:

> Fatty fatty two by four
> Can't get through the bathroom door.
> So, he did it on the floor,
> Licked it up and did some more.

(We don't say that where the teacher can hear us!)

So, in the end, I have learned that children will gladly share their lore with adults who are attentive. I have also learned that if we really want to know what the children say, it is best to listen closely while the children play.

Thank You Notes

First, thank you to the children whose voices are heard in the pages of this work. I feel I was privileged to be the person who recorded these talented entertainers. I believe that the preservation of the lore of children adds a level of appreciation for the music, poetry, and the spoken culture of south Louisiana. I was aided in this long-term study by the principals and teachers in schools, public and private, in south Louisiana. They allowed me to tape record students in classrooms and on playgrounds and encouraged students to participate in my taping sessions.

Second, thank you to the readers who have read this book, I hope the memories these children's words have evoked have filled you with nostalgia. I also realize that, for some, what the children say fills you with horror. In recording the words of children, I have chosen to report *all* that they said, without "cleaning it up." Children, I have learned over the years, listen and imitate, and say much the same things adults say.

Any other thank yous must go back in time more than fifty years. I am deeply indebted to many people. I begin with my parents, grandmothers, and fourteen aunts and uncles who all were funds of storytelling, jokes, pranks, rhymes, and games recalled from their childhoods. Next are notable teachers and principals who welcomed me into classrooms and schoolyards. Thanks to Mrs. Howard Samuel, of Baton Rouge, who handed me my first quality tape recorder and ushered me out to collect for the Bicentennial Commission of Baton Rouge. Special thanks to James Isenogle, who gave me my first grant to assemble a Cultural Resources Management Study for the Jean Lafitte National Park, and the Committee on Ethnicity in New Orleans (1980). Thanks to John Cooke of the University of New Orleans who secured a grant for Archeological and Cultural Research through "Perspectives on Ethnicity in New Orleans" (1980). I hope my writings meet the expectations of Dr. George Reinecke, Dr. Patricia Rickels, Dr. Marcia Gaudet, and Dr. Sylvia Iskander,

who read my scribblings, made excellent suggestions for improvement, cor-
rected my loose punctuation, and encouraged, encouraged, encouraged.

Thank you to Anne Rogers, for her careful editing of my writing in my
first book; Margaret H. Lovecraft, for her suggestion that I compile this set
of transcriptions; and Laura Westbrook for her comments and emendations.

Most of all, thanks to my children and grandchildren, who all have become
collectors and contributors—Ida Eve, Richard, Virginia, Monique, Mason,
Guillaume, Leyla, and Max.

Notes

Introduction

1. William Wells Newell, the founder of the American Folklore Society (1888), started children's folklore collecting off with a bang in the nineteenth century. His *Games and Songs of American Children* (1883), includes games and tunes with lyrics and was the first collection of folk rhymes and music of American children. Newell was also one of the first children's folklore collectors to assert, erroneously, that child lore had to be collected soon, because "The vine of oral tradition . . . is perishing at the roots." Across the Atlantic, Lady Alice B. Gomme produced her monumental, two volume *The Traditional Games of England, Scotland, and Ireland* in 1894 and 1898. Lady Gomme tapped into a network of mostly adult correspondents who supplied hundreds of games, songs, and rhymes they remembered from their childhoods. In the twentieth century, collectors such as Peter and Iona Opie, Brian Sutton-Smith, and Roger Abrahams, turned to the children themselves, tape recording much of their children's lore collecting. The Opies concentrated their questionnaires on schools and playgrounds of England, Scotland, and Ireland. Brian Sutton-Smith, a New Zealand–born psychologist and educator, explored children's games in New Zealand, as well as in the United States and other countries. Roger Abrahams was an American folklorist whose specific interests rested with collecting child lore and African American spoken events.

2. Elizabeth Tucker notes in her introduction to *Children's Folklore: A Handbook* that "Some children's folklore has circulated for centuries" and that "Internet technology offers just one of many expressions of the rich array of games, songs, rhymes, jokes, riddles, tales, legends, pranks, toys, and other amusements that comprise children's folklore" (1–2); see also Niall Ferguson, *The Square and the Tower: Networks and Power, from the Freemasons to Facebook*," for a fascinating discussion of the "less visible social networks that are the true drivers of change."

3. The names have been changed.

4. Tucker, 1.

5. Enwikipedia.org—Blind man's buff (Feb. 10, 2019) traces the game from Ancient Greece to modern Marco Polo played in the swimming pool. See also Brian Sutton-Smith, *The Games of New Zealand Children*, 129–32, for a discussion of "Knucklebones" as played by both European and Maori children in the nineteenth and twentieth centuries.

Chapter 1

1. The most comprehensive collection of children's counting-out formulas, *The Counting-Out Rhymes of Children*, was written in 1888 by Henry Carrington Bolton. Bolton compiled eight

hundred and seventy-seven counting-out rhymes in various languages and attempted to trace the historical background for many of them. Bolton believed that counting-out rhymes were used for divination and as a method of choosing victims for sacrifice. Much of his theory is no longer felt to be valid. Folklorists today seldom attempt to link child lore to mystical divination or witchcraft. Bolton's collection, however, even with its faults, remains a classic in children's folklore. It can be found online at archive.org. In 1980, ninety-two years after Bolton's work, Roger D. Abrahams and Lois Rankin published *Counting-Out Rhymes: A Dictionary*, which contains five hundred and eighty-two rhymes in the English language. It is a good source book for further study for anyone who finds counting-out rhymes of interest.

2. For a discussion of racist elements in children's counting-out rhymes, see Knapp, Mary and Herbert, *One Potato, Two Potato*, "Prejudices: Blacks" 190–98. The Knapps also compiled further reading references to "Prejudice: Blacks," *One Potato, Two Potato*, 232–33; see also Bolton, Henry Carrington, *The Counting-Out Rhymes of Children: Their Antiquity, Origin, and Wide Distribution: A Study in Folk-Lore*, 46–51. Bolton states, "Apparently the doggerel which is the favorite among American Children to-day is the senseless jingle:—Eeny, meeny, miny, mo / Catch a ****** by the toe! / If he hollers let him go! / Eeny, meeny, miny / mo. At all events this has actually been reported orally and by letters from the states of New Hampshire, Massachusetts, Connecticut, Rhode Island, New York, New Jersey, Pennsylvania, Maryland, Virginia, North Carolina, South Carolina, Florida, Illinois, Iowa, Nebraska, Minnesota, Wisconsin, Colorado, Missouri, Tennessee, Louisiana, Nevada, California, and Oregon, as well as Dakota Territory and Ontario, Canada (46). Bolton includes a section in "Rhymes and Doggerels" (103–6), "Eeney, meenie, mony, my," where he lists fifty-one variations of "Eeny, meenie, minie, moe." See also Sherman, Josepha, and W. T. K. Weisskopf, *Greasy Grimy Gopher Guts*, 114, 138–40; Bronner, Simon J., *American Children's Folklore*, 55; Abrahams, Roger D., and Lois Rankin, *Counting-Out Rhymes: A Dictionary*, 45–68. Abrahams and Rankin describe counting-out rhymes beginning "Eena, meena" to "Eeny, weeny" and include notes from every English-speaking land; Opie, Peter and Iona, *Children's Games in Street and Playground*, 36, 40–45; Sutton-Smith, Brian, *The Games of New Zealand Children*, 70; Newell, William Wells, *Games and Songs of American Children*, 199–200.

3. The taped interviews with schoolchildren from the New Orleans area were collected under the auspices of the Jean Lafitte National Historical Park and the National Park Service, and the Committee on Ethnicity in New Orleans and the Archaeological and Cultural Research Program, University of New Orleans.

4. Abrahams, Roger D., and Lois Rankin, eds., *Counting-Out Rhymes: A Dictionary*, 78–80; Opie, Peter and Iona, *Children's Games in Street and Playground*, 58, 59.

5. Peter and Iona Opie noted in the *The Lore and Language of School Children* (1959):

> The faithfulness with which one child after another sticks to the same formulas even of the most trivial nature is remarkable. A meaningless counting-out phrase such as "Pig snout, walk out," sometimes adapted to "Boy scout, walk out," or a tag for two balls like "Shirley Temple is a star, s-t-a-r," is apparently in use throughout England, Scotland, and Wales. (4)

6. Bolton (1888) 95, 98, 99, 102, 104, 109, 111, 115. Henry Carrington Bolton's *The Counting-Out Rhymes of Children: Their Antiquity, Origin, and Wide Distribution (1888)* . . . can be accessed at https://Archive.org/details/countingoutrhymeOObolt. The entire book is online; see also Abrahams, Roger D., and Lois Rankin, *Counting-Out Rhymes: A Dictionary*, 38–39, 343.

7. Abrahams, Roger D., *Counting-Out Rhymes: A Dictionary*, 120.

8. Soileau, Jeanne P., *Yo' Mama, Mary Mack, and Boudreaux and Thibodeaux*, 136; Sherman, Josepha, and T. K. F. Weisskopf, *Greasy Grimy Gopher Guts*, 91; Bronner, Simon J., *American Children's Folklore*, "Policeman, policeman / Do your duty," 72.

9. Soileau, Jeanne P., *Yo' Mama, Mary Mack, and Boudreaux and Thibodeaux*, 141.

10. Opie, Peter and Iona, *Children's Games in Street and Playground*, 54; Abrahams, Roger D., and Lois Rankin, eds. *Counting-Out Rhymes: A Dictionary*, 164–65 (with many references); Knapp, Mary and Herbert, *One Potato, Two Potato*, 25.

Chapter 2

1. Lady Alice B. Gomme devotes four pages to "Drop Handkerchief" in *Traditional Games of England, Scotland, and Ireland* Vol. 1. 109–12. The game appears again in Lady Gomme's *Traditional Games* Vol. 1 under the name "Lubin," 352–61. See also J. O. Halliwell Phillips, *Popular Rhymes and Nursery Tales (1849)*, 129, "Dancing Looby"; J. O. Halliwell-Phillips, *Nursery Rhymes of England (1886)*, "Now we dance looby looby," 190–91; Opie, Peter and Iona, *Children's Games in Street and Playground*, 198–202; Sutton-Smith, Brian, *The Games of New Zealand Children*, "Drop the Handkerchief," 20; Newell, William Wells, *Games and Songs of American Children*, 169.

2. Knapp, Mary and Herbert, *One Potato, Two Potato*, 147; Abrahams, Roger D., and Lois Rankin, *Counting-Out Rhymes: A Dictionary* (as a counting-rhyme), 147.

3. Opie, Iona and Peter, *The Singing Game*, "Okey Kokey," 391–98—with extensive notes; Newell, William Wells, *Games and Songs of American Children*, "Right Elbows In," 131; Sutton-Smith, Brian, *Games of New Zealand Children*, "Baloo Baloo Balight," 13.

4. Knapp, Mary and Herbert, *One Potato, Two Potato*, 132.

5. Bronner, Simon J., *American Children's Folklore*, "Punchanella," 58; Opie, Peter and Iona, *The Singing Game*, 25, 391, 412–13; Sutton-Smith, Brian, *The Games of New Zealand Children*, "Look who is here, Punchinello, funny fellow," 30.

6. https://en.wikipedia.org/wiki/Soul-Train. "Soul Train is an American music-dance television program which aired in syndication from October 2, 1971 to March 27, 2006. In its 35-year history, the show primarily featured performances by R&B, soul, dance/pop and hip-hop artists, although funk, jazz, disco and gospel artists also appeared. The series was created by Don Cornelius, who also served as its first host and executive producer." Web.

7. Knapp, Mary and Herbert. *One Potato, Two Potato*, for a discussion of "Rhymes about Orientals," 198–99; Sherman, Josepha, and T. K. F. Weisskopf, *Greasy Grimy Gopher Guts*, 92; Opie, Peter and Iona, *Lore and Language of Schoolchildren*, 22, 85, 94. On the playground at St. Genevieve (1940s) we jumped rope to "Ching Chong Chinaman / Eats dead rats / Swallows them down like gingersnaps."

8. Knapp, Mary and Herbert. *One Potato, Two Potato*, 127–28. The Knapps describe one variant of the game of "categories": "The players sit in a circle; they clap their hands on their thighs, twice; clap their hands together, twice; then snap their fingers, first those of one hand, then those of the other. Between the first finger-snap and the second, the person who begins names a category—usually cars, trees, or animals. The next player says the name of a member of the category beginning with the letter *a*. The next names one beginning with *b*, and so on, always between finger-snaps" (127).

9. Gomme Alice B. *Traditional Games of England, Scotland, and Ireland*, Vol. 2. 362—374. Lady Gomme included thirteen variations of "When I Was a Young Girl." She found it especially interesting and examined it extensively. Her words:

It will be seen, from the description of the way this game is played, that it consists of imitative actions of different events in life, or of actions imitating trades and occupations. It was probably at one time played by both girls and boys, young men and young women. . . . Young girl, sweetheart, or going courtin', marriage, birth of children, loss of baby and husband, widowhood, and the occupations of washing and cleaning, exactly sum up the principal and important events in many working women's lives—comprising, in fact, the whole. (372)

See also Mona Lisa Saloy, "Sidewalk Songs, Jump-Rope Rhymes, and Clap-Hand Games," 38–40; Newell, William Wells, *Games and Songs of American Children*, "When I was a Shoemaker," 88; Soileau, Jeanne P., *Yo' Mama, Mary Mack, and Boudreaux and Thibodeaux*, 64–70; Tucker, Elizabeth, *Children's Folklore: A Handbook*, 58; Rosen, Michael. *The Penguin Book of Childhood*, 191–92; Sutton-Smith, Brian. *The Games of New Zealand Children*, 19.

Chapter 3

1. I was one of those "working-class" children running the streets. My family moved to Lafayette, Louisiana, when I was four, but we returned to New Orleans to spend every birthday, wedding, funeral, and holiday with our relatives. We never missed Mardi Gras. My Grandmother Pitre lived on Banks Street in Mid-City, and it was the hub of visiting festivities. Whenever we arrived, everyone gathered at Grandma's house, and the children were ushered out to "go play."

2. When I was a third grader in Lafayette, Louisiana, in 1949, we also jumped rope to the word "Mississippi." We jumped hunched over on the letter "M"; straight up on the letter "I"; we said "crooked letter, crooked letter" for the "S S"; then crouched over for the "P P"; and finally, straight up tall for the final "I." See also Abrahams, Roger D., ed. *Jump-Rope Rhymes: A Dictionary*, 123; Knapp, Mary and Herbert, *One Potato, Two Potato*, 117–18 (with directions for play).

3. "I like coffee / I like tea / I like the boys / And the boys like me." This short, but memorable, verse appears again and again in my collection. My mother skipped to it in the 1920s at Crossman School in Mid-City, New Orleans. I skipped to it in the 1940s in Lafayette, Louisiana. I collected it from multiple sources in south Louisiana from the early 1970s to 2017. I entered "I like coffee / I like tea—children's rhyme" on the Internet search bar December 14, 2017, and at least fifteen sites discussed the jingle; some exploring it for a racist additional line I had never encountered—"I like coffee / I like tea / I like to sit on the black man's knee." YouTube.com features the doo-wop singing quartet, the Ink Spots, utilizing the first line in their song "Java Jive (I like coffee / I like tea) 1940. See also thechocolatetease.blogspot.com, where "I like coffee / I like tea," is listed among eleven other games played in Detroit, Michigan; Soileau, Jeanne, *Yo' Mama, Mary Mack, and Boudreaux and Thibodeaux*, 57–59; Knapp, Mary and Herbert, *One Potato, Two Potato*, 14; Opie, Peter and Iona, *Lore and Language of Schoolchildren*, 117, 121.

4. Opie, Peter and Iona, *The Oxford Dictionary of Nursery Rhymes*, 333–34; Halliwell-Phillips, J. O., *The Nursery Rhymes of England* (1886), 17; *One, Two, Buckle My Shoe* (1940), mystery novel by Agatha Christie.

5. Knapp, Mary and Herbert, *One Potato, Two Potato*, 117. I searched the Internet for "Policeman, Policeman do your duty" on December 15, 2017, and an interesting site came up: "The James T. Callow Computerized Folklore Archive: UDM Libraries / Instructional / Design Studio." Several variants of "Policeman, Policeman do your duty" listed as being heard or recorded in Detroit, Michigan.

6. Entered "Teddy Bear, Teddy Bear jump rope" into the search bar, and the Internet revealed seven sites listing "Teddy Bear, Teddy Bear" and "Ladybug." All sites, from "Canadian Children's Songs," to "Christian Home Education," utilized the refrain to instruct jumpers to follow the Teddy Bear's varied motions. See also Soileau, Jeanne, *Yo' Mama, Mary Mack, and Boudreaux and Thibodeaux*, 102–3; Bronner Simon, *American Children's Folklore*, 71; Knapp, Mary and Herbert, *One Potato, Two Potato*, 117; Abrahams, Roger D., ed. *Jump-Rope Rhymes: A Dictionary*, 186–89 (with copious notes).

7. For "Down in the valley where the green grass grows," see Gomme, Alice B., *The Traditional Games of England, Scotland, and Ireland*, Vol. 1, 99–100, and Vol. 2, 416–18. "Down in the valley" is one of many rhymes sung and chanted by twentieth-century children that appear in the works of Alice B. Gomme and other English collectors. See also Knapp, Mary and Herbert, *One Potato, Two Potato*, 116; Opie, Peter and Iona, *Lore and Language of Schoolchildren*, 364; Bronner, Simon, *American Children's Folklore*, 71; Abrahams, Roger D., ed. *Jump-Rope Rhymes: A Dictionary*, 40–43 (several variants with notes).

8. Tucker, Elizabeth, *Children's Folklore: A Handbook*, 57.

9. Opie, Peter and Iona, *Lore and Language of Schoolchildren*, under heading "Friendship and Fortune," 339.

10. This is another of the many jump-rope rhymes I remember from my own childhood. Wikipedia—"Pretty Little Dutch Girl" provides a lengthy article, including 1. History; 2. Story within the song; 3. Origins and distribution; and 4. Use in children's media. See also Bronner, Simon J., *American Children's Folklore*, 59–60 (as a handclap), 70 (as jump rope); Opie, Peter and Iona, *The Singing Game*, 450–52, with excellent notes; Abrahams, Roger D., ed. *Jump-Rope Rhymes: A Dictionary*, 70–71.

11. Bronner, Simon J., *American Children's Folklore*, 70; Opie, Peter and Iona, *Lore and Language of Schoolchildren*, 23; Abrahams, Roger, D., and Lois Rankin, *Counting-Out Rhymes: A Dictionary*, 134; Abrahams, Roger D., ed. *Jump-Rope Rhymes: A Dictionary*, 110–11 (with notes).

12. I was taught to play "Jacks" ("Knucklebones") by my grandmother. She had a soft leather bag with ten knucklebones of a sheep in it. She did not use a ball; instead, she threw one of the sheep bones up, picked up one bone off the table, then caught the bone she had thrown in the air. She then picked up two, then three, etc. She would not play on the floor, as we did at school. My grandmother said in French, "Young ladies do NOT sit on the floor!" Learning from her, I got pretty good at playing on a tabletop without a ball. See also the painting "Children's Games," by Pieter Bruegel the Elder (1560), where in the lower, right-hand corner, two girls play with knucklebones.

Chapter 4

1. The first part of the hand-games collection, those from Baton Rouge and those from Camp Ruth Lee, were recorded under the aegis of the Bicentennial Project, a folklore enterprise headed by Mrs. Howard Samuel (now deceased). I met Mrs. Samuel while I was teaching at Louisiana State University in 1973, when I answered an ad asking for volunteers to interview Baton Rouge businessmen for the bicentennial celebration of the United States. Mrs. Samuel gave me my first tape recorder and instructed me how to use it. She sent me out to gather the reminiscences of prominent businessmen from Baton Rouge. I interviewed two businessmen, and found myself only mildly interested in interviewing them. Every day, I passed public schools on my way to work at Louisiana State University and saw the children playing at handclaps and ring games on the grounds. They looked as though they were having as much fun as the

children I had observed playing in New Orleans when I taught there. I asked Mrs. Samuel if I could collect children's schoolyard lore instead of gathering the memories of businessmen. She looked at me quizzically at first and then agreed. Thus began my nearly fifty-year collection of schoolyard verbal lore.

2. "Money Honey" is a popular song from the 1950s. Two notable versions exist on YouTube. There is Sheila Gernon—"Money Honey" Cool Records (403 No. 4th Street, Harrison, N.J.) 2, 615 views as of January 21, 2019; and Elvis Presley—" Elvis Presley - Money Honey - 1956," 399,479 views as of January 21, 2019. A note following the Elvis Presley video is written by Cesare Vesdani, November 4, 2014. Vesdani states, "Money Honey" written by Jesse Stone, was released in September 1953 by Clyde McPhatter backed for the first time by the newly formed Drifters . . ."

3. "Apple on a stick," Tucker, Elizabeth, *Children's Folklore: A Handbook*, 57, with notes on other collected versions, and possible meaning; Abrahams, Roger D., *Jump-Rope Rhymes: A Dictionary*, 11.

4. Opie, Peter and Iona, *The Singing Game*, 445, 467–68.

5. "Long-legged spider"—Opie, Peter and Iona, *The Singing Game*, 456–57, with notes; Knapp, Mary and Herbert, *One Potato, Two Potato*, 129; Langstaff, John and Carol, *Shimmy Shimmy Coke-Ca-Pop*, 76.

6. Wikipedia.org (12 / 15 / 2017) said of "Pretty Little Dutch Girl": "Pretty Little Dutch Girl is a children's nursery rhyme, clapping game, and jump-rope rhyme. It has a Roud Folk Song Index number of 12986." Wikipedia supplied eleven variations of "Little Dutch Girl" gathered from the United States and England. In these variants, there was incorporation of lines from other handclaps, and the origin of the boyfriend changed all the time. Wikipedia also noted that the author was unknown and that the song seemed to have appeared in 1940. See also Opie, Peter and Iona, *The Singing Game*, 450–52; Bronner, Simon J., *American Children's Folklore*, 59–60; Knapp, Mary and Herbert, *One Potato, Two Potato*, 115 as jump rope rhyme, and 123, where transferred phrases are discussed; Abrahams, Roger D., *Jump-Rope Rhymes: A Dictionary*, 69 (as jump rope); Winslow, David J., "An Annotated Collection of Children's Lore: Part Three of Oral Tradition among Children in Central New York State," *Keystone Folklore Quarterly*, Vol. II (Fall) 1966, 155, 160; Wikipedia.org (12/17/2017) "I Am a Pretty Little Dutch Girl" nine variations listed.

7. Sherman, Josepha, and T. K. F. Weisskopf, *Greasy Grimy Gopher Guts*, "Ms. Lucy had a steamboat . . ." 33–35; Bronner, Simon, *American Children's Folklore*, "Lulu had a steamboat," 61; Soileau, Jeanne P., *Yo' Mama, Mary Mack, and Boudreaux and Thibodeaux*, 141.

8. "Mary and John sitting in a tree . . ." Sherman, Josepha, and T. K. F. Weisskopf, *Greasy Grimy Gopher Guts*, 41–42; Knapp, Mary and Herbert, *One Potato, Two Potato*, 87–88.

9. "Miss Mary Mack" . . . Langstaff, John and Carol, *Shimmy Shimmy Coke-Ca-Pop!*, "Old Lady Mac," 80–81; Bronner, Simon J., *American Children's Folklore*, "Oh Mary Mack Mack Mack," 65; Knapp, Mary and Herbert, *One Potato, Two Potato*, 136–37; Opie, Peter and Iona, *The Singing Game*, 469–70; Soileau, Jeanne P., *Yo' Mama, Mary Mack, and Boudreaux and Thibodeaux*, 133, 169; Sherman, Josepha, and T. K. F. Weisskopf, *Greasy Grimy Gopher Guts*, 87; Gaunt, Kyra, *The Games Black Girls Play*, 20–21, 63–68.

10. Undoubtedly one of the most commonly repeated handclaps of my collection, I feel that a bit of history of "Miss Suzy" is helpful. Peter and Iona Opie, in *The Singing Game* (1985), researched the origin of this ditty, and tell us:

The first eight lines can be recognized as part of a bawdy song about a whore called Lulu, who had a baby which "was an awful shock, She couldn't call it Lulu' cos, The bastard had a cock." In the 1920s Lulu and her baby featured in one of the joke verses popular at the time, in which the rude words are never actually said; it was sung to the 'Soldiers' Chorus' from Gounod's *Faust*:

> Lulu had a baby, she called it Sunny Jim,
> She took it the bathroom to see if it could swim.
> It swam to the bottom, it swam to the top,
> Lulu got excited and grabbed it by the—
> Cocktails, ginger ale, two and six a glass . . . (473)

The Opies, who were British, then traced the game rhyme's appearance in the United States to a jump-rope verse recorded in 1920 in West Medford, Massachusetts:

> In goes the doctor, in goes the nurse,
> In goes the lady with the big black purse;
> Out goes the doctor, out goes the nurse,
> Out goes the lady in the big black hearse. (473)

At some time in its history, a clever child poet added the "alligator purse," thus making this little song one of the most widely distributed of all handclaps.

Also in *The Singing Game*, the Opies recorded it as "The Johnsons Had a Baby." While the first line is different, the body of the chant uses "Tiny Tim," and the ubiquitous "lady with the alligator purse," 472–73. See also Knapp, Mary and Herbert, *One Potato, Two Potato*, 113; Opie, Peter and Iona, *Lore and Language of Schoolchildren*, 34; Wikipedia.org (12/17/2017) "Miss Lucy had a baby" for the rhyme's history in America; Sherman, Josepha, and T. K. F. Weisskopf, *Greasy Grimy Gopher Guts*, 39, 40; Langstaff, John and Carol, *Shimmy, Shimmy Coke-Ca-Pop*, 54; Abrahams, Roger D., *Jump-Rope Rhymes: A Dictionary*, 126–2,8 where references are given for "The lady with the alligator purse."

11. I read this collection of hand games to Francis A. de Caro, who was teaching folklore at Louisiana State University in the early 1970s. When I sang "Rubber Dolly," he asked me if I would like to hear a recording of a song by the same name. I said yes, and a few days later, he brought in "Rubber Dolly Rag," recorded by Uncle Bud Landress and the Georgia Yellow Hammers. It was available on Old Timey LP 101, "Old-Time Southern Dance Music: The String Bands," Vol. 2. The record cover had no information on the song, but the tune Bud Landress sang was essentially the same as the one sung by the African American girls at McKinley Junior High, University Terrace, and Camp Ruth Lee.

"Rubber Dolly" appears on YouTube.com. The first video I viewed was by the Belle Stars. It was titled "The Clapping Song, 1982," and as of August 12, 2017, it had 402, 737 views. Sung by four white girls and one black singer, it came off as bland. There was no handclapping, though all the words were there. A further search turned up a video by Shirley Ellis, "The Clapping Song" (Shivaree-March 20, 1965). Shirley Ellis supplies a livelier version, and she and her background singers demonstrate hand-clapping motions (159,985 views August 21, 2017). An included note about Shirley Ellis written July 8, 2014, states, "New York vocalist and composer Shirley Ellis was in the Metronomes before earning fame as co-composer and performer of some enjoyable soul novelty tunes in the mid-'60s. These included the Top Ten R&B hits 'The Nitty Gritty' and 'The Name Game.' 'The Name Game' was co-written with her manager and husband Lincoln Chase, and peaked at number 4 R&B and number Three (sic) pop in 1965. She and Chase also collaborated on the follow-up, 'The Clapping Song (Clap Pat Clap Slap),' which reached number 16 R&B, but also represented the end of the creative line for the trend . . ." Ron Wynn, Rovi.

12. Wikipedia.org (12/12/2017) tells us "(Oh Baby Mine) I Get So Lonely" is a popular song. It was written by Pat Ballard and was published in 1953. It was recorded by a number of artists, including Bing Crosby accompanied by Guy Lombardo and his Royal Canadians (1954). The biggest hit version was done by the Four Knights, on Capitol Records in 1954." The "biggest hit version" can be found on YouTube.com—The Four Knights—Oh Baby Mine (I Get So Lonely).

13. I Googled "Children's song "Twilight Forever." Under the heading Google answers: answers.google.com/answersthreadview?id=235768, several variants of the song "Twilight Forever" were given. One post recalled the hand motions used by players in Brooklyn (12/17/2017). See also Knapp, Mary and Herbert, *One Potato, Two Potato*, 134–36; Bronner, Simon J., *American Children's Folklore*, 63–65.

14. "Crazy old man from China"—pancocojams.blogspot.com (9/3/2013) "Racially Derogatory Variants of Old Shoe Boots and Leggings," ed. Azizi Powell. It states:

"In 2004, I started a Mudcat [folk music] discussion thread about "Songs Your Parents Didn't Allow." http://mudcat.org/thread.cfm?threadid=73889. The first song that I posted to that thread was one whose title I knew as "The Little Baldheaded Chinese." Shortly after I posted the lyrics to that song, Joybell, a commentator from Australia, indicated that the song I had posted was a variant of song "Old Shoe Boots And Leggings." Prior to reading that comment, I had never heard of that song by that title, or any other title.

Here's the lyrics of that song which I had somehow learned as a child but definitely not from my parents:

> My mother she told me to open the door.
> The little bald headed Chinese nese nese
> I opened the door.
> He fell on the floor.
> The little bald-headed Chinese nese nese . . .

This example of the "Crazy Old Man From China" is then compared with the lyrics from an "Old Shoe Boots and Leggings" variation:

"With His Old Gray Beard a Shining" Cat. #0217 (MFH #687)—As sung by Mrs. Laura McDonald and Reba Glaze, Springdale, Arkansas, on July 23, 1958:

> There was an old man, lived over th lea
> I hope, but I won't have 'im
> Came over th lea, a courtin with me
> With his old gray beard a shining . . .

15. "Istrouma" is the local Indian word for "Red Stick." The French explorers translated it to "Baton Rouge." The mascot of the Istrouma football team is an Indian warrior chief.

16. Opie, Peter and Iona, *The Singing Game*, "There's a big fat teacher," 478; Soileau, Jeanne P., *Yo' Mama, Mary Mack, and Boudreaux and Thibodeaux*, 137.

17. Soileau, Jeanne P., *Yo' Mama, Mary Mack, and Boudreaux and Thibodeaux*, note, 180; Knapp, Mary and Herbert, *One Potato, Two Potato*, 163–64; Bronner, Simon J., *American Children's Folklore*, 109–10; Sherman, Josepha, and T. K. F. Weisskopf, *Greasy Grimy Gopher Guts*, 151–53.

18. Soileau, Jeanne P., *Yo' Mama, Mary Mack, and Boudreaux and Thibodeaux*, 172; Bronner, Simon J., *American Children's Folklore*, "My mother gave me a nickel," 62; Knapp, Mary and Herbert, *One Potato, Two Potato*, 115.

19. Soileau, Jeanne P., *Yo' Mama, Mary Mack, and Boudreaux and Thibodeaux*, "Tweedle tweedle dee," "Rockin' Robin," 94–105.

20. "Crazy old man from China"—China and Chinamen appear often in children's verse. My friends and I jumped rope to "Ching chong Chinaman / Eats dead rats / Swallows them down like gingersnaps" (1940s). See also Knapp, Mary and Herbert, *One Potato, Two Potato*, "Rhymes about Orientals" under "prejudice against," 198–200, and 118–19 "Chinese Jump-rope" with illustrations; Opie, Peter and Iona, *Lore and Language of Schoolchildren*, "Chinese torture," 202–3; Langstaff, John and Carol, *Shimmy Shimmy Coke-Ca-Pop!*, 55.

21. "3-6-9 the goose drank wine." Peter and Iona Opie, in *The Singing Game*, note that, "The clapping rhyme was known in Britain in the late 1950s, and in America as a 'narrative' rhyme in the 1930s, when it began 'Once upon a time':

> Once upon a time, the goose drank wine,
> The monkey chewed tobacco on the street car line; . . . 449–50.

Soileau, Jeanne P., *Yo' Mama, Mary Mack, and Boudreaux and Thibodeaux*, 158; Abrahams, Roger D., *Jump-Rope Rhymes: A Dictionary*, 145.

22. Knapp, Mary and Herbert, *One Potato, Two Potato*, 180; Abrahams, Roger D., *Jump-Rope Rhymes: A Dictionary*, 98.

23. Opie, Peter and Iona, *The Singing Game*, 476–77; Knapp, Mary and Herbert, *One Potato, Two Potato*, 128–29.

24. Peter and Iona Opie, in their introduction to *The Singing Game*, comment on the tendency children have to mix and mingle parts of one game with another: "Tattered lines from old game-songs combine to make patchwork songs of strange beauty. Actions change, and are transferred from one game to another. The stronger and simpler actions and tunes oust the weaker," 29.

25. Langstaff, John and Carol, *Shimmy Shimmy Coke-Ca-Pop*, 78.

26. Wikipedia.org "Playmates Song" lists several versions of the song. See also YouTube "Playmates Song by the Fontane Sisters (1955), uploaded August 2, 2011. [45,401 views as of Dec. 17, 2019]; Opie, Peter and Iona, *The Singing Game*, 474–75; Knapp, Mary and Herbert, *One Potato, Two Potato*, 131; Soileau, Jeanne P., *Yo' Mama, Mary Mack, and Boudreaux and Thibodeaux*, 168; Bronner, Simon J., *American Children's Folklore*, 61–62.

27. Wikipedia.org (12/16/2017)—"Take Me out to the Ball Game" is a 1908 Tin Pan Alley song by Jack Norworth and Albert Von Tilzer . . . The song's chorus is traditionally sung during the middle of the seventh inning of a baseball game." Under *History of the Song*, Wikipedia also states, "The most famous recording of the song was credited to 'Billy Murray and the Haydn Quartet,' even though Murray did not sing in it. The confusion, nonetheless, is so pervasive that, when 'Take Me Out to the Ball Game' was selected by the National Endowment for the Arts and the Recording Industry Association of America as one of the 365 top 'Songs of the Century,' the song was credited to Billy Murray, implying his recording of it as having received the most votes among songs from the first decade."

28. For two quite different renditions of "Under the Bamboo Tree," see YouTube.com, and view "Under the Bamboo Tree" with Judy Garland." This features Judy Garland and Margaret O'Brien singing and dancing in the movie "Meet Me in St. Louis" (1944). For a much more nostalgic trip (at least for me) go to YouTube.com "Under the Bamboo Tree" Lyrics by the Vaudeville star Marie Cahill (Song by Bob Cole and J. Rosamund Johnson.) This recording sung in Ms. Cahill's lovely soprano voice on a somewhat scratchy disk, had only 7,045 views when I listened to it August 14, 2017. It should be heard more! The writer of the song, J. Rosamund Johnson (August 11, 1873–November 11, 1954) was an African American composer and singer during the Harlem Renaissance. He composed "Lift Every Voice and Sing," what has come to be known as the "Negro National Anthem." For more information on J. Rosamund Johnson, see Wikipedia.com.

The phrase "Under the bamboo tree" is one of those lines one does not readily forget. I remember hearing, early one morning, while driving to work, a very tinny recording played by Bob Ruby on "Mornings with Ruby," WWL Radio, New Orleans. The singer sang a song beginning "Under the bamboo tree," and the tune stayed with me. When I heard the children sing "Under the bamboo tree," I recognized the closeness to the words, though the melody was modified considerably. Bob Ruby, who on the WWL New Orleans radio program *Mornings with Ruby*, used to play many early recordings, discussed "Under the Bamboo Tree." He recalled that the song was written in 1902, for the show "Sally in Our Alley." Ruby stated, "The song concerns a 'dusky maid' and a 'Zulu from Matabooloo.'" The Zulu sings:

> If you lak-a-me, lak I lak-a you
> And we lak-a-both the same,
> I lak-a-say, this very day,
> I lak-a-change your name;
> 'Cause I love-a-you and love-a-you true
> And if you-a-love-a-me
> One live as two, two live as one
> Under the bamboo tree.

I looked up "Under the bamboo Tree" and found a variant on Nonesuch records *H 71304 After the Ball: A Treasury of Turn-of the Century Popular Songs*.

I asked Francis de Caro, who was teaching folklore in the English Department at the same time I was working at Louisiana State University, if he recognized the song "Under the Bamboo Tree." He referred me to T. S. Eliot "Sweeny Agonistes," where Eliot lampoons the song (On the Internet at: T. S. Eliot Fragment of an Agon https://genius.com>T>T.S. Eliot).

Eliot's lines are:

> Song by Wauchope and Horsfall
> Swarts as Tambo. Snow as Bones
> Under the bamboo
> Bamboo bamboo
> Under the bamboo tree
> Two live as one
> One live as two
> Two live as three
> Under the bam

Under the boo
Under the bamboo tree

Where the breadfruit fall
And the penguin call
And the sound is the sound of the sea
Under the bam
Under the boo
Under the bamboo tree.
. . . . (*T. S. Eliot Collected Poems 1909–35*)

Is there any connection between the song the children sing and the song from "Sweeny Agonistes"? It is hard to say there is a link, because the children's song contains only two lines, which are identical, but the theme is the same in both.

29. Bronner, Simon J., *American Children's Folklore*, 63–65.

30. J. S. Udal, in "Dorsetshire Children's Games, Etc.," *The Folk-Lore Journal* 7 (January–December, London Elliot Stock, 1889) supplies this elegant version on pp. 218–19:

The children form a circle, and moving round and round to the right, sing:

When first we went to school—to school—to school
How happy was I!
(Each girl here takes the side of her dress or skirt by the right hand and just lifts it,
singing the while:)
'Twas this way, and that way,
How happy was I!

Next I went to service—to service—to service—
How happy was I!
(The dress is now let go, and sometimes an imitation of scrubbing
or sweeping with a long broom is introduced, as they sing:)
'Twas this way, and that way,
How happy was I!

Next I had a sweetheart—a sweetheart—a sweetheart—
How happy was I!
(Here they break the ring, and walk around in couples, singing:)
'Twas this way, and that way,
How happy was I!

Next I got married—got married—got married—
How happy was I!
(Still walking round in couples.)
'Twas this way, and that way,
How happy was I!

Next I had a baby—a baby—a baby—
How happy was I!

(Here their arms swing to and fro as they walk round, as if nursing or trying to qui-
eten a baby.)
'Twas this way, and that way,
How happy was I!
(At the conclusion of this verse the circle is re-formed.)

Next my husband died—he died—he died—
How sorry was I!
(Here they put their pinafores to their eyes, crying.)
'Twas this way, and that way,
How sorry was I!

Next my baby died—she died—she died –
How sorry was I!
(Still crying.)
'Twas this way, and that way,
How sorry was I.

31. J. S. Udal was not the only English folklorist to collect "When I was a baby." Lady Alice B. Gomme, in her classic *"The Traditional Games of England, Scotland*, and *Ireland,"* recorded fourteen variations of "When I Was a Young Girl" in Volume 2, pages 362–74. Each of her vari-ants is slightly different; some are told from a female perspective, while others present stanzas from a male perspective. Gomme also included five pages of explanatory notes and alternate tunes to which the performance was sung. Lady Gomme published her collection in London in 1898. Here in the United States, William Wells Newell had already published his *Games and Songs of American Children* in 1884. He included "When I Was a Shoemaker," which begins with the words "When I was a shoemaker / And a shoemaker was I, / This way, and that way, / And this way went I." Newell's note to "When I was a Shoemaker" makes it clear that the song was not then new. He states, "As with most street-games, further inquiry has shown us that the song is old in America" (88).

Variations of "When I Was a Young Girl," Gomme, Alice B., *Traditional Games of England, Scotland, and Ireland*, 362–74; See also Soileau, Jeanne P., *Yo' Mama, Mary Mack, and Boudreaux and Thibodeaux*, 64–72; Opie, Peter and Iona, *The Singing Game*, "When I Was a Lady," 294–97, "Mary Was a Bad Girl," 301–6, and "When Susie Was a Baby," 458–61, with notes 461. Compare with the earlier handclap given by white girls at Happy Face Day Nursery: "When Courtney had a baby"; Rosen, Michael, ed., *The Penguin Book of Childhood*, "When Suzy was a baby," 191–92; Newell, William Wells, *Games and Songs of American Children*, "When I was a shoemaker," 88; Tucker, Elizabeth, *Children's Folklore: A Handbook*, "Miss Suzie was a baby . . ." 58.

32. Bronner, Simon J., *American Children's Folklore*, "Fudge fudge call the judge," 71–72; Abrahams, Roger D., *Jump-Rope Rhymes: A Dictionary*, 51–52 (with many notes); Rosen, Mi-chael, ed. *The Penguin Book of Childhood*, 162; Sherman, Josepha, and T. K. F. Weisskopf, *Greasy Grimy Gopher Guts*, 42–43; Winslow, David J., "An Annotated Collection of Children's Lore: Part Three of Oral Tradition among Children in Central New York State," *Keystone Folklore Quarterly* 2 (Fall) 1966. 158.

33. Soileau, Jeanne P., *Yo' Mama, Mary Mack, and Boudreaux and Thibodeaux*, 104, 105, 132, 133; Sherman, Josepha and T. K. F. Weisskopf, *Greasy Grimy Gopher Guts*, 42.

34. Soileau, Jeanne P., *Yo' Mama, Mary Mack, and Boudreaux and Thibodeaux*, "C C C / I don't want to go to / College any more more more," 136–37.

35. Gaunt, Kyra D., *Games Black Girls Play*, 24–33, discussion of "slide," and how its rhythm changes.

36. Soileau, Jeanne P., "Children's Cheers as Folklore," *Western Folklore* 39, no. 3 (July 1980), 232–47; Soileau, Jeanne, P., *Yo' Mama, Mary Mack, and Boudreaux and Thibodeaux*, 145–48; Sherman, Josepha, and T. K. F. Weisskopf, *Greasy Grimy Gopher Guts*, 94–95.

37. Search Internet "Four white horses up the river," and several sites appear. One, bethsnotes. com, supplies the musical notation, and identifies the game as a "fun handclapping game from the Caribbean."

38. Soileau, Jeanne P., *Yo' Mama, Mary Mack, and Boudreaux and Thibodeaux*, 94–104, for variations on the theme of "Tweedle tweedle dee" and "Rockin' Robin."

39. Song "Nice & Slow" by Usher. Album, *My 7*.

40. YouTube.com The Puppies-Funky Y-2-C (1994) performed at https://www.youtube. com/watch?v=HdVPZQRO4lo.) The dance the children perform on the video is the same dance the third graders "shake their booty to" in the classroom. The words to "Funky Y-2-C" are partly derived from lines lifted from children's handclaps and jump rope chants played throughout the United States and beyond. This phenomenon is explored eloquently in Kyra D. Gaunt's book, *The Games Black Girls Play: Learning the Ropes from Double-Dutch to Hip-Hop*.

41. Girls are singing excerpted lines from "Shawty Got Moves." "Shawty Got Moves" by Get Cool on YouTube.com. Again, this song uses well-known lines familiar from jump-rope chants and handclaps.

42. "Let me Ride that Donkey Lyrics" 69boyz YouTube.com.

43. Gomme, Alice B., *Traditional Games of England, Scotland, and Ireland*, "Bingo" Vol. 1, 29–33; Sutton-Smith, Brian, *Games of New Zealand Children*, 21.

44. Opie, Peter and Iona, *Children's Games in Street and Playground*, "Slappies," 224–25

45. Tucker, Elizabeth, *Children's Folklore: A Handbook*, 32–33.

46. Thomas Kochman, in *Rappin' and Stylin' Out* states:

> In Black culture the focus is also on "what you do," but because the *do* here is *personal* (rather than *promotional*—as is the case in mainstream culture), the *concern* is also with how you do it and how well you do it: style and skill manifested in performance. Therefore, the culture, in a very traditional way, promotes the development and demonstration of those skills which reflect on an individual's underlying intelligence, verbal ability, speed, strength, agility and endurance. As any or all of these qualities become manifest in a variety of cultural activities, such as "gaming," "rapping," singing, dancing, fighting, ball-playing, etc., they are appropriately judged and appreciated.

Kochman, Thomas, *Rappin' and Stylin' Out*, 19

Chapter 5

1. Bronner, Simon J., *American Children's Folklore*, 56; Abrahams, Roger D., ed. *Jump-Rope Rhymes: A Dictionary*, 149–50; Abrahams, Roger D., and Lois Rankin, *Counting-Out Rhymes: A Dictionary*, 174.

2. Bronner, Simon J., *American Children's Folklore*, "On Top of Old Smoky," 99–100; Knapp, Mary and Herbert, *One Potato, Two Potato*, 174–76, 177–78; Soileau, Jeanne P., *Yo' Mama, Mary Mack, and Boudreaux and Thibodeaux*, 160–62; Sherman, Josepha, and T. K. F. Weisskopf, *Greasy Grimy Gopher Guts*, 110–12; Tucker, Elizabeth, *Children's Folklore: A Handbook*, 64.

3. Sherman, Jopsepha, and T. K. F. Weisskopf, *Greasy Grimy Gopher Guts*, 106–8; Soileau, Jeanne P., *Yo' Mama, Mary Mack, and Boudreaux and Thibodeaux*, 162; Bronner, Simon J., *American Children's Folklore*, 97–99; Knapp, Mary and Herbert, *One Potato, Two Potato*, 173–74; Opie, Peter and Iona, *Lore and Language of Schoolchildren*, 374.

4. Bronner, Simon J., *American Children's Folklore*, "Lulu had a steamboat," 61; Sherman, Josepha, and T. K. F. Weisskopf, *Greasy Grimy Gopher Guts*, 33, 34, 35.

5. Wikipedia.org "Anti-Barney Humor" (12/15/2017). See also: Elizabeth Tucker. *Children's Folklore: A Handbook*, 64–65; Sherman, Josepha, and T. K. F. Weisskopf, *Greasy Grimy Gopher Guts*, "The Life & Deaths of Barney," 192–200; Sullivan, C. W. III, "Children's Oral Poetry: Identity and Obscenity," *Children's Folklore Review*, Vol. 31. (2008–2009), 71.

6. Sherman, Josepha, and T. K. F. Weisskopf, *Greasy Grimy Gopher Guts*, 58–60; Bronner, Simon J., *American Children's Folklore*, 108; Knapp, Mary and Herbert, *One Potato, Two Potato*, 58–59.

7. Knapp, Mary and Herbert, *One Potato, Two Potato*, 61; Bronner, Simon J., *American Children's Folklore*, 74.

8. "Political Rhymes" Knapp, Mary and Herbert, *One Potato, Two Potato*, 206–11; Sherman, Josepha, and T. K. F. Weisskopf, *Greasy Grimy Gopher Guts*, 130–38.

9. Sherman, Josepha, and T. K. F. Weisskopf, *Greasy Grimy Gopher Guts*, 168–69; Knapp, Mary and Herbert, *One Potato, Two Potato*, 164; Opie, Peter and Iona, *The Singing Game*, 471–72; Bronner, Simon J., *American Children's Folklore*, 109.

10. Sherman, Josepha, and T. K. F. Weisskopf, *Greasy Grimy Gopher Guts*, 116; Bronner, Simon J., *American Children's Folklore*, 77.

11. Knapp, Mary and Herbert, *One Potato, Two Potato*, 173; Bronner, Simon J., *American Children's Folklore*, 97–99; Sherman, Josepha, and T. K. F. Weisskopf, *Greasy Grimy Gopher Guts*, 103–6.

12. See: "Go to Bed, Now You're Dead": Suffocation Songs and Breath Control Games," Elizabeth Tucker, *Children's Folklore Review* Vol. 31 2008–2009, 45–58; Sherman, Josepha, and T. K. F. Weisskopf, *Greasy Grimy Gopher Guts*, 71–74; Knapp, Mary and Herbert, *One Potato, Two Potato*, 253.

13. We sang this "Comet" song on the playground at St. Genevieve in Lafayette, La. in the late 1940s. One line was "Comet, it tastes like kerosene"; Sherman, Josepha, and T. K. F. Weisskopf, *Greasy Grimy Gopher Guts*, 162–63; Bronner, Simon J., *American Children's Folklore*, 80.

14. Sherman, Josepha, and T. K. F. Weisskopf, *Greasy Grimy Gopher Guts*, 74–77; Bronner, Simon J., *American Children's Folklore*, 81.

15. Wikipedia.org (12 / 1 / 2117)—"I'm Looking over My Dead Dog Rover." Under "Arrangements" section is the note "My Dead Dog Rover" by Hank Stu Dave and Hank (Hank Landsberg and Dave Whited) from 1977, which appears on the Dr. Demento 25th Anniversary Collection— The parody version "I'm Looking Over My Dead Dog Rover" was played on Dr. Demento's show for a time"; Sherman, Josepha, and T. K. F. Weisskopf, *Greasy Grimy Gopher Guts*, 27–29.

16. YouTube.com has a video of Smiley Lewis singing "I Hear You Knocking," accompanied by Huey "Piano" Smith. The piano accompaniment is that distinctive sound, later associated closely with Fats Domino. Wikipedia.org (12/12/2017) states "I Hear You Knocking"—Smiley Lewis recorded "I Hear You Knocking" with Dave Bartholomew's band at J&M Studios in New

Orleans, owned by Cosimo Matassa. Beginning with his signing by the Los Angeles-based Imperial Records in 1950, Smiley Lewis was one of the main proponents of the emerging New Orleans rhythm and blues style, along with Fats Domino, Lloyd Price, Dave Bartholomew, and Professor Longhair."

17. Bronner, Simon J. *American Children's Folklore*, "Come up, come up, come up, dear dinner, come up."103; Sherman, Josepha, and T. K. F. Weisskopf, *Greasy Grimy Gopher Guts*, 64–65.

18. wwwnola.com (11/4/2017)—Regal Beer—"Falstaff moved into Louisiana in 1936 by buying the local National Brewing Co., and dominated sales in the 1950s and 60s. During that time, Falstaff, Dixie, Jax and Regal held 80 percent of the local beer market . . . Regal was made popular by its jingle, "Red beans and rice and Regal on ice." It was produced at the American Brewing Co. brewery on Bienville Street, today the site of the Royal Sonesta Hotel. The American Brewery closed in 1962; See also: Sherman, Josepha, and T. K. F. Weisskopf, *Greasy Grimy Gopher Guts*, 68.

19. Soileau, Jeanne P., "Children's Cheers as Folklore," *Western Folklore* 39, no. 3 (July 1980): 235.

20. Soileau, Jeanne P., "Children's Cheers as Folklore," *Western Folklore* 39, no. 3 (July 1980): 232–47.

More Camp Songs

1. Searched the Internet for "Hands on Myself, What Have I Here?" and a site "Mamalisa. com" featured "funny" accents—mock German and baby-talk (1/9/2018).

2. Knapp, Mary and Herbert, *One Potato, Two Potato*, 164, 184, 188; Sherman, Josepha, and T.K.F. Weisskopf, *Greasy Grimy Gopher Guts*, 168–69; Opie, Peter and Iona, *The Singing Game*, 471–72.

3. Searched Internet for "Oh she sailed away on a happy summer's day" (1/9/2018). Eleven sites referred to the line "Oh she sailed away . . ." The sites included YouTube, where a delightful older lady demonstrated the hand motions.

4. Langstaff, John and Carol, *Shimmy Shimmy Coke-Ca-Pop*, 78 (with music); Gaunt, Kyra D., *The Games Black Girls Play*, 94–95, Gaunt's discussion of the game and its appearance in popular music, 97–98.

5. Searched "Rise and shine and you got the glory," and various sites appeared (1/9/2018). Referred to as "Rise and Shine" and "The Arky, Arky song," there were YouTube presentations, and references to "Scout songs," and "Songs for teaching," and "Dionne Warwick Lyrics." A spritely rendition is found at https://www.youtube.com/watch?v=DSxd9JVE3r4 web uploaded by Apple Crisol.

6. I love the way Carol sings of the cow as "him." "Did you feed my Cow?" Did Google search (1/9/2018). Song is featured on YouTube, and discussed as a song for very small children in at least ten sites, including Smithsonian Folkways, and Wikipedia.

7. Two nine-year-old girls from Happy Face Nursery in Chalmette, Louisiana, sang "I picked a peanut" which varied somewhat from that sung at the St. Joan of Arc bingo babysitting session. Beginning with the following:

Called the doctor
Called the doctor
Called the doctor just now
Oh, just now called the doctor
Called the doctor just now

The doctor said I wouldn't die . . .
I died anyway . . .
I went to heaven . . .
I kicked an angel . . .
Went to hell . . .
Slapped the devil . . .

See also Sherman, Josepha, and T. K. F. Weisskopf, *Greasy Grimy Gopher Guts*, 69–71; Soileau, Jeanne P., *Yo' Mama, Mary Mack, and Boudreaux and Thibodeaux*, 151–52.

8. According to Wikipedia.org (2017), "Flamin' Mamie" is a 1925 jazz classic composed by Paul Whiteman and Fred Rose as a "Fox Trot Song" on Jazz Age themes relying on the 1920s image of a vamp: "A Red Hot Stepper." It was one of the top hits of 1925." Here it is, still alive, being "vamped" around the bonfire by older Girl Scouts. YouTube has a version sung by Aileen Stanley (1925) that embodies the heart of the song.

9. Knapp, Mary and Herbert, *One Potato, Two Potato*, "Hail, Mary, full of grace . . . "171–72; Sherman, Josepha, and T. K. F. Weisskopf, *Greasy Grimy Gopher Guts*, "Jesus hates you this I know . . . ," 127.

10. I gave a lecture on Children's Folklore at the Baton Rouge Book Festival, October 2017. In the audience were a man and his wife from Chalmette, Louisiana. After the fifteen minutes or so that I spoke, the man and his wife added several chants they remembered to my collection. His version of "One bright day in the middle of the night" was amazingly close to the one given at Ursaline:

Two dead boys got up to fight
Back to back they faced each other
Drew their swords and shot each other
A deaf policeman heard the noise
And came to save the two dead boys
If you're not sure this tale is true
Ask the blind man, he saw it too.

The informant was in his sixties and had learned his speech at grade school in Chalmette, Louisiana, 1950s. See also Bronner, Simon J., *American Children's Folklore*, 78; Sherman, Josepha, and T. K. F. Weisskopf, *Greasy Grimy Gopher Guts*, 100–102, 127–28; Knapp, Mary and Herbert, *One Potato, Two Potato*, 97–98; Opie, Peter and Iona, *Lore and Language of Schoolchildren*, 25; Opie, Peter and Iona, *I Saw Esau*, 29.

11. Sherman, Josepha, and T. K. F. Weisskopf, *Greasy Grimy Gopher Guts*, 117–19.

12. Skylighters.org—Skylighters, The Web Site of 225th AAA Searchlight Battalion: Music of the WWII years—Roll Me Over in the Clover. "Roll Me Over in the Clover" was a randy little number that was hugely popular in England in 1944. The lyrics, for the time, were extremely racy and the subject matter was, well, sex." Web 2017.

13. Wikipedia.org. "Hallelujah I'm a Bum." According to Wikipedia (1/12/2018), Ruthanna is singing the refrain of a song "sung to the tune of the Presbyterian hymn "Revive us again." For various explanations of the origin of the song and its uses, see "Hallelujah I'm a Bum" Wikipedia.org.

14. Wikipedia.org. (1/10/2018) states, "This Old Man" is an English language children's song, counting and nursery rhyme with a Roud Folk Song Index number of 3550." Under "Origins

and history," Wikipedia says, "The origins of this song are obscure. The earliest extant record is a version noted in Anne Gilchrist's *Journal of the English Folk Dance and Song Society* (1937), learnt from her Welsh nurse in the 1870s under the title 'Jack Jintle'..."

15. At https://campsongs.wordpress.com/2012/07/19/weenie-man, two camp counselors (?) sing a shortened "weenie man" song.

16. When I typed "Rise and Shine" into the Internet search bar, various sites popped up. The first (11/29/2017) was "scoutsongs.com." Web. Then there followed three references to YouTube uploads. Then came "Rise and shine (folk)- Jewish Learning Matters" and "Ultimate Camp Songs Resource." It seems as though all sorts of religious and camp venues lay claim to this song.

Chapter Six

1. wikiHow.com. Web. "How to Play Dreidel" provides directions for play, as well as pictures. Wikipedia.org. Web. "Dreidel," supplies description of dreidel. It also supplies a discussion of the dreidel's origins, history, and symbolism.

2. Knapp, Mary and Herbert, *One Potato, Two Potato*, 25. The Knapps also discuss various ways counting out can be manipulated by the counter, 25–28; Abrahams, Roger D. and Lois Rankin, *Counting-Out Rhymes: A Dictionary*, 164–65; Opie, Peter and Iona, *Children's Games in Street and Playground*, 54; Sutton-Smith, Brian, *The Games of New Zealand Children*, 68.

3. Opie, Peter and Iona, *Children's Games in Street and Playground*, "underground tig," "if he tick you you have to stand still with your legs open and somebody has to go under your legs and then you are free," 111.

4. Sutton-Smith, Brian, *Games of New Zealand Children*, "touch touch," 57.

5. "King of the mountain" was a favorite game played on the "monkey bars" at Andrew Jackson Elementary in New Orleans in 1970. The monkey bars were made of metal and rose to almost ten feet off the ground. The game had to be banned because it became so rough. The boys would scramble up, pushing one another fiercely out of the way so that only one boy reached the top. Once there, he had to fight to defend his "throne." He was attacked and pushed off, so another boy could assume the "king" place. I saw the identical game played later in time, on a less lofty "monkey bar," in 2017, at Epiphany Day School, in New Iberia, Louisiana. See also Opie, Peter and Iona, *Children's Games in Street and Playground*, 233–34; Knapp, Mary and Herbert, *One Potato, Two Potato*, "King of the hill," 52; Sutton-Smith, Brian, *Games of New Zealand Children*, "King of the Castle," 147.

6. Knapp, Mary and Herbert, *One Potato, Two Potato*, 20, 251–52; Opie, Peter and Iona, *Children's Games in Street and Playground*, "Old man in the well," 305–6; Sutton-Smith, Brian, *Games of New Zealand Children*, "Dialogue Games," 32–33.

7. "Kiss and Chase" dominated some playgrounds in the New Orleans area in the late 1960s and early 1970s. I observed it at Lacoste Elementary in Chalmette and at Dwight D. Eisenhower Elementary, Algiers, Louisiana; Opie Peter and Iona, *Children's Games in Street and Playground*, 169–70.

8. Langstaff, John and Carol, *Shimmy Shimmy Coke-Ca-Pop*, 47; Bronner, Simon J., *American Children's Folklore*, 184; Opie, Peter and Iona, *Children's Games in Street and Playground*, 239–41 (with notes and further references). "Red Rover" was played on the playground at St. Genevieve School, Lafayette, Louisiana, where I was a student in the late 1940s.

9. We played "Ghost in the Graveyard" both in New Orleans, and in Lafayette, Louisiana, during the nineteen forties and fifties. We played at night in Cypress Grove Cemetery in New Orleans and at a secluded graveyard near the municipal airport in Lafayette, Louisiana, until

we were spotted and run off by caretakers. See also Knapp, Mary and Herbert, *One Potato, Two Potato*, 250–51; Sutton-Smith, Brian, *Games of New Zealand Children*, 32–33; Opie, Peter and Iona, *Children's Games in Street and Playground*, 307.

10. Wikipedia.org (1/12/2018) says "Blind man's buff or blind man's bluff is a variant of tag in which the player who is 'it' is blindfolded." In the game's history Wikipedia supplies versions played in China, Ancient Greece, and the Tudor period. In Pieter Bruegel's painting "Children's Games" (1560), a blue hooded figure chases her friends in the left, bottom, quadrant of the painting. See also Opie, Peter and Iona, *Children's Games in Street and Playground*, 6, 9, 117–20, 302–3; Gomme, Alice B., *Traditional Games of England, Scotland, and Ireland*, Vol. 1, 37–40; Bronner, Simon J., *American Children's Folklore*, 178.

11. "Giant steps and Baby steps" was the name my friends and I gave to this game in the nineteen forties. See also Bronner, Simon J., *American Children's Folklore*, 181–82; Opie, Peter and Iona, *Children's Games in Street and Playground*, "May I?" 187–90; Sutton-Smith, Brian, *Games of New Zealand Children*, "Giant Steps," "Giant Strides," 49.

12. Langstaff, John and Carol, *Shimmy Shimmy Coke-Ca-Pop*, 64; Knapp, Mary and Herbert, *One Potato, Two Potato*, 262.

13. It is interesting that this game, where an object is passed around the circle, and the guessing must utilize Hebrew words, is played in Metairie, Louisiana, in a synagogue school. We played the same game in New Orleans and Lafayette, but we were encouraged to speak French when playing. My grandmother called it "Cache, Cache la bague." See also: Gomme, Alice B., *Traditional Games of England, Scotland, and Ireland*, Vol. 1, "Diamond Ring," 96; Sutton-Smith, Brian, *Games of New Zealand Children*, 105–6; Newell, William Wells, *Games and Songs of American Children*, "Hold fast my gold ring," 150.

14. Gomme, Alice, B., "Witch, The," a number of games involving witches and wolves— *Traditional Games of England, Scotland, and Ireland*, Vol. 2, 391–99; Langstaff, John and Carol, *Shimmy Shimmy Coke-Ca-Pop!*, 84.

15. "Scissors, Paper, Rock" was played on the underground when I visited Seoul, Korea, in 2001. Pairs of children huddled together engaged in "Scissors, Paper, Rock" from the moment they entered the underground, until they got off at their stop. See also Tucker, Elizabeth, *Children's Folklore: A Handbook*, 33, where she traces the game to nineteenth century Japan; Opie, Peter and Iona, *Children's Games in Street and Playground*, discuss "Scissors, Paper, Rock," and other finger and hand games, 26–28; Sutton-Smith, Brian, *Games of New Zealand Children*, 132.

16. My brother and I would lick our thumb, "stamp" the thumb into our palm, and hit the thumb tip with our fist to count the VW "bugs" when we went on car trips. On country rides we "stamped" white horses and hawks.

17. See Norman Douglas, *London Street Games*, for a strange, but interesting, collection of the games played by boys on the streets of London. The book *London Street Games*, available free at archive.org, is best described in its dedication—"To his friend L. K. This Breathless Catalogue." Douglas was a novelist and travel writer whose contribution to game lore rests with this book, in which he records boys' stream-of-consciousness descriptions, which, when read aloud, take on a poetic, surreal, aspect.

18. Lady Alice B. Gomme wrote of this game as "Drop Handkerchief" in *Traditional Games of England, Scotland and Ireland*, Vol. 1, 109–12; Bronner, Simon J., *American Children's Folklore*, 181; Sutton-Smith, Brian, *Games of New Zealand Children*, 20; Abrahams, Roger D., ed. *Jump-Rope Rhymes: A Dictionary*, 13 (a parody); Opie, Peter and Iona, *Children's Games in Street and Playground*, 198–203 (with history and notes); Opie, Peter and Iona, *The Singing Game*, 125, 239, 359.

19. Langstaff, John and Carol, *Shimmy Shimmy Coke-Ca-Pop!* 49 (with photo illustrations).

20. Opie, Peter and Iona, *Lore and Language of Schoolchildren*, 200–201 (discussion of what they term "Patty Whack").

21. Knapp, Mary and Herbert, *One Potato, Two Potato*, "Tag Kiss," 217–18; Opie, Peter and Iona, *Lore and Language of Schoolchildren*, 142.

22. Bronner, Simon J., *American Children's Folklore*, 184.

23. Bronner, Simon J., *American Children's Folklore*, 179.

24. I Google-searched "Painting—'Pop the Whip,'" on the Internet, and two delightful depictions of the game appeared: "Pop the Whip" (1973) Carroll Cloar, and "Snap the Whip" (1872) Winslow Homer.

25. We played this game in an old graveyard near the Municipal airport in Lafayette, Louisiana, when I was a teenager in the late 1950s. My mother heartily disapproved.

26. Opie, Peter and Iona, *Children's Games in Street and Playground*, "Dead Man Arise," 106.

27. In The *Traditional Games of England, Scotland, and Ireland*, Vol. 2, Gomme records several variants of tag games involving a wolf, "Sheep, sheep, come home," 396–98; "Wolf and Lamb," 399; Opie, Peter and Iona, *Children's Games in Street and Playground*, "What's the time, Mr. Wolf?" 102–3, "Sheep, Sheep, Come Home," 131–32; Sutton-Smith, Brian, *Games of New Zealand Children*, "Run, Sheepie, Run," 67.

28. Opie, Peter and Iona, *Children's Games in Street and Playground*, "Coloured Birds," 288–90; Sutton-Smith, Brian, *Games of New Zealand Children*, "Colours," 66; Newell, William Wells, *Games and Songs of American Children*, "Hawks and Chickens," 155–56.

29. This is a short version of the game "Mother, Mother, the Pot Boils Over," Gomme, Alice B. *Traditional Games of England, Scotland, and Ireland*, Vol. 1, 396–401, in which the mother has various children named after the days of the week, and they get stolen by a witch and eaten. Gomme states in her notes that William Wells Newell, the founder of the American Folklore Society, had collected some versions of this game in the United States. See Newell, William Wells, *Games and Songs of American Children* (1883), "Old Witch," 215–21, and "Bloody Tom" (a wolf and chickens game), 117–18; Opie, Peter and Iona, *Children's Games in Street and Playground*, "Mother the cake (pot) Is burning," 317–29 (with added notes and variants).

30. Gomme, Alice B., *Traditional Games of England, Scotland, and Ireland*, Vol. 1, 396–401 (citing several variants of the game); Opie, Peter and Iona, *Children's Games in Street and Playground*, "The Old Man in the Well," 305–7, and "Mother, the Cake Is Burning," 317–29; Bronner, Simon J., *American Children's Folklore*, "Old Lady Witch," 182. "Witch in the Well" is closely related to both "Mother, Mother the Pot Boils Over" and another game Lady Gomme collected, called "Ghost at the Well." *Traditional Games of England, Scotland, and Ireland*, Vol. 1, 149–50. See also Winslow, David J. "An Annotated Collection of Children's Lore: Part Three of Oral Tradition among Children in Central New York State," *Keystone Folklore Quarterly* 2 (Fall) 1966, 151–202.

31. Gomme, Alice B., *Traditional Games of England, Scotland, and Ireland*, "Ghost at the Well," 149–50; Sutton-Smith, Brian, *Games of New Zealand Children*, "Ghost in the Garden," 32; Newell, William Wells, *Games and Songs of American Children*, "Ghost in the Cellar," 223.

Chapter Seven

1. Sullivan, C. W. III, "Children's Oral Poetry: Identity and Obscenity," *Children's Folklore Review* 31 (2008–2009): 69.

2. Sherman, Josepha, and T. K. F. Weisskopf, *Greasy Grimy Gopher Guts*, 58, 81.

3. Bronner, Simon J., *American Children's Folklore*, 86–88; Opie, Peter and Iona, *Lore and Language of Schoolchildren*, 48, 237, 171, 177.

4. Sherman, Josepha, and T. K. F. Weisskopf, *Greasy Grimy Gopher Guts*, 24–25.

Chapter Eight

1. In *Social and Emotional Development in Infancy and Early Childhood*, one passage gives an example of a preschooler's struggle to repeat a riddle:

The humor of a riddle such as, "Why did the girl salute the refrigerator? Because it was General Electric" is derived from the conceptual incongruity of the term 'general'. If one does not have the knowledge base to understand why a general should be saluted and that the phrase is also the name of a refrigerator maker, the riddle is not funny. After her older sister told that riddle, a preschool-age child then told this riddle: "Why did the boy salute the refrigerator? Because he was hungry." The child had the form of the riddle but was missing the conceptual incongruity dimension. Of course, the adults who heard her pre-riddle followed the social convention of laughter at the pre-riddle. This learning of the humor form of riddle and joke telling is an important stage because it then leads to the ability to tell real riddles and jokes a later age. Benson, Janette B., and Marshall M. Haith. Eds. *Social and Emotional Development in Infancy and Early Childhood*, 192.

2. Opie, Peter and Iona, *The Lore and Language of Schoolchildren*, 82; Bronner, Simon J., *American Children's Folklore*, "Joking Questions," 116–18.

3. Bronner, Simon J., *American Children's Folklore*, "Knock-Knock Jokes," 118–19; Tucker, Elizabeth, *Children's Folklore: A Handbook*, 51–52; Knapp, Mary and Herbert, *One Potato, Two Potato*, 94.

4. Wikipedia.org (12/15/2017)—"The Monkey's Paw." Published in 1902, "The Monkey's Paw" is the work of W. W. Jacobs. Jacobs was a humor writer but is best known for several ghost stories. "The Monkey's Paw" is a classic 'be careful what you wish for' tale." The story has seen many film, television, and theater adaptations. See Wikipedia, "List of Adaptations of the Monkey's Paw." I have viewed three movies made on this theme. Chiller Films (2013), *The Monkey's Paw*, directed by Brett Simons, and starring C. J. Thomason and Stephen Lang, is my favorite. It is set in and around New Orleans and has the look of authenticity.

5. Verses that expand on "I like Coffee": Opie, Peter and Iona, *Lore and Language of Schoolchildren*, 117; Knapp, Mary and Herbert, *One Potato, Two Potato*, 14, 116; Soileau, Jeanne P., *Yo' Mama, Mary Mack, and Boudreaux and Thibodeaux*, 57–59; Sutton-Smith, Brian, *Games of New Zealand Children*, 79.

6. Bronner, Simon J., *American Children's Folklore*, 156.

7. Bronner, Simon J., *American Children's Folklore*, "Playful Horror Tales," 154–59.

8. Bronner, Simon J., *American Children's Folklore*, 156; Tucker, Elizabeth, *Children's Folklore: A Handbook*, 82–83.

9. When I was in grade school, our choice for a joke centering on silly names often featured the Cajun twins Pee Pee and Poo Poo LeBlanc. See also Bronner, Simon J., *American Children's Folklore*, 135; Soileau, Jeanne P., *Yo' Mama, Mary Mack, and Boudreaux and Thibodeaux*, 36–37, 40, 45.

10. For Cajun jokes, see cajunguy20.tripod.com (1/23/2018) for a few of the jokes usually told with a heavy Cajun accent.

11. Bronner, Simon J., *American Children's Folklore*, 116–18; Knapp, Mary and Herbert, *One Potato, Two Potato*, 104–11 (examples and discussion).

12. Rosen, Michael, ed., *The Penguin Book of Childhood*, "My friend Billy's got a ten foot willy," 160.

13. Soileau, Jeanne, P., *Yo' Mama, Mary Mack, and Boudreaux and Thibodeaux*, 159; Bronner, Simon J., *American Children's Folklore*, 80–81.

14. Soileau, Jeanne P., "Aspects of Ethnicity as Expressed in Children's Folklore," 79–92. *Perspectives on Ethnicity in New Orleans: A Publication of the Committee on Ethnicity in New Orleans*, 1980, ed. John Cooke.

15. Wikipedia.org (12/13/2017) "Alphonse and Gaston"—The "politeness" jokes are a variation on the theme utilized by "Frederick Burr Opper in his comic strip 'Alphonse and Gaston.' These two Frenchmen were so polite that they could never get anything done they were so busy saying, "After you, my dear Alphonse." And "No, after you, my dear Gaston." My grandmother used to say, "You first, my dear Gaston," whenever we bunched up trying to go through a doorway.

16. Sacred Heart Academy is the second oldest Roman Catholic institution of learning west of the Mississippi River. At the time of this taping it educated girls in day school and as boarders.

Conclusion

1. Iona and Peter Opie were English child lore collectors who wrote three lengthy and carefully researched books in the twentieth century: *The Lore and Language of Schoolchildren* (1959), *Children's Games in Street and Playground* (1969), and *The Singing Game* (1985).

Works Cited

69 Boyz. "*Let Me Ride That Donkey (Old School) 12 Gauge.*" YouTube.com. 5,574,521 views. Apr 2010. Accessed Apr. 1, 2016. Web.

1950srockabilly. "Sheila Gernon—Money Honey." YouTube.com. 2,791 views. Dec. 4, 2010. Accessed Feb. 2, 2020. Web.

Aarne, Antti, and Stith Thompson. *The Types of the Folktale: A Classification and Bibliography.* Helsinki: Suomalainen Tiedeakatemia, 1961. Print.

Abrahams, Roger D., and Lois Rankin. "Black Talking on the Streets." *Explorations in the Ethnography of Speaking.* ed. Richard Bauman and Joel Sherzer. New York: Cambridge UP, 1989. Print.

Abrahams, Roger D., and Lois Rankin. *Counting-Out Rhymes: A Dictionary.* Austin: U of Texas P, 1980. Print.

Abrahams, Roger D., and Lois Rankin. *Deep Down in the Jungle.* New York: Aldine, 1963. Print.

Abrahams, Roger D., and Lois Rankin. "Joking: Training of the Man of Words in Talking Broad." "*Rappin' and Stylin' Out.*" Kochman 215–40. Print.

Abrahams, Roger D., and Lois Rankin. *Jump-Rope Rhymes: A Dictionary.* Austin: U of Texas P, 1969. Print.

Abrahams, Roger D., and Lois Rankin. "Negotiating Respect: Patterns of Presentation among Black Women." *Journal of American Folklore* 88 (1975): 58–79. Print.

Abrahams, Roger D., and Lois Rankin. "Playing the Dozens." *Mother Wit from the Laughing Barrel.* Dundes 295–309. Print.

Abrahams, Roger D., and Lois Rankin. *Positively Black.* Englewood Cliffs: Prentice, 1970. Print.

Abrahams, Roger D., and Lois Rankin. *Singing the Master.* New York: Pantheon, 1992. Print.

Abrahams, Roger D., and Lois Rankin. *Talking Black.* Rowley, MA: Newberry, 1976. Print.

Abrahams, Roger D., and Lois Rankin. "The Training of the Man of Words in Talking Sweet." *Verbal Art as Performance.* ed. Richard Bauman. Prospect Heights, IL: Waveland, 1977. 117–32. Print.

"Anne and Virginia playing 'Say Say Say Playmate.'" YouTube.com. MyLorgan. 305,028 views. Dec. 26, 2013. Accessed Jan. 20, 2018. Web.

Anti-Barney Humor—Wikipedia. en.wikipedia.org. > wiki > Anti-Barney_humor. Accessed Dec. 15, 2017. Web.

Alphonse and Gaston—Wikipedia. en.wikipedia.org > wiki > Alphonse_and_Gaston. Web.

Apte, Mahadev L. *Humor and Laughter: An Anthropological Approach.* Ithaca: Cornell UP, 1985. Print.

Aries, Philippe. *Centuries of Childhood: A Social History of Family Life.* Trans. Robert Baldick. New York: Random, 1962. Print.

Avedon, Elliott M., and Brian Sutton-Smith. *The Study of Games.* New York: Wiley, 1971. Print.

"Average Television Viewing Time, May 1999." *World Almanac and Book of Facts.* 1999 Ed. Print.

Babcock, W. H. "Carols and Child-Lore at the Capitol." *Lippincott's Monthly Magazine* 38 (1886): 320–42. Print.

Babcock, W. H. "Games of Washington Children." *American Anthropologist* 1 (1888): 243–64. Print.

Babcock, W. H. "Song Games and Myth Dramas at Washington." *Lippincott's Monthly Magazine* 37 (1886): 239–57. Print.

Ballard, Pat. (*Oh Baby Mine*) *I Get So Lonely.* Wikipedia.org. Web.

Bankston, Carl L., and Stephen J. Caldas. *A Troubled Dream: The Promise and Failure of School Desegregation in Louisiana.* Nashville: Vanderbilt UP, 2002. Print.

Bascom, William R. "The Four Functions of Folklore." *Journal of American Folklore* 67 (1954): 333–49. Print.

Bateson, Gregory. *Steps to an Ecology of Mind: Collected Essays in Anthropology.* New York: Ballantine, 1972. Print.

Bauman, Richard, ed. *Folklore, Cultural Performance, and Popular Entertainments.* New York: Oxford UP, 1992. Print.

Bauman, Richard, ed. *Verbal Art as Performance.* Prospect Heights, IL: Waveland, 1997. Print.

Bauman, Richard, ed., and Charles L. Briggs. "Poetics and Performance as Critical Perspectives on Language and Social Life." *Annual Review of Anthropology* 19 (1990): 59–88. Print.

Benson, Janette B., and Marshall M. Haith. eds. *Social and Emotional Development in Infancy and Childhood.* San Diego: Academic P. 2009. Print.

Beresin, Ann Richman. "Double Dutch and Double Cameras: Studying the Transmission of Culture in an Urban School Yard." Sutton-Smith, *Source Book.* 75–92. Print.

Beresin, Ann Richman. *Recess Battles.* Jackson: U of Mississippi P, 2010. Print.

Berry, Jason, Jonathan Foose, and Tad Jones. *Up from the Cradle of Jazz: New Orleans Music Since World War II.* Lafayette: U of Louisiana P. 2009. Print.

Blank, Trevor J., ed. *Folk Culture in the Digital Age: The Emergent Dynamics of Human Interaction.* Logan: Utah State UP, 2012. Print.

Blank, Trevor J., ed. *Folklore and the Internet: Vernacular Expression in a Digital World.* Logan: Utah State UP, 2009. Print.

"Blind Man's Buff." en.wikipedia.org. Web.

Bogle, Donald. *Toms, Coons, Mulattoes, Mammies, and Bucks: An Interpretive History of Blacks in American Films.* 1973. Rev. Ed. New York: Viking, 1999. Print.

Bolton, Henry Carrington. "The Counting-Out Rhymes of Children: Antiquity, Origin, and Wide Distribution." *Journal of American Folklore* 1 (1880): 31–37. Print.

Bolton, Henry Carrington. *The Counting-Out Rhymes of Children: Antiquity, Origin, and Wide Distribution.* London: Elliot Stock, 1888. https://Archive.org./details/countingoutrhyme oobolt. Web.

Brady, Margaret K., and Rosalind Eckhardt. *Black Girls at Play: Perspectives on Child Development.* Austin: Southwest Educational Development, 1975. Print.

Brewster, Paul G. *American Non-Singing Games.* Norman: U of Oklahoma P, 1953. Print.

Brewster, Paul G. "Children's Games and Rhymes." *The Frank C. Brown Collection of North Carolina Folklore.* ed. Paul G. Brewster. Vol. 1, Durham: Duke UP, 1952. 29–219. Print.

Bridges, Ruby. *Through My Eyes*. New York: Scholastic, 1999. Print.

Bronner, Simon J. *American Children's Folklore*. Little Rock: August, 1988. Print.

Bronner, Simon J. "Digitizing and Virtualizing Folklore." *Folklore and the Internet: Vernacular Expression in a Digital World*. ed. Trevor J. Blank. Logan Utah: Utah State UP. 2009.

Brown, H. Rap. *Die Nigger Die*. New York: Dial, 1969. Print.

Bruegel, Pieter. "Children's Games." artandculture.google.com. Web.

Bynum, Russ. "Georgia Schools Want to Crack Down on Sexy Cheerleading." Nov. 3, 2001. 1–2. Http://detnews.com/2001/schools/0111/03/schools-334455.htm. Web.

Bynum, Russ. "Rah Rah Raunch?" *Sunday Advertiser*. 4 Nov. 2001: D1, D3. Print.

Cajun Jokes. Cajunguy20.tripod.com. Web.

Chagall, Irene. *Let's Get the Rhythm: A Video by Irene Chagall and City Lore*. American Folklore Society Annual Meeting. New Orleans, La. 2012. Video.

Children's song "Twilight Forever." Answers.google.com/answersthreadview?Id=235768. Web.

Clemens, Samuel Langhorne. *Adventures of Huckleberry Finn*. 2nd Ed. New York: Norton, 1977. Print.

Cloar, Carroll. "Pop the Whip 1973." Remembering a master—Memphis. Memphismagazine .com. Web.

Clotfelder, Charles T. *After "Brown": The Rise and Retreat of School Desegregation*. Princeton N.J.: Princeton UP, 2006. Print.

"Commercial Broadcast Stations on the Air." *World Almanac and Book of Facts*. 1972 Ed. Print.

Cooke, Benjamin G. "Nonverbal Communication among Afro-Americans: An Initial Classification." *Rappin' and Stylin' Out*. Urbana: U of Illinois P, 1972. Print.

Costa Rica Rich. "Rockin' Robin Hand Game 2017." YouTube.com. Jan. 6, 2017. 50,292 views. Accessed Mar. 20, 2019. Web.

"Crazy old man from China." Pancojams.blogspot. Web.

Crisol, Apple. "The Arky Arky Song (Rise and Shine)—Heritage Kids Lyrics." YouTube. 2,755,447 views. Jul. 24, 2016. Accessed Jun. 2, 2019. Web.

Dance, Daryl Cumber. *Honey Hush: An Anthology of African American Women's Humor*. ed. Daryl Cumber Dance. New York: Norton, 1998. Print.

Dance, Daryl Cumber. *Shuckin' and Jivin': Folklore from Contemporary Black Americans*. Bloomington: Indiana UP, 1978. Print.

Dates, Jannette L., and William Barlow. *Split Image: African Americans in the Mass Media*. Washington: Howard UP, 1993. Print.

DeCaro, Frank, and Rosan Jordan. "In This Folk-Lore Land: Race, Class, Identity, and Folklore Studies in Louisiana." *Journal of American Folklore* 109 (1996): 31–59. Print.

Degh, Linda. *American Folklore and the Mass Media*. Bloomington: Indiana UP, 1994. Print.

"Did you feed my cow?" YouTube. Smithsonian Folkways Recordings. Ella Jenkins. 107,500 views. May 21, 2015. Folkways.si.edu > did-you-feed-my-cow > childrens > music > track. Accessed Feb. 13, 2020.

Dollard, John. "The Dozens: Dialect of Insult." Dundes, 277–94. Print.

Douglas, Norman. *London Street Games*. archive.org > details > londonstreetgameoodoug. Web.

Doyle, Audrey. "Sound Effects." *Computer Graphics World*. Apr. 2000: 10 pp. <http://ehost vgw6.epnet.com/fulltext.asp?resultSetId=ROOOOOOOO&hitNum=1&booleanTerm= . . . > Web.

Drake. "Tuesday ft. Makonnen (lyrics)." YouTube. 3,952,706 views. Aug. 12, 2014. Accessed Feb. 20, 2019. Web.

Dreilinger, Danielle. Nola.com. The Times Picayune. "How one New Orleans Neighborhood worked to reopen its school—and lost." Posted Jul. 31, 12:08 p.m. Updated Jan. 06, 2015. 5:10 p.m. Web.

Dundes, Alan, ed. *Mother Wit from the Laughing Barrel*. Englewood Cliffs: Prentice, 1973. Print.

"Early Break Dancing." *Library of Congress Online*. Nov. 19, 2001: 1 p. <http://www.americasli brary.gov/pages/jp_dance_break_1html>. Web.

Ellis, Shirley. "The Clapping Song (Shivaree—Mar. 20, 1965). YouTube.com. 285, 509 views. Jul. 28, 2014. Accessed Jul. 09, 2017. Web.

Eckhardt, Rosalind, and Margaret K. Brady. "From Hand Clap to Line Play." *Black Girls at Play: Perspectives on Child Development*. Austin: Southwestern Educational Development, 1975. 57–101. Print.

Eliot, T. S. "Sweeny Agonistes." T. S. Eliot Fragment of an Agon. https:// genius.com > T > T. S. Eliot. Web.

En.wikipedia.org. "*Pretty Little Dutch Girl*." Accessed Jan. 10, 2019. Web.

Ferguson, Nial. *The Square and the Tower: Networks and Power, from the Freemasons to Face- book*. New York: Penguin Press, 2018. Print.

Ferris, William Reynolds. *Black Folklore from the Mississippi Delta*. Ann Arbor: University Microfilms, 1969.

Fine, Elizabeth C. "Performance Approach." *American Folklore: An Encyclopedia*. New York: Garland, 1996. Print.

Fine, Gary Alan. "Children and Their Culture: Exploring Newell's Paradox." *Western Folklore* 39 (1980): 170–83. Print.

"Flamin' Mamie." en.wikipedia.org. > wiki > Flamin > Mamie.

Fluent-C., Toze, and Zia. "Breakdancing Breakdown-UK." *Bomb Hip-Hop Magazine* 46 (Apr./ May 1996): 1–6. Print.

Ford, Robert. *Children's Rhymes Children's Games Children's Songs Children's Stories: A Book for Bairns and Big Folk*. Paisley: Gardner. 1904. Web.

"Four White Horses." *Beth's Notes: Supporting & Inspiring Music Educators*. bethsnotesplus. com. Accessed Feb. 11, 2020. Web.

Gatesofprayer.org. Web.

Gaunt, Kyra D. *The Games Black Girls Play: From Double Dutch to Hip-Hop*. New York: New York UP, 2006. Print.

Georges, Robert A., and Michael Owen Jones. *Folkloristics: An Introduction*. Bloomington: Indiana UP, 1995. Print.

Get Cool. "Shawty Got Moves." YouTube. 185,769 views. Dec. 30, 2011. Accessed Apr. 10, 2018.

Glassie, Henry. Address. Deep South Writer's Conference. Alumni House, Lafayette, La. Oct. 13, 2000.

Goffman, Erving. *Behavior in Public Places: Notes on the Social Organization of Gatherings*. New York: Free, 1963. Print.

Goffman, Erving. *Forms of Talk*. Philadelphia: U of Philadelphia P, 1981. Print.

Goffman, Erving. *Frame Analysis*. New York: Harper, 1974. Print.

Goffman, Erving. *Interaction Ritual*. Garden City: Anchor, 1967. Print.

Goffman, Erving. *The Presentation of Self in Everyday Life*. Garden City, NY: Doubleday, 1959. Print.

Gomme, Alice B. *Old English Singing Games*. London: Nutt, 1900. Print.

Gomme, Alice B. *Traditional Games of England, Scotland, and Ireland.* 2 vols. London: Nutt, 1894, 1898. Print.

Goodwin, Marjorie Harness. "Accomplishing Social Organization in Girls' Play: Patterns of Competition and Cooperation in an African American Working-Class Girls' Group," Hollis 149–65. Print.

Gracyk, Tim. "Aileen Stanley "Flamin' Mamie" Victor 19828 (October 5, 1925) Biography of Aileen Stanley." YouTube.com. 2,143 views. Jun. 8, 2013. Accessed Feb. 18, 2020. Web.

Grau, Shirley Ann. *The Keepers of the House.* 1963 New York: Knopf, 1978. Print.

Grider, Sylvia Ann. "The Study of Children's Folklore." *Western Folklore* 39 (1980): 159–69. Print.

Grider, Sylvia Ann. "Who Are the Folklorists of Childhood?" Sutton-Smith, *Source Book*, 11–18. Print.

"Hallelujah I'm a Bum—Wikipedia" en.wikipedia.org > wiki > Hallelujah_I'm _a_Bum.

Halliwell-Phillips, J. O. *The Nursery Rhymes of England.* London: John Russell Smith, 1886. *Archive.org.* Web. Feb. 1, 2017.

Halliwell-Phillips, J. O. *Popular Rhymes and Nursery Tales: A Sequel to the Nursery Rhymes of England.* London: John Russell Smith, 1849. *Archive.org.* Web. Feb. 1, 2017.

Hank, Stu, Dave, and Hank (Hank Lansberg and Dave Whited) "I'm Looking over My Dead Dog Rover." Wikipedia.org. Web.

Haskins, Jim. *Richard Pryor: A Man and His Madness.* New York: Beaufort, 1984. Print.

Hixon, Martha. *Awakenings and Transformations: Re-Visioning the Tales of "Sleeping Beauty," "Snow White," "The Frog Prince," and "Tam Lin."* Dissertation. University of Southwestern Louisiana. Lafayette, LA: 1997. Print.

Hollis, Susan Tower, Linda Pershing, and M. Jane Young, eds. *Feminist Theory and the Study of Folklore.* Urbana: U of Illinois P, 1993. Print.

Homer, Winslow. "Snap the Whip "(1872). (Metropolitan Museum of Art, NYC)—Canvas print. Canvasprint.com. Web.

"Households with Television Sets by Percentage." *The World Almanac and Book of Facts.* Ed. Luman H. Long. New York: World Almanac Education Group, 1972. Print.

"How to play Apple on a stick clapping game." YouTube.com. Kidspot. 199, 529 views. May 23, 2013. Accessed Jan. 20, 2018.

"How to Play Dreidel: 6 Steps (with pictures)"—wikiHow.com. Jan 5, 2020. Accessed Feb. 14, 2020. Web.

Huffingtonpost.com / national-trust-for-historic-preservation / neworleans. Web.

Hughes, Langston. *The Big Sea.* New York: Knopf, 1940. Print.

Hughes, Linda. "Children's Games and Gaming." Sutton-Smith, *Source Book* 93–120. Print.

Hughes, Linda. "You Have to Do It with Style: Girls' Games and Girls' Gaming." Hollis 130–48. Print.

Hurston, Zora Neale. *Dust Tracks on a Road.* 1942. Rev. text. New York: Lippincott, 1995. Print.

Hurston, Zora Neale. *Go Gator and Muddy the Waters: Writings by Zora Neale Hurston from the Federal Writer's Project.* ed. Pamela Bordelon. New York: Norton, 1999. Print.

Hurston, Zora Neale. *Mules and Men.* 1935. New York: Harper, 1990. Print.

Hurston, Zora Neale. "My People! My People!" Dundes 22–23. Print.

Hurston, Zora Neale. *Their Eyes Were Watching God.* New York: Penguin, 1995. Print.

Hymes, Dell. *"In Vain I Tried to Tell You": Essays in Native American Ethnopoetics.* Philadelphia: U of Pennsylvania P, 1981. Print.

"I Am a Pretty Little Dutch Girl." en.wikipedia.org > wiki > Pretty_Little_Dutch_Girl.Web.

"Ink Spots Live 1941—Java Jive—YouTube." YouTube.com. > watch. 1,026,342 views. Jul 12, 2008. Accessed Jan 10, 2019. Web.

Jabr, Ferris. "Can You Really Be Addicted to Video Games?" *The New York Times Magazine*, 36–41; 54–55. October 27, 2019. Print.

Jackie Chan: Stuntman to Superstar. Dir. Bill Harris. ABC Productions for A&E Network. Videocassette, Blockbuster. 1996. Video.

Jackson, Michael. *Moonwalk*. New York: Doubleday, 1988. Print.

Jacobs, W. W. "The Monkey's Paw." en.wikipedia.org > wiki > The_Monkey's_Paw. Web.

James T. Callow Computerized Folklore Archive: UDM Libraries / Instructional / Design Studio. libraries. udmercy.edu.Web. Accessed Feb. 9, 2020.

Jeansonne, Glen. *Leander Perez: Boss of the Delta*. Baton Rouge: Louisiana State UP. 1982. Print.

Johnson, Guy. "Double Meaning in the Popular Negro Blues." Dundes 258–66.

Johnson, J. Rosamond. Wikipedia.com. Web.

Jones, Bessie, and Bess Lomax Hawes. *Step It Down: Games, Plays, Songs, and Stories from the Afro-American Heritage*. New York: Harper, 1972. Print.

"Judy Garland under the Bamboo Tree—YouTube." YouTube.com. MyMusicalSoul941.

Keyes, Cheryl L. "We're More Than a Novelty, Boys: Strategies of Female Rappers in the Rap Music Tradition." *Feminist Messages: Coding in Women's Folk Culture*. ed. Joan Newton Radner. Urbana: U of Illinois P, 1993. 205–20. Print.

"Killer Sticks." *Newsweek* 15 Oct. 1973: 67. Print.

Kingsolver, Barbara. *Prodigal Summer*. New York: HarperCollins, 2000. Print.

Kinney, Jeff. *Diary of a Wimpy Kid Old School*. New York: Abrams, 2015. Print.

Knapp, Mary, and Herbert Knapp. *One Potato, Two Potato: The Folklore of American Children*. New York: Norton, 1976. Print.

Kochman, Thomas. *Black and White Styles in Conflict*. Chicago: Chicago UP, 1981. Print.

Kochman, Thomas, ed. *Rappin' and Stylin' Out*. Urbana: Illinois UP, 1972. Print.

"The Kung Fu Craze." *Newsweek* 7 May 1973: 76. Print.

Landress, Uncle Bud. "Rubber Dolly Rag (feat. The Georgia Yellow Hammers.) "*Gimme Dat Harp Boy*" Roots of the Captain. Play.google.com. Web.

Langstaff, John, and Carol Langstaff. *Shimmy Shimmy Coke-Ca-Pop: A Collection of City Children's Street Games and Rhymes*. New York: Doubleday, 1973. Print.

Legman, Gershon. *Rationale of the Dirty Joke*. 2 vols. New York: Grove, 1968, 1975. Print.

Labov, William. *Language of the Inner City: Studies in the Black English Vernacular*. Philadelphia: U of Pennsylvania P, 1972. Print.

Labov, William. "Rules for Ritual Insults." *Rappin' and Stylin' Out*. ed. Thomas Kochman. Urbana: U of Illinois P, 1972. 265–314. Print.

Lisa, Mama. "Mama Lisa's World International Music & Culture Teddy Bear, Teddy Bear, Turn Around Songs and Rhymes from Canada." Mamalisa.com. Web.

Lisa, Mama. "Mama Lisa's World International Music & Culture My Hand on Myself Action Song." Mamalisa.com. Web.

Lofznmuzik. "Fats Domino I Hear You Knocking." YouTube.com. 1,144,680 views. Aug. 29, 2014. Web.

Lord, Albert. *The Singer of Tales*. Cambridge: Harvard UP, 1960. Print.

Macdonald, J. Fred. *Blacks and White TV: African Americans in Television Since 1948*. 2nd ed. Chicago: Nelson-Hall, 1972. Print.

Maic Mc. "The Belle Stars—The Clapping Song Video." Youtube.com. 807,207 views. Mar. 2, 2006. Accessed Feb. 2, 2020. Web.

"Martial Arts." *BellSouth: The Real Yellow Pages: New Orleans.* New Orleans: BellSouth Advertising and Publishing, 2000. 737–38. Print.

McDowell, John H. "The Transmission of Children's Folklore." Sutton-Smith, *Source Book.* 49–62. Print.

McLuhan, Marshall. *Understanding Media: The Extensions of Man.* New York: Mentor, 1966. Print.

McLuhan, Marshall, and Quentin Fiore. *The Medium Is the Massage.* New York: Random, 1967. Print.

McMahon, Felicia R., and Brian Sutton-Smith. "The Past in the Present: Theoretical Directions for Children's Folklore." Sutton-Smith, *Source-Book.* 293–308. Print.

McNeil, W. H. Introduction to *American Children's Folklore.* By Simon Bronner. Little Rock: August House, 1988. 11–12. Print.

Mechling, Jay. "Children's Folklore." *Folk Groups and Folklore Genres.* ed. Elliott Oring. Logan: Utah State UP, 1986. Print.

Meisenhelder, Susan. "Conflict and Resistance in Zora Neale Hurston's *Mules and Men." Journal of American Folklore* 109 (1996): 289–307. Print.

Melnick, Mimi Clar. "I Can Peep through Muddy Water and Spy Dry Land: Boasts in the Blues." Dundes, 267–68. Print.

"Miss Lucy had a baby". en.wikipedia.org >wiki > Miss_Lucy_had_a_baby. Accessed Dec. 17, 2017. Web.

Mitchell-Kernan, Claudia. "Signifying." Dundes 310–28. Print.

The Monkey's Paw (2013 film). en.wikipedia.org > wiki > The_Monkey's_Paw_(2013_film). Web.

Morris, Joan, and William Bolcom. *After the Ball: A Treasury of Turn-of-the-Century Popular Songs.* LP. Vinyl. Amazon Music. Amazon.com.

Morton, Laura E. *Louisiana Folklife* Special Issue: *Toys, Games, and Play in Louisiana and the Southeast.* Vol. 18. 1994. Print.

Morton, Laura E., ed. *Louisiana Toys and Games: The Makers and The Players.* Winning Entries from the Louisiana Toys and Games Contest. The Louisiana Folklife Center, 1994. Print.

"My Dead Dog Rover." YouTube. 169,460 views. May 11, 2009. Accessed Feb. 11, 2020.

Newell, William Wells. *Games and Songs of American Children.* New York: Dover, 1883. Print.

NOLA.com. www.nola.com/timespic/stories/index.ssf?/base/news-3/117938579301370. Web. NOLA.History: 6 New Orleans Schools of Historic Interest.

Norworth, Jack, and Albert Von Tizler. "Take Me Out to the Ball Game." en.wikipedia.org > wiki > Take_Me_Out_to_the_Ball_Game. 1908. Accessed Dec. 16, 2017. Web.

Old-new-orleans.com/NO_konos.html. Web.

Opie, Iona. *The People in the Playground.* Oxford: Oxford UP, 1994. Print.

Opie, Peter, and Iona Opie. *Children's Games in Street and Playground: Chasing, Catching, Seeking, Hunting, Racing, Dueling, Exerting, Daring, Guessing, Acting, Pretending.* Oxford: Clarendon, 1969. Print.

Opie, Peter, and Iona Opie. *The Classic Fairy Tales.* New York: Oxford UP, 1974. Print.

Opie, Peter, and Iona Opie. *I Saw Esau: Traditional Rhymes of Youth.* London: Williams and Norgate, 1947. Print.

Opie, Peter, and Iona Opie. *Lore and Language of Schoolchildren.* Oxford: Clarendon, 1959. Print.

Opie, Peter, and Iona Opie. *The Singing Game.* Oxford: Oxford UP, 1985. Print.

Paredes, Amerigo. "*Folklore and Culture on the Texas Mexican Border.*" Center for Mexican American Studies. Austin: U of Texas P, 1993. Print.

Patriot 420. "Shirley Ellis the Clapping Song (clap-pat-clap-slap)". YouTube.com. 1,915,714 views. Aug. 13, 2009. Accessed Feb 13, 2020. Web.

Pbs.org/wnet/african-americans-many-rivers-to-cross/video. Web.

"Planet Hip-Hop." *Gear.* 3. 12 (2002): 81. Print.

Playmates. "*The Fontane Sisters—Playmates (1955).*" 46,994 views. Aug. 2, 2011. Youtube.com Accessed Mar. 3, 2017. Web.

"Playmates (Song)—Wikipedia." en.wikipedia.org. Web.

Powell, Azizi. "Racially Derogatory Variants of the Song 'Old Shoe Boots and Leggings.'" pan cojams.blogspot.com. Sep. 3, 2013. Accessed Jan. 1, 2017. Web.

Presley, Elvis. "Money Honey—1956." YouTube.com. 519,244 views. Nov. 13, 2014. Accessed Feb. 9, 2020. Web.

"Pretty Little Dutch Girl." en.wikipedia.org. Pretty_Little_Dutch_Girl. Web.

The Puppies. "*Funky Y-2-C* (Video)." YouTube. 664,107 views. Mar. 23, 2016. https://www.you tube.com/watch?v=HdVPZQRO4lo. Accessed Feb 9, 2019. Web.

Rainey, Richard. Nola.com. The Times Picayune. "Before Lee Circle, New Orleans schools soul-searched their own Ties to slavery." Nola.com. Posted Jun. 25, 2015 at 1:30 a.m. Web.

"Rise and Shine." Cedarmont Kids—Rise and Shine (Arky Arky) [Official video]. YouTube . 1995. 3,534,584 views. Oct. 17, 2015. Accessed Feb. 14, 2020. Web.

Roemer, Danielle M. "Riddles." Sutton-Smith, *Source Book* 161–92. Print.

"Roll Me Over in the Clover." www.skylighters.org > ww2music > rollmeover. Web.

Rosen, Michael, ed. *The Penguin Book of Childhood.* London: Penguin, 1995. Print.

Rosevear, Dany. "Oh she sailed away on a happy summer's day—an action song." YouTube .com. Feb. 14, 2013. 18, 870 views. Accessed Feb. 13, 2020. Web.

Ross, Michael A. *The Great New Orleans Kidnapping Case: Race, Law, and Justice in the Recon-struction Era.* New York: Oxford UP, 2015. Print.

Rouse, Deborah. "The Artistic Realm of Music Video." *American Visions.* June 2000: 2 pp.http://www.findarticles.com/cf_dis/m1546/3_15/62724398/print.jhtml. Web.

Rover (song). En.wikipedia.org > wiki > Rover (song). Accessed Feb 10, 2020. Web.

"Rubber Dolly Rag." Uncle Bud Landress and the Georgia Yellow Hammers. Old Timey LP 101, "Old-Time Southern Dance Music: The String Bands." Vol. 2.

"Sales of Recorded Music and Music Videos, by Units Shipped and Value, 1990–98." *World Almanac and Book of Facts.* 1999. Print.

Saloy, Mona Lisa. "Sidewalk Songs, Jump-Rope Rhymes, and Clap-Hand Games of African American Children." *Children's Folklore Review.* Vol. 33. 2011. 35–43. Print.

Scott, Mike. "*Remembering when Regal Beer reigned over New Orleans beers: Sprawling French Quarter plant is now home to a major hotel.*" Nola.com. Feb. 5, 2020. 10:00 a.m. Accessed Feb. 12, 2020. Web.

Sherman, Josepha, and T. K. F. Weisskopf. *Greasy Grimy Gopher Guts: The Subversive Folklore of Childhood.* Little Rock: August House, 1995. Print.

Slim, Iceberg. *Airtight Willie and Me.* Los Angeles: Holloway, 1979. Print.

Slim, Iceberg. *Doom Fox.* New York: Grove, 1998. Print.

Soileau, Jeanne. *African American Children's Folklore: A Study in Games and Play.* (Disserta-tion). Spring 2002. Ann Arbor: ProQuest/UMI, 2002. 3057548. Print.

Soileau, Jeanne. *Black Children's Folklore in New Orleans*: A Cultural Resources Management Study for the Jean Lafitte Historical Park and the National Park Service. 1980. Print.

Soileau, Jeanne. "Children's Cheers as Folklore." *Western Folklore* 39 July (1980): 232–47. Print.

Soileau, Jeanne. "Media Influences on the Play of New Orleans Children." *Perspectives on Ethnicity in New Orleans: A Publication of the Committee on Ethnicity in New Orleans.* eds. John Cooke and Mackie Blanton. 1981. 32–37.

Soileau, Jeanne. *Yo' Mama, Mary Mack, and Boudreaux and Thibodeaux.* Jackson: U of Mississippi P, 2016. Print.

"Soul Train." Wikipedia.org. > wiki > Soul_Train. Web.

Spaeth, Sigmund. *A History of Popular Music.* New York: Random, 1948.

Splash Games. "Hand Clapping Game Slide—YouTube." YouTube.com. Jun. 10, 2009. 1,317,409 views. Accessed Feb. 2, 2020. Web.

"Styles—B-Boying (Breaking)." Nov. 10, 2001: 1p. <http://www.meu.edu./user/okmurak/styles/breakinghtml/>. Web.

Stevenson, Robert Louis. *A Child's Garden of Verses.* New York: Scribner, 1885. Print.

Sullivan, C. W., III. "Children's Oral Poetry: Identity and Obscenity." *Children's Folklore Review* 31 (2008–2009): 67–77.

Sutton-Smith, Brian. "Children's Folkgames as Customs." *Western Folklore* 47 (1989): 33–42. Print.

Sutton-Smith, Brian. *Children's Folklore: A Source Book.* ed. Brian Sutton-Smith, Jay Mechling, Thomas W. Johnson, and Felicia R. McMahon. New York: Garland, 1995. Print.

Sutton-Smith, Brian. *A Children's Games Anthology: Studies in Folklore and Anthropology.* New York: Arno, 1976. Print.

Sutton-Smith, Brian. *The Folk Games of Children.* Austin: U of Texas P, 1972. Print.

Sutton-Smith, Brian. *The Folkstories of Children.* Philadelphia: U of Pennsylvania P, 1981. Print.

Sutton-Smith, Brian. *The Games of New Zealand Children.* Berkeley: California UP, 1959. Print.

Sutton-Smith, Brian. "Play Theory and the Cruel Play of the Nineteenth Century." *The World of Play.* ed. Frank E. Manning. West Point, NY: Leisure, 1983. Print.

Sutton-Smith, Brian. "Shut Up and Keep Digging: The Cruel Joke Series." *Midwest Folklore* 10 (1960): 11–22. Print.

Sutton-Smith, Brian, and Diana Kelly-Byrne. *The Masks of Play.* New York: Birch, 1991. Print.

Sutton-Smith, Brian, John Grestmyer, and Alice Meckley. "Playfighting as Folkplay amongst Preschool Children." *Western Folklore* 47 (1988): 161–76. Print.

Sutton-Smith, Brian, Jay Mechling, Thomas W. Johnson, and Felicia R. McMahon, eds. *Children's Folklore: A Source Book.* Logan: Utah State UP, 1999. Print.

Taraborrelli, J. Randy. *Michael Jackson: The Magic and the Madness.* New York: Birch, 1991. Print.

Taraborrelli, J. Randy. *Michael Jackson—The Magic, the Madness, the Whole Story.* New York: Grand Central P, Rev Upd Ed., 2010. Print.

"Teddy Bear Teddy Bear Jump Rope Variations." Christian Home Education. http://www.homeschool.co.uk. Web. "theitem.com. *38th Annual Double Dutch Championships.*" YouTube. 1.3 M views. Jun. 17, 2011. Web.

Theitemdotcom. "38th Annual Double Dutch Championships." YouTube.com. Jun. 17, 2011. 1,336,198 views. Accessed Feb. 2, 2020. Web.

TheMasterOfJukeBox. "The Four Knights—*Oh Baby Mine (I Get So Lonely).* "Youtube.com. 217 views. Feb 21, 2015. Accessed Feb. 9, 2020. Web.

"This Old Man." en.wikipedia.org. > wiki > This_Old_Man. Web.

Tucker, Elizabeth. *Children's Folklore: A Handbook.* Westport, CT: Greenwood. 2008. Print.

Tucker, Elizabeth. "Go to Bed, Now You're Dead": Suffocation Songs and Breath Control Games." *Children's Folklore Review.* Vol. 31. 2008–2009. 45–57. Print.

Tucker, Elizabeth. "Tales and Legends." Sutton-Smith, *Source Book.* 193–212. Print.

"Twilight Forever." *Old Children's Song "Twilight Forever."* answers.google.com > answers > threadview. Accessed Jan. 20, 2019. Web.

Udal, J. S. *"Dorsetshire Children's Games, Etc."* *The Folk-Lore Journal* 7, no. 3. (January–December, 1889), London: Elliot Stock. Print.

"U.S. Commercial Radio Stations, by Format, 1993–99." *World Almanac and Book of Facts.* 1999 Ed. Print.

"U.S. *Television* Set Owners." *World Almanac and Book of Facts.* 1999 Ed. Print.

Vaudeville Star Marie Cahill Sings "Under the Bamboo Tree" 1917. gallerydreams.YouTube. Jul 4, 2011. 16, 439 views. Accessed Feb. 10, 2020. Web.

Usher. *"Nice & Slow* (Official video)"—YouTube. 1997. 35, 393, 145 views Oct. 25, 2009. Accessed Jan. 2, 2019. Web.

Vesdani, Cesare. "Elvis Presley—Money Honey—1956." YouTube.com. 521,625 views. Nov. 13, 2014. Accessed Feb. 2, 2020. Web.

Waterman, Richard Alan. "African Influence on the Music of the Americas." Dundes 81–94. Print.

"Weenie Man." https://campsongs.wordpress.com weenie man.

Wgno Web Desk. WGNO.com. "News with a Twist: Valena C. Jones Elementary was a 'sacred space' for children of the 7th Ward." Posted Feb. 23, 2018 at 3:36 p.m. Web.

Wikipedia.org. "Holy Cross School New Orleans." Enwikipedia.org > wiki > Holy_Cross_School_New_Orleans. Web.

Wikipedia.org. "John McDonogh." Web.

Winslow, David J. "An Annotated Collection of Children's Lore: Part Three of Oral Tradition among Children in Central New York State." *Keystone Folklore Quarterly* 2 (Fall 1966). Web.

Wolf, Howlin'. "I Have a Little Girl." *More Real Folk Blues* (MCA CHD) 9279. 1955. Recording.

Wolfenstein, Martha. *Children's Humor: A Psychological Analysis.* Bloomington: Indiana UP, 1954. Print.

Wolfenstein, Martha, and Nathan Leites. *Movies: A Psychological Study.* New York: Hafner, 1971. Print.

www.cbn/special/BlackHistory/underGod-RubyBridges.aspx Web.

www.nola.com/politics/index.ssf/2010/11/fifty_years_later_students_rec.html Web.

Xhenryxspencerx. "Smiley Lewis—I Hear You Knockin'." YouTube.com. 343,169 Views. Oct. 26, 2011. Accessed Feb. 10, 2020. Web.

Zumwalt, Rosemary. "The Complexity of Children's Folklore." Sutton-Smith, *Source Book* 23–48. Print.

Appendix: Annotated List of Collection Sites

1. Adolph Meyer Elementary School, 2013 General Meyer Ave. Algiers, La. Adolph Meyer Elementary, named for a Confederate officer and later a congressman, was renamed for the abolitionist Harriet Tubman in the 1990s. (For information on the renaming of schools in New Orleans in the 1990s, see—Rainey, Richard, NOLA.com The Times Picayune "Before Lee Circle, New Orleans schools soul-searched their own ties to slavery" posted on June 25, 2015 at 1:30 A.M. Web).

2. Andrew Jackson Elementary School—now International School of Louisiana: Camp Street Campus (French and Spanish) 1400 Camp Street, New Orleans La. 70130. In the 1970s, Andrew Jackson Elementary School served hundreds of children drawn from the Lower Garden District. Much of my early folklore collecting featured the students from Andrew Jackson Elementary.

3. Baker Middle School, 5903 Groom Rd. Baker, La. 70714. The girls who were recorded were campers at Camp Ruth Lee.

4. Beauregard Junior High School. "NOLA History: 6 New Orleans Schools of Historic Interest—GoNOLA.com." Web. gives the following history of Beauregard Junior High School. "The school was originally named for P. G. T. Beauregard, who was an American Army officer, then a Confederate General, and later an influential private citizen of New Orleans. In the 1990s, the Orleans Parish School Board began a program to rename a number of its schools, to make those names more meaningful to the overwhelmingly African-American student population. Beauregard Middle School (as it had become) was renamed for US Supreme Court Justice Thurgood Marshall. Since Hurricane Katrina, the building is now home to two charter schools, Pierre Capdeau Early College High School, and Langston Hughes Academy."

5. Beechwood Elementary School, 2555 Desoto Drive, Baton Rouge, La.

6. Benjamin Franklin High School, 2001 Leon C. Simon Dr. New Orleans, La. 70122. "Ben Franklin" was founded in 1957 as a public school for gifted children.

7. Birthday party, Chalmette, La. (2007) This birthday party was the first occasion for those close friends of my family to reunite following the devastation of Hurricane Katrina. Every member of the birthday party had had to relocate temporarily due to flooding. I took the opportunity to collect children's games learned during the "exile," and the flood remembrances of both children and adults.

8. Broadmoor High, Baton Rouge, La. 10100 Goodwood Blvd. 70815. Broadmoor Senior High School is a fully accredited high school located on a thirty-acre campus in the historic Broadmoor Neighborhood.

9. Camp Ruth Lee, Norwood, La. 70761. Camp Fire was organized in 1910 and was originally chartered in Baton Rouge in 1939. Girls from kindergarten to twelfth grade attended Camp Ruth Lee in the early 1970s, regardless of race, creed, or color.

10. Chalmette High School, 1100 Judge Perez Dr., Chalmette, La.

11. Charles Gayarre Elementary, 2515 N. Robertson Street, New Orleans, La. Built in 1920, Charles Gayarre Elementary was named for a lawyer and writer and the grandson of Etienne de Bore, the first mayor of New Orleans. Charles Gayarre Elementary was renamed in the 1990s for Oretha Castle Haley, a civil rights leader. The school was closed as a result of Hurricane Katrina, and as of 2017, it remained shuttered. NOLA.com. Rainey, Richard. "Before Lee Circle, New Orleans schools soul-searched their own ties to slavery." The Times Picayune. Posted on June 25, 2015 at 1:30 a.m. Web.

12. Crocker Elementary School (Lawrence D. Crocker), 2301 Marengo Street, New Orleans, La. 70115–5838. Located uptown, near Tulane University, Crocker Elementary is today listed as a "college prep, Charter school." Before Hurricane Katrina, Crocker drew from the neighborhood of Tulane University, and its diverse and vocally adept students contributed much lore to my collection.

13. Dalton Elementary School, 3605 Ontario Street, Baton Rouge, La. 70805.

14. Delmont Elementary School, 5300 Douglas Ave., Baton Rouge, La. (closed 2016).

15. Dunbar Camp. Held at Dunbar School in the Hollygrove neighborhood of New Orleans, Dunbar Camp provided summer recreation for children of the neighborhood. See NOLA.com The Times Picayune. Dreilinger, Danielle. "How one New Orleans neighborhood worked to reopen its school—and lost." Posted Jul. 31, at 12:08 pm. Updated Jan 06, 2015 at 5:10 p.m. Web.

16. Eden Park Academy, 1650 North Acadian Thruway East, Baton Rouge, La. 70802. Girls from Eden Park contributed cheers and jump rope games to my collection.

17. Dwight D. Eisenhower Elementary School, 3700 Tall Pines Dr. New Orleans, LA. 70131. Located in Algiers, on the West Bank of the Mississippi, Eisenhower Elementary has been renamed Dwight D. Eisenhower Academy of Global Studies post Hurricane Katrina.

18. Gates of Prayer Hebrew Synagogue, 4000 W. Esplanade Ave., Metairie, La, 70002. The web site gatesofprayer.org says, "Congregation Gates of Prayer is a strong, vibrant and active Reform Jewish synagogue located in Metairie, La. We offer a full range of programs for all ages from young children to our oldest adults." I found the children I interviewed there to be well informed about their faith as well as about child lore.

19. Happy Face Nursery School, Chalmette, La. My search for Happy Face Nursery School came to naught when I searched the name in 2017. Happy Face was the place where I dropped off my children when I went to work in New Orleans from 1970 to 1974. Hurricane Katrina may have wiped the school off the map along with many other locations in St. Bernard Parish.

20. Holy Cross High School. Wikipedia.org "Holy Cross School New Orleans" gives a history of the school from which my son graduated. "Holy Cross School is a high school and middle school founded in 1849 by the Congregation of the Holy Cross in New Orleans, Louisiana . . . In 1849 the Brothers, Priests and Sisters of Holy Cross arrived in New Orleans, after having established the University of Notre Dame in South Bend, Indiana, and took over an orphanage for the boys and girls who survived a plague. This orphanage, along with the first Ursaline School for Girls (the oldest Catholic School in America), was destroyed to make room for the 1923 Industrial Canal (the same Industrial Canal which experienced levee failures that flooded large parts on New Orleans twice, with Hurricane Betsy in 1965 and Hurricane Katrina in 2005). Since Hurricane Katrina, Holy Cross School has been relocated to 5500 Paris Ave, the former campuses of St. Francis Cabrini Parish and Redeemer—Seton High School. Its former location in 4950 Dauphine Street, Arabi, La. has been designated a Federal Historic District."

21. International Year of the Child Celebration (1979), Lafayette Square, New Orleans, La. I interviewed children who were waiting in line to get their faces painted.

22. Isidore Newman School, 1903 Jefferson Ave, New Orleans, La. 70115. Isidore Newman School is considered to be an elite private institution. The campus is uptown near both Tulane University and Loyola University.

23. Istrouma High School, Baton Rouge, La. Located 3730 Winbourne Ave, Baton Rouge, LA 70805. Istrouma was founded in 1917, and its name is a local Indian word for "Red Stick" (in French, "Baton Rouge.") Closed in 2014 for renovation, Istrouma reopened in 2017.

24. J. W. Faulk Elementary, 711 East Willow Street, Lafayette, La. 70501. It was here that boys gleefully delivered clean "dozens" on the schoolground, and girls sang popular songs.

25. John Dibert Elementary School, 4217 Orleans Ave., New Orleans, 70119. When I collected in its fifth- and sixth-grade classrooms, John Dibert was probably the most diverse school I had encountered. The student-teacher ratio was high; the enrollment was well racially mixed; and the enthusiasm of both teachers and students energetic. John Dibert School was closed in 2015. It was relocated and renamed Phillis Wheatley Community School.

26. Lacoste Elementary School, 1625 Missouri Street, Chalmette, LA. 70043. Because of Hurricane Katrina, Lacoste Elementary has been relocated to the site formerly occupied by St. Mark Catholic Church. I collected at its old location, on Judge Perez Drive.

27. Landmark of Acadiana Nursing Home, 1710 Smede Hwy, St. Martinville, La., 50582.

28. La Salle Elementary (Lasalle), 8000 Lasalle Ave, Baton Rouge, La. 70806. Children from LaSalle contributed cheers and jump-rope games.

29. Louise Day Care Center, 1205 Louisiana Ave New Orleans, La. 70115. Some of the youngest girls I recorded performed handclaps at Louise Day Care.

30. Louisiana State University, Baton Rouge, La. 70803. Freshman students contributed written games and rhymes.

31. Lusher Elementary School (Now Lusher Charter School) 7315 Willow St., New Orleans, La. 70118.

32. Magrauder Center, Desire Project. When I asked certain children I was tape recording where they had learned their lore, I was told "At the Magrauder Center in the Desire." I have searched everywhere for Magrauder Center and have found no reference to it in the list of New Orleans Recreation Department sites or anywhere else.

33. Mandeville High School, 1 Skipper Dr. Mandeville, La. 70471. Several of my informants from LSU were graduates of Mandeville High School.

34. Mayfair Elementary School, 9880 Hyacinth Ave. Baton Rouge, La. 70810 (closed in 2007). Mayfair girls were lively contributors to my Baton Rouge collection.

35. McDonogh High School, 2426 Esplanade Ave. New Orleans, La. 70119. Some of my high school age students came from McDonogh High. For information on John McDonogh and his generous educational legacy, see Wikipedia—John McDonogh.

36. McKinley Junior High School, 1550 Eddie Robinson, Sr. Drive, Baton Rouge, La. 70802. Children from McKinley Junior High School contributed cheers and playground lore in writing and on tape. The teachers there were very helpful.

37. Meraux Elementary School, 200 East St. Bernard Highway, Chalmette, La. 70043–5162. The children who were recorded from this school were attending Happy Face Day Care (Nursery) in Chalmette. The original school in Meraux was lost in Hurricane Katrina.

38. Metairie Park Country Day School, 300 Park Rd. Metairie, La. 70005. The students knew a great deal of playground lore. They were shy but willing to share.

39. Myrtle Place Elementary, 1100 Myrtle Place, Lafayette, La. 70506. The recordings done here took place in the cafeteria, a loud, echoing venue, but the children energetically performed.

40. Northside Elementary School, 1090 Robbie Street, Denham Springs, La. 70726.

41. Northwestern Middle School, 5200 E. Central Ave. Zachary, La. 70791. Most of the girls I interviewed who attended Northwestern Middle School were day campers at Camp Ruth Lee. One tape, however, was recorded by a teacher at Northwestern Middle School. She had her students use tape recording as a class project.

42. Prescott Junior High School, 4055 Prescott Rd., Baton Rouge, La. (closed 2016).

43. Redeemer High School, 1453 Crescent Street, New Orleans. Redeemer High, where I taught during the early 1980s, and where I recorded ninth graders telling jokes, was the only racially diverse, co-educational private Catholic school in New Orleans. It was closed after Hurricane Katrina damaged the campus in 2005.

44. Sacred Heart Academy, Grand Coteau, La. 70541. A Catholic boarding and day school for girls, Academy of the Sacred Heart is the second oldest institution of learning west of the Mississippi. Five generations of girls in my family attended Sacred Heart. The last to attend was my daughter, Ida, who recorded boarding-school stories.

45. Samuel J. Peters Junior High School, New Orleans, La. (closed since Hurricane Katrina). Samuel J. Peters is the school where WGNO television videotaped young football players participating in handclap games with girls their age. The school was once quite beautiful.

46. Sherwood Forest Elementary School, Baton Rouge (now closed).

47. St. Benilde Catholic School, 1803 Division Street, Metairie, La. 70001. The children I interviewed from St. Benilde were at the International Year of the Child Celebration in Lafayette Square, New Orleans (1979).

48. St. Catherine of Siena Girl Scout meeting, Old Metairie, La.

49. St. Genevieve School, 201 Elizabeth Ave., Lafayette, La., 70501. I recorded children second to sixth grade here.

50. St. Joan of Arc bingo babysitting, 8321 Burthe Street, New Orleans, La. 70118. There, two teenagers, Carol, and Gregory, conducted a babysitting venue for parents playing bingo at the church.

51. St. Joseph's Academy, 3015 Broussard Street, Baton Rouge, La. 70808.

52. St. Louise De Marillac Catholic School, 1914 Aycock St., Arabi, La., 70032.

53. St. Rita Catholic School, 194 Ravan Ave., Harahan, La, 70123 and at another location at 65 Fontainbleu Dr., New Orleans, La, 70125.

54. Tara High School, 9002 Whitehall Ave., Baton Rouge, La. 70806. Several of the Camp counselors I interviewed at Camp Ruth Lee graduated from this school.

55. Tulane University, 6828 St. Charles Ave., New Orleans, La. 70118.

56. University Terrace Elementary School, 575 W. Roosevelt St., Baton Rouge, La. 70802. This was the site of one of my earliest taping sessions.

57. Ursaline Academy, 2635 State St., New Orleans, La., 70118. The sisters watched the interviewees carefully.

58. Valena C. Jones Elementary School (closed 2018). See WGNO.com, "Valena C. Jones Elementary was a 'sacred space' for the 7th Ward," posted 3:36 p.m., February 23, 2018, by WGNO Web Desk.

59. Valley Park Junior High School, 4510 Bawell St., Baton Rouge, La. Campers from this school contributed cheers and handclaps to the collection.

60. Walnut Hills Elementary School, Baton Rouge, La. Part of the Janice Pierce Collection.

61. Xavier University, 1 Drexel Dr., New Orleans, La. 70125.

62. Zachary Elementary School, 3775 Hemlock Street, Zachary, La. 70791.

General Index

Index of First Lines and Titles

About the Author

Photo by Monique Soileau

Jeanne Pitre Soileau was born in New Orleans and taught in Louisiana for forty-seven years. Though retired, she is still actively collecting folklore. She is author of *Yo' Mama, Mary Mack, and Boudreaux and Thibodeaux: Louisiana Children's Folklore and Play,* which won the 2018 Opie Prize and the 2018 Chicago Folklore Prize.

9 781496 835741